The
COCKTAIL
DRESS

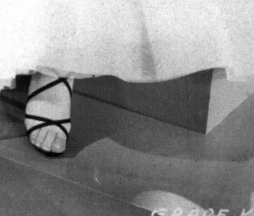

The COCKTAIL DRESS

Laird Borrelli-Persson

COLLINS DESIGN

An Imprint of HarperCollins Publishers

HarperCollins books may be purchased for educational, business,
or sales promotional use. For information, please write: Special
Markets Department, HarperCollins*Publishers*, 10 East 53rd Street,
New York, NY 10022.

First published in 2009 by:
Collins Design
An Imprint of HarperCollins*Publishers*
10 East 53rd Street
New York, NY 10022
Tel: (212) 207-7000
Fax: (212) 207-7654
collinsdesign@harpercollins.com
www.harpercollins.com

Distributed throughout the world by:
HarperCollins*Publishers*
10 East 53rd Street
New York, NY 10022
Fax: (212) 207-7654

Library of Congress Control Number: 2008935842

ISBN: 978-0-06-153613-7

BOOK DESIGN BY SHUBHANI SARKAR

Printed in China
First Printing, 2009

FOR CFP

ACKNOWLEDGMENTS

Thanks and skål—to my husband, Carl F. Persson; my dear
parents; Dr. Valerie Steele; the HarperCollins team:
Elizabeth Viscott Sullivan, Dinah Fried, Signe Bergstrom,
Ilana Anger, Roni Axelrod, Diane Aronson, and
Shubhani Sarkar; Candy Pratts Price; Michael Vollbracht;
Nancy MacDonell; Alexander Terexov, Arnold Scaasi,
and Parker Ladd; Catherine Malandrino, Chris Benz,
Cynthia Rowley, Isaac Mizrahi, Peter Som, and
Sarah Singh; Don Ashby and Lyndsay Black at firstView;
Ron Mandelbaum and F. Victor Burgos at Photofest;
Sherly Rabbani, and Josephine Solimene; and all who
have contributed to this project.

THE COCKTAIL DRESS, BE IT DECADENT OR DEMURE, MERGES FESTIVITY WITH SEX APPEAL. DESPITE ITS UBIQUITY, THE COCKTAIL DRESS HAS A SHORT HISTORY. ALTHOUGH THE WORD *COCKTAIL* ENTERED THE LEXICON IN 1803, *COCKTAIL PARTY*— THE REASON FOR THE DRESS—WASN'T INTRODUCED UNTIL 1928. NO CORSETED VICTORIAN MATRON OR WHOLESOME GIBSON GIRL would have dreamed of dressing specifically to drink anything but tea, and she would usually do that within the confines of home. In contrast, a flapper wouldn't have dreamed of staying in. Cocktail dresses, most often worn for going out, are sartorial symbols of women's greater freedom, both of action and being. Like the classic martini, which critic and wit H. L. Mencken described as "the only American invention as perfect as the sonnet," the cocktail dress will never be out of fashion. But history shows us that its potency and popularity is strongest in times that are really shaken—not merely stirred—with major social change.

Cocktail culture started to take root before World War I, but was to flower only in a postwar era in which "earthquakes shook the social fabric," according to contemporary observer Michael Arlen, a novelist of the smart set. Cocktail parties—which Parisian author and style expert Genevieve Antoine Dariaux described as "a sort of unorganized receiving line . . . that liquidates social obligations to an unlimited number of people"—have always had a democratic appeal. With alcohol flowing in abundance, the mood of these parties was lighthearted, loose, and less exclusive; people from different classes mingled—just as they had in the trenches.

In *The Women We Wanted to Look Like*, Brigid Keenan writes that "The war years of unhappiness and pent-up tension were over and relief exploded like fireworks. Not for nothing were they known as the Roaring Twenties.

Everyone went a little crazy—they kicked up their legs doing the Charleston, they sipped cocktails for the first time, they danced cheek to cheek in nightclubs. They were jazz-mad party-mad, and like exuberant children enjoyed dressing up and playing pranks." Fast flappers like Zelda Fitzgerald (who once jumped fully clothed into the fountain outside of the Plaza Hotel in New York City) forcefully rejected staid Victorian convention. "The day of the wax-doll debutante that squeaked 'Ma-ma' if ever so lightly pressed is over," declares the protagonist of Emily Post's satiric 1928 novel, *How to Behave—Though a Debutante*. "The baby doll of to-day [sic] has a smooth-working dynamo under her indestructible exterior instead of a little squeak bellows buried in her sawdust!" In other words, the world was her oyster—at least in comparison to the world that her mother or grandmother knew. The New Woman—who was likely to work and live away from home—was able to exercise choice.

In 1920, just one year after Paul Poiret shackled women's legs with his hobble skirt, the Nineteenth Amendment—which had been fought for long and hard by women in corsets and crinolines—was passed in the United States, giving women the right to vote. (French women waited until 1944 for the same privilege.) At the same time, Sigmund Freud gave them other liberties: "Freud and sex were all the thing then!" exclaim Angus Wilson and Philippe Jullian in *For Whom the Cloche Tolls*, their satirical take on the Jazz Age. According to journalist Helen Rowland, the New Woman was no "longer Man's plaything, but his playmate." This equality found visual expression in a sort of androgyny. Not only did women crop their hair, but they bound their breasts. The ideal figure was boyish, emphasized by straight, cylindrical frocks worn with rolled stockings (into which a flask was sometimes tucked). For evening, lustrous silks might be embroidered or beaded with glittering Art Deco motifs. These unrestrictive ensembles made it easy to move freely with a drink in hand—often served in a tea cup in an attempt to foil the police during Prohibition in the United States (1920–1933)—and dance the Charleston into the night. Knee-length hems exposed the legs—strident symbols of women's liberation as well as greater social and sexual mobility.

If Poiret, the so-called King of Fashion, dominated fashion with his dazzling, exotic, and sometimes impractical Orientalism in the prewar era, his nemesis Gabrielle "Coco" Chanel set the standard of postwar style with her sporty and sophisticated fashions. After all, new types of

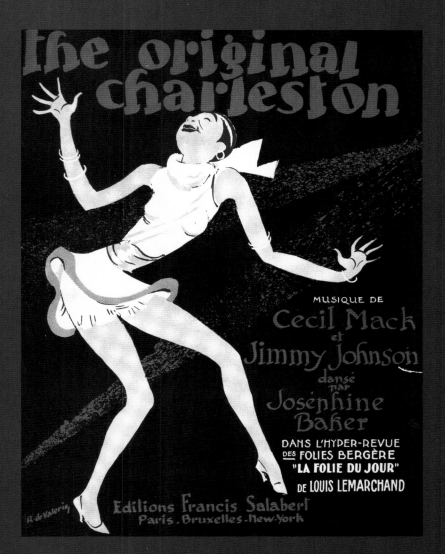

entertainment, like the cocktail party, called for a new kind of semiformal sartorial expression. Unlike the dance dress, which needed to flow, or the gown, which had to impress, the cocktail dress was short and sweet, offering a bite-sized taste of seduction—but not without a twist of practicality. In 1926, Chanel famously showed a simple drop-waisted ebony frock embellished only with seams and worn with a head-encasing cloche, which *Vogue* described as "a sort of uniform for all women of taste," and dubbed fashion's "Ford," a term that reflected the decade's fascination with technology and machines. Like Henry Ford's Model T, the simple and elegant little black dress was an instant hit, and it has remained a classic cocktail dress style. In fact, two very famous cocktail dresses—the form-fitting Givenchy number Audrey Hepburn sports as Holly Golightly for her visit to Sing Sing in *Breakfast at Tiffany's* (1961), and the full-skirted taffeta dress Elizabeth Taylor as Gloria Wandrous wears in the sexually charged bar scene in *Butterfield 8* (1960)—are little black dresses.

The black dress's adaptability and easy transition from day to evening are some of its best qualities. Black is simple and conservative at the office and chic and sophisticated for happy hour or an evening at the theater. The quickest way to transform a little black dress into a personal fashion statement is through creative accessorizing, which has always been an important aspect of cocktail dressing. In her 1959 book *Wife Dressing*, designer Anne Fogarty writes, "I believe in accessories as the prime factor for cocktail garb. Satin shoes. Marvelous jewelry. White kid shorties. Festive handbag. These can transform a simple, uncluttered wool or silk into a gala ensemble." And none other than Christian Dior enthused that "cocktail hats are the fanciest hats of all." A change of accessories, rather than dress, most commonly transforms the sober worker bee into a sparkling creature of the night.

Thirteen long years of Prohibition did little to stop high jinks and alcohol consumption but rather galvanized America's obsession with drinking—after all, *the* novel of the decade, F. Scott Fitzgerald's *The Great Gatsby,* opens with a cocktail party. Dressing especially for drinking became the norm—be it in a dress glittering with Egyptian-style embellishments inspired by the Tut mania that accompanied the discovery of the Egyptian pharaoh's tomb in 1922; something chic and silky by Lucien Lelong (whose second wife, Princess Natalie Paley, was often featured in *Vogue*); or a dress by Callot Soeurs, the go-to designers for lace- and flower-trimmed confections.

Over time the tea gown gave way to the cocktail dress, a term that was first used, appropriately, in the post-Prohibition year of 1935.

There was little to celebrate in the years of the Great Depression (1929–1939). *New York Times* critic Humphrey Doulens wrote, "The campus boys and girls have turned serious. Life to them no longer means a lot of frills, nightclubs and necking. They think of life now as a problem of social and economic adjustments. They've discovered that the world's problems are, in fact, their own, and they cannot find escape from the world in a spirit of abandon." Rather than drowning their sorrows in drink, many turned instead to the silver screen as a powerful form of escapism. Sartorially speaking, the thirties are often referred to as the "Glamour Years." Styles then were long, languorous, and lovely—and heavily influenced by Hollywood. Screen idols such as Marlene Dietrich, Greta Garbo, and Jean Harlow became fashion icons, just as costume designers like Gilbert Adrian, Jean Louis, and Travis Banton became arbiters of style, influencing clothing choices of women worldwide.

Youth was no longer glorified as it had been in the twenties, which was evident in the clothes that people wore. Cylindrical frocks that skimmed boyish figures, anchoring only at the hips, gave way to slim, bias-cut dresses that emphasized grown-up, womanly figures. Madeleine Vionnet is credited with pioneering the bias technique, in which fabric is cut on the diagonal, allowing it to stretch and cling like a second skin. An innovative designer in many ways, Vionnet, whose outlook was more classical than cyclical, considered herself to be "an enemy of fashion." This explains why her name has less currency than that of Mainbocher, who described himself as "the Rolls-Royce of the fashion trade." Mainbocher made fashion history in 1937 when he dressed Wallis Simpson, the woman for whom Edward VIII abdicated the British throne, for her wedding. Only the filthy rich could afford Mainbocher's outrageously expensive yet exceptionally sober designs. Their strict, often monochromatic propriety was appropriate to depressed times in which there was little place for ostentatiousness.

Though subtle sartorial expressions were Chanel's forte, in 1934, *Time* chose her rival Elsa Schiaparelli for its cover, heralding her as being "madder and more original than most of her contemporaries." Chanel referred to her as "the Italian artist who makes clothes"; art and humor were the weapons with which Schiaparelli confronted the absurdity of contemporary reality.

In 1930, for example, she showed a porcelain "aspirin necklace"; one can imagine the Crash had caused many a headache. Among her other outré sartorial landmarks are a surrealistic hat in the shape of an upside-down shoe, a perfume bottle based on Mae West's hourglass silhouette, and novelty prints. She collaborated with artists such as Alberto Giacometti, Christian "Bébé" Bérard, and Salvdaor Dalí, who designed a dress with a large lobster printed on it for her line.

Thirties glamour gave way to utility, the byword of forties fashion. Wartime fabric restrictions kept the silhouette short and narrow, though stronger, broader shoulders gave it shape. "The mood of life," noted Grace Margaret Morton, a University of Nebraska home economics professor, in her 1948 style guide, "tends to make for a more realistic attitude toward clothes. Economic pressures of today demand sanity, the elimination of extravagant frou frou and a return to sound buying principles with emphasis on quality." The strain of the war had an appropriately sobering effect on cocktail dressing. In 1941, just three years after publishing a spread on the idle rich that read, "They pay high for clothes. They spend time on them. They lunch in groups, then on to shopping, bridge, or the hairdresser. They know every restaurant, night-club, and show in town," *Vogue* published a special "Women in Defense Work" feature to appeal to women entering the workforce to replace men, who were away at war. Women no longer needed party clothes but work wear, be it a tailored suit, a "Rosie the Riveter" jumpsuit, or a uniform.

During the war, the American fashion industry, which until that point had largely followed the lead of Paris, needed to fend for itself. With most of the French couture ateliers closed and no new styles to copy, New York City's fashion district, Seventh Avenue, introduced American sportswear. Claire McCardell is credited as one of sportswear's pioneers, and one of her sartorial innovations was to work "poor" fabrics—like calico, denim, and ticking—into simple separates like jumpers and wrap dresses, which she called "popovers." According to costume designers at the Metropolitan Museum of Art, "In Utility achieved with ingenuity, McCardell found synergy." Her designs were particularly suited to the more casual American lifestyle—encompassing suburban barbecues and country club mixers—which was to flourish in the fifties and sixties.

"The real masterpieces of American design," said Christian Dior in his 1957 autobiography, *Dior by Dior*, "are the cocktail dresses, the cocktail being the symbol par excellence of the American way of life." Far from being tradition-bound, the cocktail party brings people of all classes together for two hours of happy flux. "For cocktail parties," Anne Fogarty writes, "I like dresses I can 'lean' in, a silhouette that looks well standing or mingling with groups of people." In other words, for drinks, one should look like a long, cold drink of water while sipping something decidedly more intoxicating.

Alluring as cocktail dresses of the fifties were, they were not overtly revealing. Knees so daringly on view in the Jazz Age were conspicuously absent from the picture in this postwar period, a decade dominated by two designers: Cristóbal Balenciaga and Christian Dior. Though Christian Dior was to become famous for the rapidity with which he altered his silhouettes—creating A-lines one season and trapezes the next—his most lasting contribution to fashion, dubbed the "New Look" by *Harper's Bazaar* editor Carmel Snow, was created not with dance-mad adventurers in mind, but rather a staid *femme fleur* clad in long, Edwardian-influenced dresses with full skirts and cinched waists. The hourglass became and remains one of the most classic of cocktail silhouettes. Widely copied, the New Look was worn across the globe.

Of course, not everyone was sporting Christian Dior—or the Dior copies that Seventh Avenue churned out. The fashion elite, such as renowned fashion editor Diana Vreeland and Countess Mona von Bismarck (who is said to have ordered 150 dresses from the couturier in one sitting after a railroad accident destroyed many of her clothes), favored the work of Balenciaga, who found elegance in simplicity with "a structure that is often more significant than the body," as *New Yorker* columnist Kennedy Fraser put it. By ingeniously cutting an asymmetric hem into a taffeta dress, paring a neckline just so, or adding subtle jet beading as decoration, Balenciaga achieved a kind of fashion Zen.

The French didn't have a hegemony on occasion dressing. Simonetta and Fontana put Italy on the fashion map with flirty, feminine creations— some featuring raffia embellishments, others brilliant beadwork. And in the United States, the cocktail creations of Ceil Chapman—a favorite of Marilyn Monroe—were popular, as were the designs of the Academy Award–winning Helen Rose, whose costumes for Elizabeth Taylor in *Cat on a Hot Tin Roof* (1958)—a pleated V-neck chiffon in white—and *Butterfield 8* (1960)—a lace-trimmed slip worn as a dress and accessorized with a high-ball, as well as a black taffeta décolletage number accessorized with proper pearls—are

unforgettable. Another indelible image is that of Anouk Aimée in a form-fitting black dress in Federico Fellini's masterpiece *La Dolce Vita* (1960). Though the dress doesn't reveal a lot of skin, its body-loving lines are as femme fatale as the more overtly seductive design of the strapless gown worn by Anita Ekberg in the same film.

In 1964, Dariaux wrote that "The dress worn by a guest at a cocktail party should be scarcely décolleté at all, and should always be accompanied by a hat." Propriety was still a byword of fashion in the first half of the sixties, and no one embodied its principles more keenly than Jacqueline Kennedy. A true fashion icon throughout her life, as First Lady of the United States in the early sixties, she favored monochromatic dressing, boxy suits and A-line shifts, pill-box hats, and white gloves. In 1961, Oleg Cassini, the Principal State robe designer, said, "We are on the threshold of a new American elegance thanks to Mrs. Kennedy's beauty, naturalness, understatement, exposure and symbolism." As much as Kennedy loved French couture—and allegedly had Cassini copy it—it's difficult to imagine her in an alligator biker jacket designed by Yves Saint Laurent, fashion's young dauphin, who "shook up" the house of Christian Dior in 1960. The uproar this collection caused probably had less to do with the actual clothes and more to do with the approach. Instead of following the trickle-down system of high fashion, which cast the designer in the role of dictator, Saint Laurent, always one step ahead of the crowd, embraced the influence of the street, and thus challenged the established order of things.

A more significant threat to the status quo than Saint Laurent's black turtlenecks was the legalization of oral contraceptives in 1960, which, like suffrage in the twenties, dramatically changed the lives of women. The cocktail dress, the *Times* reported in the thirties, "retains its skirt about 12 inches from the ground." In the sixties, lengths crept way upward of that thanks to the miniskirt, which, like the flapper dress before it, became the symbol of a youth-worshipping age. This decade's fashion icon was one Lesley Hornby, aka Twiggy, a gawky, cropped-top British model with endless legs.

Diana Vreeland coined the term "Youthquake" to describe the rumblings of revolt that originated in London, the movement's fault line. Mary Quant, who really shook things up when she dressed models with long fake eyelashes in bright, colorful tights and miniskirts, described her boutique as "a kind of permanently running cocktail party." Saint Laurent, who showed his iconic Mondrian dress in 1965, wasn't the only designer to be influenced by art. Designer Rudi Gernreich was tuned in to the contemporary art scene, designing abbreviated Op Art–patterned pieces. Space exploration also ignited the imagination of designers such as André Courrèges, who worked in a predominately white and silver palette; Pierre Cardin, who showed stiff A-lines in materials like vinyl, Perspex, and a self-invented fabric called Cardine that could hold three-dimensional shapes; and Paco Rabanne, who outfitted Jane Fonda in *Barbarella* and made some memorably outrageous and revealing cocktail numbers from linked plastic discs.

As the decade came to a close, styles started coming down to earth, reflecting public concern for the environment, racism, materialism, and the Vietnam War. The hippie movement was in full swing, with a stronghold in San Francisco's Haight-Ashbury district that resonated nationwide. Denim-clad youth wearing tie-dyed T-shirts and flowers in their hair attended huge protests and politically-minded gatherings. They experimented with psychedelic drugs, often lived and worked together on communes, and promoted peace, love, and happiness. But a recession in the early seventies diminished much of the hippies' idealism, paving the way for an era often referred to as the "Me Decade." Self-obsession, women's lib, bell-bottoms, maxiskirts, and hot pants all figured large—and cocktail dresses featured small. At *Vogue*, editorial stewardship had passed from Vreeland to Grace Mirabella, who championed so-called *"real* women," the kind of woman who—stylist Polly Allen Mellen recounts—"was aware of who she was. A woman who would take a good look at herself in the morning when she got dressed and then go out and forget what she had on and live her day."

The seventies were not the heyday of the cocktail dress. "Emphasis was shifting," Kennedy Fraser explains, "from a basically formal view of clothes and the importance of their shape and fit to a more informal style of dress that began with bodies, to whose shape and movement a soft 'unobstructed' garment remained subsidiary." But cocktail dresses were not completely out of the picture; Studio 54 regulars hardly had to go naked (though some did by choice). Colorful characters like Liza Minnelli and Bianca Jagger partied in dresses by Halston, made of ingeniously cut and revealing jersey, which was also the preferred fabric of Stephen Burrows, who sold his color-blocked knits from the trendy Stephen Burrows' World boutique at Henri Bendel.

"We will have a mixture of casualness, fluidity and fantasy," retailer and designer Carole Austen told *International Textiles* magazine with foresight in 1970. Saint Laurent explored the latter with his imaginative journeys through Africa and Russia, the most memorable pieces of which were evening gowns. At the same time, Laura Ashley was going country and popularizing floral prairie dresses, while Karl Lagerfeld was whipping up romance with ruffles, jersey, and Art Deco prints at Chloé. In 1974, Diane von Furstenberg encouraged women to embrace their femininity and freedom with pride with the introduction of her iconic wrap dress. Advertisements for these figure-hugging jersey dresses featured the powerful slogan "Feel like a woman, wear a dress." The wrap dress had instant appeal, and millions have been sold since it was first introduced. One of these dresses is in the permanent collection at the Costume Institute of the Metropolitan Museum of Art, thanks to its significant influence on women's fashion.

By 1980, not only were more women in the workforce than ever before, but the economy was flourishing in a way that it hadn't since the sixties. Everything began to revolve around money. Hostile corporate takeovers were happening left and right, and people were ruthless and money-hungry, doing anything and everything they could to get to the top. "Greed is, for lack of a better word, good," or so said Gordon Gekko, the unscrupulous corporate raider played by Michael Douglas in the film *Wall Street* (1987), which is a pitch-perfect portrayal of this decade's culture. Paychecks and bank accounts got significantly bigger, and fashion mirrored this sudden economic boom. Who you were became a question of what you had, the theory being that he or she with the most toys wins. People used excessive material purchases as a means of showing off their wealth and status. High-end labels and logos loomed large as people searched for ways to ostentatiously display their wealth, creating a boom for the luxury goods houses that rule over the fashion industry today.

Style increased physically as well, a growth evident in widening shoulder widths and the presence of mega shoulder pads. Christian Lacroix's pouf skirts announced their importance with both their size and opulence. Ivana Trump, clad in Lacroix, was racking up column inches in the *New York Post*'s Page Six; and television viewers were captivated by the gaudy, shirred, and puff-sleeved costumes that Nolan Miller designed for Joan Collins, Linda Evans, and crew on *Dynasty*. In his novel *The Bonfire of the Vanities*, Tom Wolfe characterized the women who wore pouf skirts as "social x-rays," thus coining the term. The decadence of this era of greed was given sartorial expression by Thierry Mugler and Gianni Versace, who fleshed out their quasi-fetishistic fantasies on the runway. In the early eighties, when Japanese designers Rei Kawakubo, Yohji Yamamoto, and Junya Watanabe first showed their esoteric, often shroudlike fashions in Paris, they seemed wholly anomalous to prevailing trends. In retrospect, these clothes can perhaps be seen as an omen of what was to come. It wasn't long before people realized they had been dancing on the edge of a volcano. Wall Street crashed in 1987: The party was over.

In the wake of the crash, people were left in a state of shock and panic and took comfort in the past, looking back at familiar things. Designers were recalling the past with nostalgia as well, which took the name of retro. Alexander McQueen channeled Hitchcock heroines and femme fatales such as Marlene Dietrich. John Galliano favored historical romps, transforming his models—usually in bias-cut cocktail dresses and gowns— into both tsarinas and demimondaines, inspired by sources as disparate as Schiaparelli, the Maori, and Proust.

Marc Jacobs had a more jaded view. His 1993 grunge collection for Perry Ellis, inspired by Seattle rockers and the so-called heroin-chic aesthetic, was seen by many, including his employers, to be anti-fashion: It cost him his job. Miuccia Prada's approach to fashion was also revolutionary, but her assault on convention was less raw and conventionally prettier than that of Jacobs'. Although Prada touts all things jolie-laide, she filters "laide" through the fifties and sixties references she seems to have internalized, so the result is quietly subversive and always ladylike. (She excels at cocktail dresses, showing in 2002 belted pleated numbers that deflated any Marilyn Monroe bombshell connotations in favor of something more soignée and sophisticated, while in 2004 she showed printed sheaths that could have been plucked from a Cinecittà film.) Meanwhile, Jacobs resurrected his career at luxury conglomerate LVMH, where he was appointed Louis Vuitton's creative director. In recent years, the designer has been turning ducklings into swans in retro prom-style garb reimagined as modern cocktail dresses for his eponymous line and staidly chic numbers for the storied French house.

In the nineties, less became more. The exaggerated styles of the eighties gave way to an emphasis on the natural human form, perhaps best exemplified

by the work of Azzedine Alaïa. If anyone knows how to accentuate the body through clothes, it is Alaïa. He has long taken the hot air out of fashion with his focus on celebrating the beauty of the female form, whether clothing it in second-skin leopard knits or sheer black chiffons. Not surprisingly, some of his most devoted clients are supermodels, such as Stephanie Seymour and Naomi Campbell, whose allegiance to the designer has never faltered. While Alaïa's style focuses on sensuality, Tom Ford, who successfully revitalized Gucci in the early nineties, created styles that evoked raw sexuality. Alaïa's clothes caress the body; Ford's—who designed for both for Gucci and later for Yves Saint Laurent—seek to provoke with their overt exposure of the body. Some of Ford's cocktail numbers for sirens with kohl-smudged eyes were made of bandages of colored silk, or based on Asian cheongsams that exposed miles of leg balanced on knifelike stilettos.

Ford was not the only one fixated on sex. Four women named Carrie, Samantha, Charlotte, and Miranda shared his fascination with tomfoolery and fashion. The popular television series *Sex and the City*, which first aired in 1998, was a sartorial microcosm of turn-of-the-century trends, thanks to costume designer Patricia Field's keen observations and creative expression of the eclectic styles that were happening in the late nineties. Carrie's closet in particular reflected the turmoil of the times. Whether she was wearing a funky warp-print floral ensemble, a Dolce & Gabbana beaded lace slip dress, or a full-skirted raspberry cocktail dress from Oscar de la Renta's Spring 2004 collection, Carrie Bradshaw was dressed to the nines when she went out for cocktails at night at the opening of a new boutique or the trendiest nightclub. Always promising cutting-edge fashion and outlandish outfits that inspired the popular imagination, many viewers tuned in to the series each week just to see the clothes.

In this first decade of the millennium, fashion is, as ever, on the prowl for the new name and emerging talent, but today more so than ever. With new markets—such as China, India, and Russia—expanding and media outlets multiplying, fashion consciousness is increasing by the day. In this era of the Internet and reality television, even an at-home gathering might appear in a video on YouTube or in scandalous photographs on a blog. If one happens to be captured in the flash of the paparazzi, it is preferable to be clad in something by one of two of the most directional designers working today: Nicolas Ghesquière at Balenciaga or Alber Elbaz at Lanvin. Ghesquière, in keeping with the legacy of the house, is focused on the architecture of fashion, and his special talent is to infuse it with a kind of futurism. Elbaz, in contrast, is more focused on romance and *flou*. He's especially good at creating valentines of cocktail dresses with little structure but great appeal that show up everywhere from Cannes to Watermill.

Prada and Jacobs are still in the headlines, along with new names like Zac Posen, the go-to man for the artier set who aren't afraid to sizzle with a bit more sexiness, and Jack McCollough and Lazaro Hernandez at Proenza Schouler, whose bustier dresses fashion insiders and starlets like Kate Bosworth and Maggie Gyllenhaal find hard to resist. Peter Som is carrying on in the ladylike tradition of Oscar de la Renta with dreamy bow ties and taffeta cocktail numbers, while Dutch design duo Viktor & Rolf often lean toward a Saint Laurentish classicism despite the drama of their Paris presentations. Take away the masks from their 2006 collection, for example, and you have a modern take on bougie Right Bank propriety that conjures art-filled pied-a-terres, Edith Piaf songs, and glasses of Perrier-Jouet—in other words, *la vie en rose.* Now that's something to toast to.

In some ways the naughties resemble the eighties. Emerging markets are embracing logos as a way of quickly joining the establishment, and greater fashion awareness and more media outlets encourage ostentation and peacock-like display. Yet accompanying the growth of the luxury sector is that of "masstige" labels such as H&M and the general acceptance of the high-low mix, which is a way to stand out at charity events, media mingles, screenings, and other events where one hand is occupied with a beverage and one eye ever searching the crowds for the party photographer.

There is something greater than seams and fabric that connects the silken drop-waisted flapper dress worn with pearls to the short and flirty flower-trimmed number worn today. The introduction and popularity of the cocktail party necessitated a new form of sartorial expression, whose form has ebbed and flowed to mirror our forever transforming society and women's changing role in it. Sometimes a dress is not just a dress. An invitation that reads "cocktail attire" is a two-hour pass to lighthearted amusement, where a drink can be taken neat and a book judged by its cover. As Vreeland understood, "a new dress doesn't get you anywhere; it's the life you're living in the dress, and the sort of life you had lived before, and what you will do later."

THE
COCKTAIL
DRESS

"What is a cocktail dress?"

"Something to spill cocktails on."

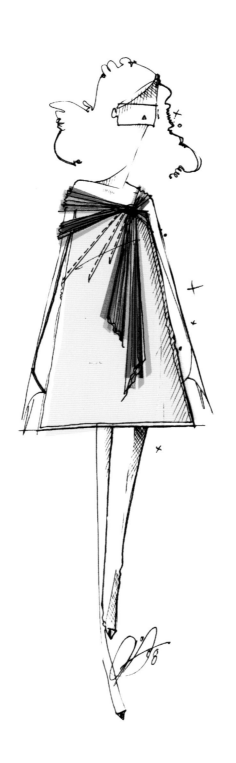

Five out o
five men
are said to
look twice
at any girl
in a black
dress.

ELIZABETH HAWES, *ANYTHING BUT*

My dear, there are some things that just aren't done, such as drinking Dom Pérignon '53 above the temperature of 38 degrees Fahrenheit.

There was music from my neighbor's house through the summer nights. In his blue gardens men and girls came and went like moths among the whisperings and the champagne and the stars.

F. SCOTT FITZGERALD, *THE GREAT GATSBY*

VOGUE

HOT WEATHER
FASHIONS
number

© THE CONDÉ NAST PUBLICATIONS INC
JULY 1·1926   35 CENTS

Navy
Sweater/Club
AllX Dress

Swin 7in
ALL X Dress

1939

1941

1938

1942

1944

1945

1946

1947

1947

1950

1952

1954

There are clothes for early morning, clothes for shopping, clothes for every type of luncheon party, the early afternoon sitabout dress . . . a cocktail time dress, a little dinner-dress . . . the quiet evening dress. . . .

DORIS LANGLEY MOORE, *PANDORA'S LETTER BOX*

Too much of anything is bad, but too much Champagne is just right.

MARK TWAIN

Something about
glamour interested me.
All my schoolbooks
had drawings of women
on terraces with a cocktail
and a cigarette.

BILL BLASS

Let there be dancing in the streets, drinking in the saloons, and necking in the parlor.

GROUCHO MARX AS OTIS B. DRIFTWOOD
A NIGHT AT THE OPERA, 1935

The dress worn by a guest at a cocktail party should be scarcely décolleté at all, and should always be accompanied by a hat.

GENEVIEVE ANTOINE DARIAUX, ELEGANCE

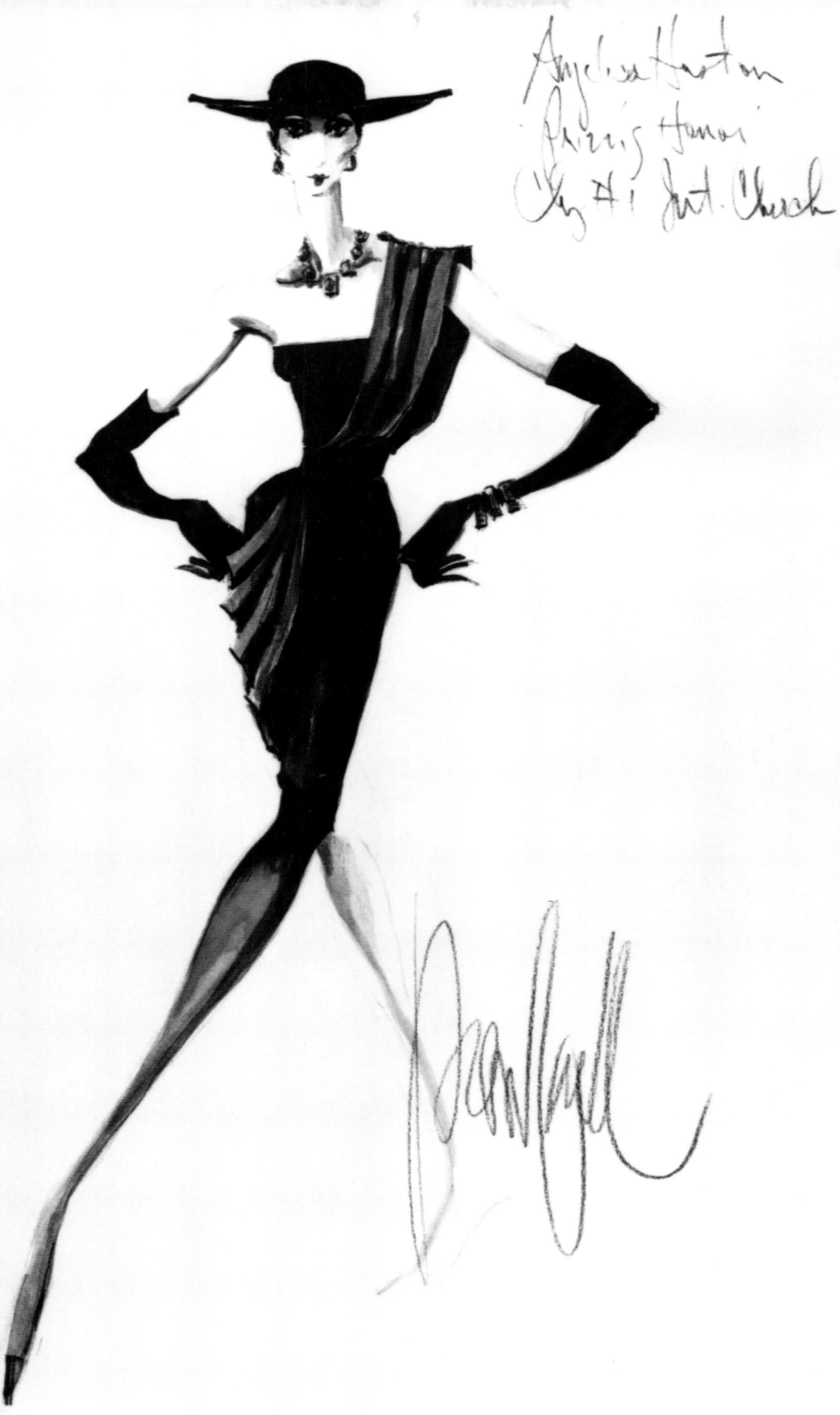
Angelica Huston
Prizzi's Honor
Chg #1 Int. Church

But in the world of smart society, clothes represent not only our ticket of admission, but our contribution to the effect of a party. What makes a brilliant party? Clothes. Good clothes.

EMILY POST, *ETIQUETTE*

ROBES DU SOIR, de JEANNE LANVIN

chez

MERCIE M^cHARDY

3, PRINCES STREET   et   240, OXFORD STREET
(OXFORD CIRCUS) LONDON W. 1.

We find that in the Twentys, a young lady full of grain alcohol had no corset to confine her, her skirt was above her knees normally, her stockings were rolled down and her hair Wind Blown, so that she was at all times in complete harmony with the natural activities of the period.

ANITA LOOS, "IT'S ALL A PLOT OF THE HAIRDRESSERS"

Sometimes she went to as many as three cocktail parties a day before heading home up the long and winding hill, driving herself in her Rolls-Royce to dress for whatever dinner was on that night.

DOMINICK DUNNE
THE WAY WE LIVED THEN: RECOLLECTIONS OF A WELL-KNOWN NAME DROPPER

It has become a well-established habit for women to drink cocktails. It is thought a smart thing to do.

THE BOSTON AMERICAN, MARCH 1910

catching fireflies

Cynth

Cocktail wear can be made of any fabric and be of almost any style design and still be appropriate.

ANNE FOGARTY, WIFE DRESSING

Samantha:
Frankly, I think it's sad, the way she's using a child to validate her existence.

Carrie:
Exactly. Why can't she just use sex and a nice cocktail like the rest of us?

SEX AND THE CITY, 1998

Black, in any case your cocktail dress, and of course you'll add the white note of your kid gloves.

ROLAND BARTHES, *THE FASHION SYSTEM*

There comes a time in every woman's life when the only thing that helps is a glass of champagne.

BETTE DAVIS AS KIT MARLOWE
OLD ACQUAINTANCE, 1943

THE
MARTINI

THE
MARTINI

THE
PIMMS
CUP

THE
GIMLET

THE
SIDECAR

COCKTAILS
WITH.
PETER SOM.
2008

ILLUSTRATION AND PHOTOGRAPHY CREDITS

GRACE KELLY IN *REAR WINDOW* (1954). Legendary costume designer Edith Head won more Academy Awards than any woman in history in the course of her career, which began in 1924 at Paramount. For Alfred Hitchcock's *Rear Window*, Head dressed Grace Kelly—who plays a socialite fashion editor—in a stunning New Look silhouette. *Photo: © Sunset Boulevard/ Corbis.*

THE ORIGINAL CHARLESTON, STARRING JOSEPHINE BAKER, C. 1926. The Charleston—a provocative-for-its-time dance most closely associated with the rebellious 1920s—originated in African-American communities and segued into the mainstream. Josephine Baker achieved instant succès de scandale in Paris in 1925 as part of La Revue Nègre. Later, she starred in her own show at the Folies-Bergère. *© Leonard de Selva/ CORBIS.*

ANN MILLING IN CHRISTIAN DIOR LONDON'S FEATHER-TRIMMED ORGANZA DRESS, 1967. Marc Bohan spent thirty-one years at Christian Dior. He began as the head of the London branch in 1958 and was named Creative Director in 1960. Rather than revolutionizing the house, Bohan's focus was on maintaining its tradition for ladylike elegant clothes, such as this swinging sixties number. *Photo: Wesley/ Getty Images.*

AUDREY HEPBURN IN GIVENCHY IN *BREAKFAST AT TIFFANY'S* (1961). "It was a warm evening, nearly summer and she wore a slim, cool black dress, black sandals, a pearl choker," wrote Truman Capote of Holly Golightly in his 1958 novella, *Breakfast at Tiffany's*. Who better than Hubert de Givenchy to give life to that vision? The designer's costumes, brought to life by Audrey Hepburn in the film, made Capote's character a touchstone of elegance. *Photo: Hulton Archive/ Getty Images.*

NEW LOOK, MONTMARTRE, PARIS 1999. Berlin-based fashion photographer Ralph Mecke captures fashion's obsession with vintage at the turn of the century in this image of a barefoot model casually wearing a structured New Look silhouette in a very unladylike pose. "Twisting" classics is a favorite trope of designers as varied as John Galliano and Miuccia Prada. *Photo: © Ralph Mecke.*

JOAN CRAWFORD IN AN ADRIAN DESIGN FOR SADIE MCKEE, 1934. Following the stock market crash in 1929, the linear, youth-centric silhouette of the Jazz Age gave way to a more mature and curvy one. Working in the 1930s, Adrian—a legendary costume designer at MGM, and later ready-to-wear designer—was known for "combining dramatic flair with subdued dignity." *Photo: Hulton Archive/Getty Images.*

QUERELLE JANSEN WEARS PRADA, FALL 2004. Miuccia Prada is often referred to as an "intellectual" designer. The house she runs "is said to be the most prominent example of a new form of inward-directed luxury." She described her Fall 2004 collection—which reconsidered fifties fashions—as expressing "romanticism between past and future." *Photo: Marcio Madeira.*

TWO MODELS IN CHRISTIAN DIOR, FEBRUARY 1951. The nip-waisted, full-skirted New Look silhouette pioneered by Christian Dior continued to dominate fashion in the fifties, but as fashion writer Caroline Rennolds Milbank notes, "It existed in tandem with a narrow, curvy style as well as a boxy look." However, it wasn't until the introduction of the sack dress in 1957 that the full-skirt hegemony was seriously threatened. *Photo: Gordon Parks/ Time & Life Pictures/Getty Images.*

LOUISE BROOKS, C. 1928. "She is so very Manhattan. Very young. Exquisitely hard-boiled. Her black eyes and sleek black hair are as brilliant as Chinese lacquer. Her skin as white as a camellia. Her legs are lyric," wrote Ruth Waterbury in *Photoplay* of Louise Brooks, the fetching, feckless, dissolute dancer-turned-actress. Brooks's signature was her fringed bob, the quintessential flapper 'do, and the subject of a 1920 short story by F. Scott Fitzgerald: *Bernice Bobs Her Hair*. *Photo: Frank Driggs Collection/Getty Images.*

PAUL NEWMAN AND ELIZABETH TAYLOR IN *CAT ON A HOT TIN ROOF* (1958). Chicagoan Helen Rose designed wedding dresses for Grace Kelly and Elizabeth Taylor, but it is this drape-front white chiffon cocktail dress, designed for *Cat on a Hot Tin Roof*, which launched her into the wholesale business, so great was the demand for it. (Even Taylor asked for one for her personal wardrobe.) *Photo: MGM Studios/ Courtesy of Getty Images.*

TWIGGY (LESLEY HORNBY) IN 1966. Just sixteen years old, five feet and six inches, and a mere ninety pounds, a waify Cockney young woman nicknamed Twiggy was named "The Face of '66" by *The Daily Express*. She was an overnight modeling sensation, at once Mod and androgynous, doll-like and droll. Twiggy, who has been called the first supermodel, became a symbol of sixties youth culture. *Photo: Popperfoto/Getty Images.*

NATASHA POLY WEARS BALENCIAGA BY NICOLAS GHESQUIÈRE, FALL 2008. Nicolas Ghesquière opened his Fall 2008 collection for Balenciaga with his take on that icon of fifties fashion—the cocktail dress—his vision of which was so austere, it is almost minimalist. Accessorized with weapon-sharp stilettos, the overall impression was one of savage grace. *Photo: Marcio Madeira.*

MODELS IN KASPER FOR JOAN LESLIE (LEFT) AND JOHN ANTHONY (RIGHT) WITH ESCORT, c. 1975. In 1971 in *The New Yorker*, Kennedy Fraser wrote that "cocktail dresses in sparkling materials—Lurex, brocade, sequins, and beaded embroideries—are around again, with all their potential vulgarity." The seventies might not have been the heyday of the cocktail dress, but these two little black dresses more than pass muster. *Photo: Bob Richardson/© Condé Nast Archive/CORBIS.*

BIANCA BALTI WEARS GIAMBATTISTA VALLI, FALL 2005. Giambattista Valli is a favorite with young socialites and celebrities. Katie Holmes, Eugenie Niarchos, Victoria Beckham, and Mary-Kate and Ashley Olsen are all huge fans. Why? As this sexy cocktail number demonstrates, Valli knows how to serve up la dolce vita glamour in spades. *Photo: firstview.com.*

IVANA AND DONALD TRUMP AT MORTIMER'S, NEW YORK CITY, MAY 11, 1988. "In the New York of the eighties, the Trumps were a force to be reckoned with," according to *Hello!* magazine—a very reputable source when it comes to socialites. An early fan of the pouf silhouette, Mrs. Trump was one of Christian Lacroix's first supporters. The drama—and the size—of these flowered sleeves is a testament to the "bigger is better" ethos of the time. *Photo: Ron Galella/WireImage.*

VERUSCHKA (VERA VON LENDORFF) IN *BLOW-UP* (1966). *Vogue*—whose cover she graced eleven times—called Verushcka (Vera von Lehndorff) "one of the wonders of the world." In 1966, the same year that a childlike Twiggy emerged on the scene, Veruschka did her first shoot wearing only body paint and played herself—quite seductively—in Michelangelo Antonioni's decadent and mysterious cult film *Blow-Up. Photo: Photofest.*

KATE MOSS, SEPTEMBER 2003. Kate Moss might not technically be the most photographed woman in the world, but she is an irresistible magnet for the camera. "I like creating images," she's said. One of her favorite "props" is a vintage or vintage-style dress, often with a twenties or fifties silhouette—as is the case with this yellow cocktail dress—that she always manages to take out of the past, making it feel totally current—and totally Kate. *Photo: James Devaney/WireImage.*

CHRIS BENZ, 2008. "Perfect imperfection" is Seattle transplant Chris Benz's motto. Trained at Parsons The New School of Design, Benz designed dresses and special-occasion wear before launching his eponymous line in 2007. Who does he design for? "An ageless sophisticate, a reckless preppy who desires nothing more than to 'keep dancing.'" *Illustration: Chris Benz specifically for The Cocktail Dress.*

SARAH JESSICA PARKER IN *SEX AND THE CITY* (2008). Sarah Jessica Parker's Carrie Bradshaw is a sex columnist with a closet as quirky as her personality. She's as likely to be wearing something street, like a gold script "Carrie" necklace or an Eiffel Tower–shaped bag, as something slinky like this gigantic flowered dress, a vintage floral cocktail dress, or something uptown from Oscar de la Renta—but always with Manolo Blahniks. *Photo: New Line Cinema/The Kobal Collection/ Craig Blankenhorn.*

GEMMA WARD WEARS GIVENCHY BY JULIEN MACDONALD, FALL 2004 No matter who is designing Givenchy, the brand's identity will always be informed by Hubert de Givenchy's relationship with ingénue Audrey Hepburn. For his final collection for Givenchy, Julien Macdonald embraced the house's history, showing truly chic, classic cocktail looks such as this bow-backed pearl gray dress. *Photo: Marcio Madeira.*

THE BLACK DRESS BY ALEX KATZ, 1960. Alex Katz's favorite model is his wife Ada, whom he painted in six poses next to a portrait of their friend the poet James Schuyler in 1960. Although Mrs. Katz has said that the dress was "nothing extraordinary," Leslie Camhi, writing in *The New York Times* in 2006, comments that this "picture of her in it summons a Platonic ideal of cocktail attire and comportment." *Art: © Alex Katz/Licensed by VAGA, New York, NY.*

KIM NOORDA WEARS VALENTINO HAUTE COUTURE, FALL 2007 Valentino Garavani not only lives the high life, but the Italian designer—who retired in 2007—spent his forty-five-year career designing dresses for it. Valentino, known especially for his glamorous occasion wear, counted Jacqueline Kennedy as a client as well as leading members of the jet set and glitterati. *Photo: Marcio Madeira.*

GIRLS IN THE WINDOWS, 1960. "A recent bride I know," Anne Fogarty recounts in *Wife Dressing,* "had a lopsided bachelor-girl wardrobe that consisted of Levis, baggy skirts, some collegiate-looking wools, and about 28 cocktail dresses." The implication is that a drinks party is good place to hook a husband. This photograph, shot during the workers' lunch break the day before the buildings were razed, includes photographer Gigli's own wife (second floor, far right). *Photo: © Ormond Gigli.*

PARIS *VOGUE* COVER, "LES MODES POUR L'AUTOMNE," JULY 1, 1926. Over time, the covers that the Spanish-born Benito contributed to *Vogue* and *Vanity Fair* became more Cubist, but this star-spangled example shows the artist working in the Art Deco style. It depicts a haughty, liberated woman in a flapper's pink fringed dress, who evidently—note the luxury yacht in the background—is going places. *Illustration: Eduardo Garcia Benito/Vogue © Condé Nast.*

MARILYN MONROE IN A PROMOTIONAL SHOT FOR *THE ASPHALT JUNGLE* (1950). "Miss Cheesecake of 1950" had a habit of turning heads, whether standing over a grate or poured into an inky cocktail number, as she is here in a promotional shot for *The Asphalt Jungle* (1950) that puts definite emphasis on the sexy starlet's décolletage and feminine curves. A simple strand of pearls completes the look. *Photo: Hulton Archive/Getty Images.*

ISAAC MIZRAHI, RIVIERA DRESS, RESORT 2009. How to capture summer in a collection? By evoking the Riviera, Cleopatra, caterpillars, and Creamsicles—in soft watercolor shades, as Isaac Mizrahi did for his Resort 2009 collection seen in these three images. "Color," he says, "is the most important luxury in a woman's life." *Illustration: Isaac Mizrahi.*

STILL NOT SURE. As the title of Ralph Mecke's moody photo—*Still Not Sure*—suggests getting ready to go out isn't always easy. But, opines Karl Silex, the German journalist and author of *John Bull at Home:* "The girl who can lay claim to a father in the City, three fine dogs, a horse, a Bentley sports car, and a young man to take her about in the evening is, of course beautifully dressed." *Photo: © Ralph Mecke.*

ISAAC MIZRAHI, RIVIERA DRESS, RESORT 2009. See above.

A BLACK TULLE EVENING DRESS BY ADRIAN, 1950. Adrian made the transition from full-time costume design to ready-to-wear in 1942 when he opened a boutique in Beverly Hills, California. In 1947, he told *Life* magazine that "American women's clothes should be streamlined in daytime, full of imagination at night." This evening dress, with its abbreviated length and tattered tiers, fulfills his mandate for the latter. *Photo: Genevieve Naylor/CORBIS.*

ISAAC MIZRAHI, RIVIERA DRESS, RESORT 2009. See above.

DESIGNS BY CRISTÓBAL BALENCIAGA, 1939–1954. In 1972, the year Cristóbal Balenciaga died, *Women's Wear Daily* proclaimed that the Spanish couturier was "the father of contemporary fashion . . . the father of tough chic . . . the father of great tailoring . . . the father of sure clothes." Here, renderings of some of his memorable designs during a fifteen-year period. *Illustration: Photofest.*

CHANEL IMAN WEARS OSCAR DE LA RENTA, FALL 2007. No one can design for an "Uptown Girl" (though downtown darlings like Sarah Jessica Parker have been known to succumb to the charms of his designs) quite like the Dominican-born Oscar de la Renta, who has been honing the well-heeled aesthetic since founding his own house in 1965. *Photo: Marcio Madeira.*

BIANCA JAGGER AT THE *VANITY FAIR* PARTY, FEBRUARY 29, 1988. Bianca Jagger plays the party animal in an animal-print ensemble. She—along with heiress Gloria Vanderbilt, novelist Jackie Collins, gossip columnist Liz Smith, and arriviste Princess Gloria von Thurn und Taxis—was among the glitterati that gathered to celebrate *Vanity Fair*'s fifth anniversary. It was a perfect eighties mix—one that could have been lifted from the pages of a Collins novel. *Photo: Ron Galella/WireImage.*

MODEL IN CHARLES JAMES FASHION SHOW, OCTOBER 1950. Charles James, the erratic Anglo-American perfectionist designer, produced less than 1,000 designs in forty-five years, yet his influence as a "sculptor" of fashion is lasting. James believed that "fashion in clothes was 'what is rare, correctly proportioned, and though utterly discreet, libidinous.' " *Photo: Eliot Elisofon/Time & Life Pictures/Getty Images.*

INÈS DE LA FRESSANGE WEARS CHANEL HAUTE COUTURE BY KARL LAGERFELD ON JANUARY 26, 1988. In 1983, Karl Lagerfeld was appointed chief designer for Chanel, which he catapulted into the powerhouse it is today. His method? Updating the house's classic DNA with pop culture references—from hip hop in 1991 to computers in Spring 2005. In this dress alone he daringly combined ladylike lace with graphic polka-dots—and tops it all off with a frilled hat. *Photo: © Pierre Vauthey/CORBIS SYGMA.*

GEOFFREY BEENE BY JOE EULA, C. 1995. Nineties fashion celebrated the body beautiful. In Paris, Azzedine Alaïa did it best, while in New York, the quiet American, Geoffrey Beene, opted for ballet dancers instead of models clad in his asymmetrically cut, pared-down modern designs. "Nothing is more admirable than the human body," he said in 1995. *Illustration: Joe Eula/Courtesy of a Private Collection.*

ARNOLD SCAASI ENSEMBLE, C. 1957. A recipient of the Council of Fashion Designers of America Lifetime Achievement Award in 1996, Arnold Scaasi, who dressed several First Ladies, was born in Canada. It's suggested that he changed his name from Isaacs to Scaasi to give it an "Italian flair." This voluminous polka-dot ensemble from 1957 screams chic in any language. *Photo: Courtesy of Arnold Scaasi.*

SARA SINGH ILLUSTRATION. "Like all social habits, entertaining has had a bearing on the clothes we wear. The cocktail dress did not exist until the cocktail party was invented, the short evening dress was dreamed up in the twenties for the new fun of night-clubbing, and the dinner dress was made for dinner parties," Brigid Keenan writes in *The Women We Wanted to Look Like*. Illustrator Sara Singh captures a decadent party mood in her emotive illustration. *Illustration: Sara Singh.*

COCKTAIL DRESSES BY RALPH LAUREN AND ISAAC MIZRAHI, JULY 1998. *Vogue* captures the celebratory spirit of occasion dressing in this lively photograph by Arthur Elgort featuring cocktail dresses by Ralph Lauren and Isaac Mizrahi—two very different but quintessentially American designers. *Photo: Arthur Elgort/Vogue © Condé Nast.*

COSTUME SKETCH BY DONFELD FOR ANJELICA HUSTON IN *PRITZI'S HONOR* (1985). Although Anjelica Huston won the Academy Award for Best Supporting Actress for her acting ability, the fact that she looked great definitely didn't hurt. The costume designer, Donfeld (a four-time Award nominee himself), costumed Huston in period looks like this asymmetrically draped cocktail number that had lines as sharp and striking as that of Huston's own beauty. *Illustration: Donfeld Lent by Mr. and Mrs. John Foreman/Photofest.*

GEOFFREY BEENE BY JOE EULA, SKETCH, c. 1995. Born in Louisiana, Geoffrey Beene studied medicine at Tulane University before changing course and opting for a career in fashion. Beene established his own house in 1963. The designer's knowledge of anatomy is evident in his body-conscious and precision-cut designs that combine severity and romance. *Illustration: Joe Eula/Courtesy of a Private Collection.*

LIFE COVER BY JOHN HELD, JR., FEBRUARY 18, 1926. The consummate Jazz Age artist John Held, Jr.'s, drawings of Betty Coed and Joe College—in other words, flappers and sheiks—are so indelible that they are said to have become "the quintessential definition of the decade's 'flaming' youth." This famous *Life* magazine cover, "Teaching old Dogs new tricks," depicts a PYT dancing the Charleston, of course. *Photo: MPI/Getty Images.*

BRUNA TENORIO WEARS JIL SANDER BY RAF SIMONS, SPRING 2007. Romance meets minimalism in this flowing purple cocktail dress designed by the Belgian Raf Simons for Jil Sander. "If I see a fashion show with literal influences, it doesn't make me think anymore. It doesn't make me dream. I fantasize about what the future could be in terms of aesthetic and psychology," Simons has said. *Photo: Marcio Madeira.*

THE DUCHESS OF WINDSOR IN VIONNET, c. 1945. "The spirit of our times has moved to more casual, easy-to-wear, functional fashions with straighter silhouettes; a streamlined svelte look—groomed to a high degree," Grace Margaret Morton wrote in *The Arts of Costume and Personal Appearance.* That's something that the strictly disciplined Duchess of Windsor understood, favoring the quietly patrician designs of Mainbocher and Madeleine Vionnet. *Photo: John Rawlings. © Condé Nast Archive/CORBIS.*

ROBES DU SOUR DE JEANNE LANVIN CHEZ MERCIE MCHARDY, ADVERTISEMENT FROM *LE GAZETTE DU BON TON,* 1920. In her heyday—the teens and twenties—milliner-turned-couturier Jeanne Lanvin was associated with mother-and-daughter dressing and with the fuller-skirted robe de style, inspired by eighteenth-century volumes. The Lanvin aesthetic was one of soft femininity expressed through soft color and delicate embellishments. *Photo: © Gianni Dagli Orti/CORBIS.*

PIERRE CARDIN SHEATH DRESS, 1964. "I was very lucky. I was part of the post-war period when everything had to be redone. Women wanted to party, to dance, to amuse themselves; there was a sexy side," said Pierre Cardin, who was head of tailoring *chez* Christian Dior when the New Look was launched in 1947. Three years later, Cardin went out on his own, and he made a name for himself with the bubble dress, Space Age fashions, and licensing. *Photo: Evening Standard/Getty Images.*

GEMMA WARD WEARS LANVIN BY ALBER ELBAZ, SPRING 2007. Greek draping met Space Age fascination in Alber Elbaz's Spring 2007 collection for Lanvin. "When you're stuck," he told fashion journalist Sarah Mower, "you go romantic. With freedom of spirit, you can go further. I wanted to touch technology, engineering, silicone, nylon, metal, and plastic. And a new place for the pragmatic." *Photo: Marcio Madeira.*

GENEVIEVE FATH IN JACQUES FATH, 1955. In 1954, designer Jacques Fath had sales second only to Christian Dior. His aristocratic wife, pictured here, modeled and had been a secretary to Gabrielle "Coco" Chanel. Hubert de Givenchy, who went to work for Fath in 1945, recalled the atmosphere of the house: "the air was perfumed," he said. "Everyone talked loudly, called each other by first names, kissed each other and then called each other 'Cheri . . . my pet.'" *Photo: John Chillingworth/Picture Post/Getty Images.*

ALEXANDER TEREXOV COCKTAIL DRESS, FALL 2007. Emerging markets may well be dominating fashion speak since the turn of the century, but few designers from Russia, China, or India have had much crossover appeal yet. The exception might be the subtle, sophisticated line designed by twenty-something Yves Saint Laurent–trained Russian prodigy Alexander Terexhov, who names Halston as his favorite American designer. *Illustration: Alexander Terexov, Courtesy of a Private Collection.*

ACTRESS LYNN FONTANNE WEARING CALLOT SOEURS, c. 1925. Lynn Fontanne, who pioneered naturalism in the theater with husband Alfred Lunt, poses in a streamlined dress by Callot Soeurs, a Parisian couture house founded by four sisters. Madeleine Vionnet, who trained there, said: "Without the example of the Callot sisters, I would have continued to make Fords. It is because of them that I have been able to make Rolls-Royces." *Photo: Edward Steichen for Vogue © Condé Nast Archive/CORBIS.*

MARIACARLA BOSCONO WEARS CHRISTIAN DIOR HAUTE COUTURE, FALL 2007. "Elegance is good taste plus a dash of daring," said Carmel Snow, the editor of *Harper Bazaar*, who rechristened Christian Dior's Corolle line the New Look. This nipped-waist look was shown at the Orangerie at Versailles, where the house's sixty-year anniversary was celebrated with an extravagance worthy of a Sun King. *Photo: imaxtree.com/Alessandro Lucioni.*

BRUNA SOTTILI WEARS MARC JACOBS, SPRING 2008. Praised by *The New York Times*'s critic Cathy Horyn for "offer[ing] an antidote to the cartoonish Jessica Rabbit sexuality," Marc Jacobs's Spring 2008 show—which was presented backward, starting with the designer's bow—in the designer's own words, was a parade of "cartoon versions of all the women I know—conservative types, vamps, everybody." *Photo: Marcio Madeira.*

PORTRAIT OF THE JOURNALIST SYLVIA VON HARDEN BY OTTO DIX, 1926. Otto Dix, the German painter, was a pioneer of the Neue Sachlichkeit (New Objectivity) movement, which was "dedicated to realistic painting that aimed to expose the corrupt nature of modern life." It is said that when Dix spotted the monocled lesbian journalist Sylvia von Harden in Berlin, he ran after her, "saying that he must paint her because she represented their era." *Art: © 2008 Artists Rights Society (ARS), New York/VG Bild-Kunst, Bonn.*

SNEJANA ONOPKA WEARS YVES SAINT LAURENT BY STEFANO PILATI, SPRING 2007. "Whatever your sexuality, fashion is female," Yves Saint Laurent Creative Director Stefano Pilati told *The New York Times*'s Lynn Hirschberg in 2008. "I know I sound contradictory, but even as a gay man, with women, my intent is in refining the curve of the female form." *Photo: Marcio Madeira.*

CAROLINE TRENTINI WEARS ZAC POSEN, SPRING 2007. Zac Posen is something of a fashion prodigy; he was just twenty-two at the time of his 2002 debut. *The New York Times* fashion critic Cathy Horyn has not only described Posen as "the embodiment of the new fixation on youth," but attributed Posen's success to his "flirty dresses with a slight attic quality." *Photo: Marcio Madeira.*

CYNTHIA ROWLEY, 2008. "In his blue gardens men and girls came and went like moths among the whisperings and the champagne and the stars," relates the narrator of F. Scott Fitzgerald's 1925 novel, *The Great Gatsby.* Cynthia Rowley's social butterflies, in their pastel mini dresses, update Jazz Age glamour for today. *Illustration: Cynthia Rowley specifically for* The Cocktail Dress.

SHALOM HARLOW WEARS MARC JACOBS, FALL 2007. Fashion "is always about today," Marc Jacobs told *The New York Times*. "For me, whether there are retro references or not, it's not nostalgic, they're just clothes." There wasn't a trace of grunge in his Fall 2007 collection, which the designer described as having "polish, finish, refinement, restraint, chic." *Photo: Marcio Madeira.*

MODEL IN A PACO RABANNE–STYLE DRESS, c. 1966. Trained as an architect, Paco Rabanne sold jewelry to couturiers such as Balenciaga and Givenchy before debuting his first fashion designs—which he called "the unwearables"—in 1965. He opened his own house the following year and became known for metal-linked (plastic-disc) dresses of which Françoise Hardy was a notable fan. *Photo: David McCabe/© Condé Nast Archive/CORBIS.*

MARIACARLA BOSCONO WEARS DOLCE & GABBANA, SPRING 2004. "Much of [Dolce & Gabbana's] signature look came from their homages to Italian movies," comments Mark Holgate in *New York* magazine in 2004 on the occasion of the designing duo's twentieth anniversary. Dolce & Gabbana might play with Italian stereotypes—like that of the black-clad Sicilian widow—but they never fail to pour on the glamour. *Photo: Marcio Madeira.*

AUDREY MARNAY PHOTOGRAPHED FOR *VOGUE*, MARCH 1999. Edouard Manet's last well-known painting, *A Bar at the Folies-Bergère* (1882), is an exemplar of his belief in "contemporary realism." It is somewhat ironic, then, that this 1999 *Vogue* shoot, which places Gaultier Paris haute couture in a constructed historical context, seems to have been inspired by a painting so shockingly modern for its time. *Photo: Arthur Elgort/Vogue © Condé Nast.*

ANNA MARIYA URAZHEVSKAYA WEARS GIAMBATTISTA VALLI, FALL 2007. Giambattista Valli, the Paris-based Roman designer, is a favorite among such paparazzi favorites as Victoria Beckham (for whom he named a sexy platform shoe) and Mischa Barton. This dress, with its bold, off-the-shoulder ruffle and graphic color blocking, hints at Valli's training at the house of Roberto Capucci. *Photo: Marcio Madeira.*

JUDITH BEDARD WEARS MALANDRINO, FALL 2008. A French expatriate, Catherine Malandrino moved to New York to work as a head designer for Diane von Furstenberg. Malandrino—who launched her own line in 1998—has had her work featured on *Sex and the City*, which makes perfect sense as her flattering draped dresses, like this one, combine classical technique with an assured, assertive sexuality. *Photo: Wendelien Daan/Courtesy of Malandrino.*

ROBES POUR L'ÉTÉ, 1920. Raoul Dufy was a truly multimedia artist, especially in the area of decorative arts. It was Paul Poiret who launched Dufy's career as a textile designer, working Dufy's "sumptuous" prints into striking fashions. Dufy went on to work with France's leading silk manufacturer, Bianchini-Férier et Cie., from 1912 to 1928. This panorama features the firm's silks worked into summer style by French houses. *Illustration: Raoul Dufy for* La Gazette du Bon Ton. *Courtesy of a Private Collection.*

RONALD PATERSON "NEW LOOK"–STYLE COCKTAIL DRESS AND HAT, 1955. Christian Dior's revolutionary New Look remained popular throughout the fifties. Copies made the style available everywhere and at all price levels. This elegant Dioresque cocktail dress and hat were designed by Ronald Paterson, who opened his own couture house in London in 1947. *Photo: Kurt Hutton/Getty Images.*

SEX AND THE CITY. Broadcast from 1998-2004, HBO's hit series *Sex and the City* offered escapism through friendship, refreshments, and fashion. Styled by Patricia Field, the characters' clothes were supplied by established designers like Oscar de la Renta and Vivienne Westwood, as well as emerging talents like Miguel Adrover and Pierrot. The D&G store in Manhattan's Soho was as an important "set" for the show as the offices of *Vogue*. *Photo: Darren Star Productions/The Kobal Collection.*

UNTITLED FROM *MEN IN THE CITIES* SERIES BY ROBERT LONGO, c. 1981 "The artist of the eighties" is the mantle bestowed upon Brooklyn-born artist Robert Longo, largely on the merit of his *Men in the Cities* series of full-length portraits of men and women in contorted poses. Fashion played a deliberate part in their conception; as Longo stated in an interview: "I'm picking an archetypal uniform or costume. Men wear suits, shirts and ties, and women wear dresses...." *Photo: © Christie's Images/CORBIS.*

SUPPER BY LÉON BAKST, 1902. Léon Bakst, the Russian Jewish painter and artistic director of the Ballets Russes, was renowned for his Orientalist sets and costumes, which had deep repercussions in the world of fashion—especially on the influential French couturier Paul Poiret. *Supper,* painted by Bakst in 1902, hints at none of this, depicting instead the voluptuous fin de siècle S-curve from which Poiret—among others—claims to have liberated women. *Photo: © The Gallery Collection/CORBIS.*

PETER SOM, 2008. In *American Language,* published in 1921, H. L. Mencken wrote: "In the department of conviviality the imaginativeness of Americans was shown both in the invention and in the naming of new and often highly complex beverages." In this delightful drawing, Peter Som imagines some of those libations, like the sidecar, as intoxicatingly lovely cocktail dresses. *Illustration: Peter Som specifically for* The Cocktail Dress.

BIBLIOGRAPHY

PUBLISHED SOURCES

Angeletti, Norberto and Alberto Oliva. *Vogue: The Illustrated History of the World's Most Famous Fashion Magazine*. New York: Rizzoli International Publications, Inc., 2006

Arlen, Michael. *"Piracy": A Romantic Chronicle of These Days*. New York: George H. Doran Company, 1923.

Armitage, Shelley. *John Held, Jr.: Illustrator of the Jazz Age*. New York: Syracuse University Press, 1987.

Barthes, Roland. *The Fashion System*. Translated by Matthew Ward and Richard Howard. Berkeley: University of California Press, 1990.

Beaton, Cecil. *The Glass of Fashion*. Garden City, NY: Doubleday, 1954.

Blum, Silys E. *Shocking! The Art and Fashion of Elsa Schiaparelli*. Philadelphia: Philadelphia Museum of Art, 2003.

Daché, Lily. *Lilly Daché's Glamour Book*. Edited by Dorothy Roe Lewis. New York: J.B. Lippincott Company, 1956.

Dariaux, Geneviève Antoine. *Elegance: A Complete Guide for Every Woman Who Wants to Be Well and Properly Dressed on All Occasions*. Garden City, NY: Doubleday & Company, Inc., 1964.

Dior, Christian. *Dior by Dior: The Autobiography of Christian Dior*. Translated by Antonia Fraser. London: V&A Publications, 2007.

————. *The Little Dictionary of Fashion*. New York: Abrams, 2007.

Dunne, Dominick. *The Way We Lived Then: Recollections of a Well-Known Name Dropper*. New York: Crown Publishers, 1999.

Eliot, Thomas Stearns. *T.S. Eliot: The Complete Poems and Plays 1909–1950*. New York: Harcourt, Brace and Company, 1952.

Fitzgerald, F. Scott. *The Great Gatsby*. New York: First Scribner Classic/Collier Edition, 1986.

Fogarty, Anne. *Wife Dressing: The Fine Art of Being a Well-Dressed Wife*. New York: Julian Messner, Inc., 1959.

Frasier, Kennedy. *The Fashionable Mind*. Boston: David R. Godine, Publisher, Inc., 1985.

Harriman, Margaret Case. *And the Price Is Right*. Illustrated by Roy Doty. New York: The World Publishing Company, 1958.

————. *Blessed Are the Debonair*. New York: Rinehart and Company, 1956.

Hawes, Elizabeth. *Anything but Love: A Complete Digest of the Rules for Feminine Behavior from Birth to Death*. New York: Rhinehart & Company Inc., 1948.

Head, Edith with Joe Hyams. *How to Dress for Success*. New York: Random House, 1967.

Herford, Oliver. *The Deb's Dictionary: The Essential A to Z Guide for the Aspiring Debutante*. New York: Welcome Books, 2007.

Keenan, Brigid. *The Women We Wanted to Look Like*. New York: St. Martin's Press, 1978.

Kimball, Robert, ed. *Cole Porter: Selected Lyrics*. New York: The Library of America, 2006.

Loos, Anita. *Fate Keeps on Happening: Adventures of Lorelei Lee and Other Writings*. New York: W. Clement Stone, P M A Communications, Incorporated, 1984.

Mencken, H. L. *The American Language: An Inquiry into the Development of English in the United States*. New York: Alfred A. Knopf, 1937.

Milbank, Caroline Rennolds. *New York Fashion: The Evolution of American Style*. New York: Harry N. Abrams, 1989.

Moore, Doris Langley. *Pandora's Letter Box: Being a Discourse on Fashionable Life*. London: Gerald Howe, 1929.

Morton, Grace Margaret. *The Arts of Costume and Personal Appearance*. New York: John Wiley & Sons, Inc., 1948.

Post, Emily. *Etiquette: In Society, in Business, in Politics and at Home*. New York: Funk & Wagnalls Company, 1924.

————. *Etiquette: The Blue Book of Social Usage*. New York: Funk & Wagnalls Company, 1932, 1949, 1955.

————. *How to Behave—Though a Débutante: Opinions by Muriel Overheard by Emily Post*. Illustrated by John Held Jr. Garden City, NY: Doubleday, Doran & Company, Inc., 1928.

Tomkins, Calvin. *Living Well Is the Best Revenge*. New York: The Modern Library, 1998.

Watt, Judith, ed. *The Penguin Book of Twentieth-Century Fashion Writing*. London: The Penguin Group, 1999.

Wilson, Angus and Philippe Jullian. *For Whom the Cloche Tolls: A Scrap-Book of the Twenties*. London: Methuen, 1953.

Worsley, Harriet. *The Hulton Getty Picture Collection: Decades of Fashion*. Cologne: Könemann, 2000.

WEB SOURCES

http://www.citypaper.net/articles/022802/nc.cocktail.shtml
http://encarta.msn.com/encnet/refpages/RefArticle.aspx?refid=761560565
http://findarticles.com/p/articles/mi_qa3724/is_20070331/ai_n18781289
http://www.infomat.com/whoswho/miucciaprada.html
http://oed.com
http://www.style.com/fashionshows/review/F2004RTW-PRADA

The Longest Whale Song

www.**kidsatrandomhouse**.co.uk

Jacqueline Wilson

The Longest Whale Song

ILLUSTRATED BY
NICK SHARRATT

DOUBLEDAY

If you would like to find out more about whales
and dolphins, please visit www.wdcs.org.uk

THE LONGEST WHALE SONG
A DOUBLEDAY BOOK
HARDBACK: 978 0 385 61815 1
TRADE PAPERBACK: 978 0 857 53005 9

Published in Great Britain by Doubleday,
an imprint of Random House Children's Books
A Random House Group company

This edition published 2010

3 5 7 9 10 8 6 4 2

The Random House Group Limited supports the Forest Stewardship
Council (FSC), the leading international forest certification organization.
All our titles that are printed on Greenpeace-appproved FSC-certified paper
carry the FSC logo. Our paper procurements policy can be found at
www.rbooks.co.uk/environment.

Mixed Sources
Product group from well-managed
forests and other controlled sources
www.fsc.org Cert no. TT-COC-2139
© 1996 Forest Stewardship Council
FSC

Set in 13/17pt Century Schoolbook by
Falcon Oast Graphic Art Ltd.

RANDOM HOUSE CHILDREN'S BOOKS
61–63 Uxbridge Road, London W5 5SA

www.**kids**at**randomhouse**.co.uk
www.**rbooks**.co.uk

Addresses for companies within The Random House Group Limited
can be found at www.randomhouse.co.uk/offices.htm

THE RANDOM HOUSE GROUP Limited Reg. No. 954009

A CIP catalogue for this book is available from the British Library.

Printed and bound by Clays Ltd, St Ives plc

*For dear June
and Georgie and Max,
Gabby, Emma and Joel,
and Anna and Georgina*

Chapter 1

'Why don't you come and help me with my breathing, Ella?' says Mum.

I stare at her. 'You don't need help *breathing*, Mum! You just do it. Like, in and out, in and out!'

'No, this is special breathing, darling. For when I have the baby.'

I wrinkle my nose. I don't really like it when she talks about the baby. I just want to forget about it. It's getting harder and harder, though, because Mum's e-n-o-r-m-o-u-s. Her tummy sticks out so far she can hardly get her T-shirt over it. I can see her tummy button through the material and it makes me shudder. When I was very, very little, I thought that was how babies were born: you just pressed the button and the tummy opened, and out popped the baby.

I wish they really were born that way. I haven't seen a real baby being born but I've seen actresses pretending on the television. They shout and scream a lot and go bright red in the face.

'Does having a baby really hurt a lot, Mum?' I ask.

'Mm, quite a lot,' says Mum. 'That's why I do the special breathing. It helps control the pain.' She holds out her hand to me. 'Come and lie on my bed with me and I'll show you.'

I hesitate. I hate going into Mum's bedroom now. It's not just hers. It's Mum-and-Jack's, and I can't stand Jack. But it's Saturday afternoon, and Jack's out at his stupid football so Mum and I can have a bit of peace together. We used to go to Flowerfields shopping centre or for a walk round Berrisford Park, but Mum's too tired to do anything much now. Imagine wanting to spend a Saturday afternoon *breathing*.

'Please, Ella,' she says softly.

I sigh and take her hand and go to her bedroom with her, because I love her so much, even though I'm still cross with her for marrying Jack.

I used to love Mum's bedroom back at our old flat. It always smelled beautifully of her scent and her soap and her hair stuff. It looked so pretty too. She had a red lampshade that made the whole room glow rose. She dangled her necklaces on her mirror and hung her prettiest dresses on the door and outside her wardrobe, so that it looked like there were Mums all around the room. She had deep pink velvet curtains right down to the floor. I used to like sitting beside them and stroking them, rubbing them over my nose like a comfort blanket. She had matching pink velvet cushions on her bed and a lovely rose-patterned duvet where we'd cuddle up together.

We hardly ever cuddle up together now because of Jack. This is a horrible, boring blue bedroom and it smells of *him*. Mum doesn't wear her perfume now because she says the smell makes her feel queasy. Well, Jack's lemony aftershave and the musty smell of his stupid short dressing gown hanging on the door make *me* feel queasy. But I lie down on the bed beside Mum, glad that I'm on *her* side, my head on *her* soft pillow. Mum's huge tummy sticks out ahead of us. It seems to grow a little more every time I look at it. If we lay here for a couple of days, maybe it would bump right up against the ceiling.

'You're so *big*, Mum,' I say.

'Don't you think I've noticed!' says Mum, rubbing her tummy. 'Still, not long now. So let's practise. When the baby starts coming, I have to do slow, steady breathing. Let's do that first.' She breathes slowly in and out, and I copy her, both of us blowing through our lips as if we're cooling giant bowls of soup.

'It's easy-peasy, isn't it?' says Mum. She chuckles. 'I think the baby's practising too – feel.'

I reach out gingerly and lay my hand very lightly on top of Mum's tummy. I can feel fluttering underneath, as if the baby is blowing bubbles inside. It's so weird to think it's swimming away in there all the time.

'Can it hear us?' I whisper.

'I think so,' says Mum. 'Why don't you have a little chat?'

I prop myself up on one elbow and put my mouth

close to Mum's tummy. 'Hello, baby. I'm Ella, your big sister. Well, not your *proper* sister. Your half-sister.'

'Which half do you want to be, top or bottom?' says Mum. 'You'll be a *whole* sister, you noodle. The baby's very, very lucky to have the best girl in all the world for a sister.'

If Mum thinks I'm the best girl in all the world, why does she want another child? Why does she want a husband, especially one like Jack? She always said she didn't miss my dad at all – she didn't care that he left us when I was a baby myself. She said she was glad we were just the two of us together. But now there are three, and very, very soon there are going to be four. What if she goes *on* having babies, filling the house with little miniature Jacks, all of them loud and laughing and making rude noises?

'I do hope the baby's a girl,' I say. 'Why didn't you ask if it was a boy or a girl when you went to the hospital for that scan thing?'

'I don't want to know. It'll spoil the surprise,' says Mum, rubbing her tummy. 'I don't mind which I have, and you won't either, not when it's born. Now, when the pain gets stronger, you do a different sort of breathing – lots of little pants, like this . . .' She makes funny quick puffing sounds, so I do too.

'Does panting like this *really* stop it hurting?' I ask.

'It's supposed to help. Perhaps it just acts as a distraction. Oh well, I'll have Jack there to distract me too.'

'Why can't *I* come?'

'Oh, darling, you don't want to be around.'

'Yes I do!'

'I don't think the hospital would let you.'

'I wish you didn't have to go to the hospital, Mum.'

'I won't be there long, I promise. Jack will drive me there when the baby starts coming, while you stay with Liz. She'll bring you to see me the next day – and then it'll be time for me to come home, right?'

'Mm. I still can't see why Jack gets to stay with you at the hospital and I can't.'

'They don't let children hang around when babies are being born, you know that.'

'The babies themselves are children. The baby will be hanging around.' *For ever*, I add mournfully, inside my head.

Mum gently pinches my nose. 'Don't be difficult, Ella,' she says.

I suck my lips in tight so that my mouth disappears. She's only started calling me difficult this past year, since she went to Garton Road and met Jack. *He's* the one who's made everything difficult.

Mum's friend Liz says it was a whirlwind romance. I think that's rubbish. It's stupid and disgusting for grown-up, quite old people like Mum and Jack to start fooling around like teenagers. Especially as they're *teachers*. Not at my school, thank goodness. I would have totally died of embarrassment if Mum and Jack taught at Greenfield Primary. I can just imagine all the rumours and gossip and giggling at Garton Road when Mum and Jack started going out together. What if anyone saw them holding hands along the corridor or kissing in a classroom?

Mum says they always acted perfectly professionally and were very discreet. They certainly *weren't* discreet when Jack started coming round to our flat every wretched weekend. I hated the way they snuggled up together on the sofa. One time I walked into the room and they were kissing in this awful slurpy way.

They must have done more than kissing at some stage, because suddenly Mum started being sick before we went to school in the morning and I got really worried that she had some awful illness. I couldn't *believe* it when she said she was going to have a baby.

Then everything *really* started changing. Mum and Jack decided we all had to live together. I wasn't asked, I was just *told*. Our flat wasn't big enough for three and a bit people, and neither was Jack's, so they sold their flats and bought this house together.

I don't like it one bit. It's miles away from my old home and my best friend, Sally. We used to live just round the corner from each other and could play any time we wanted. Now we have to wait for our mums to arrange things and drive us. It takes ages for Mum to drive me to school and we get caught up in the traffic. I've been late four times this term and I got really told off, and it's not *my* fault. I have to wait an awfully long time for Mum to finish at her school and come and pick me up in the afternoon. I did start going to after-school club, but it felt weird not having Sally with me. There's this girl, Martha, who bosses everyone around and is very mean to you if you don't do exactly what she says. Thank goodness Mum said I didn't have to go to after-school club any more after that first week.

Jack says I should swap schools altogether and go to Garton Road. I never ever want to go there, thank you. Mum says she understands, and I don't have to. I only do what Mum tells me. I don't listen to Jack, because he's not my dad.

I suppose he *is* my stepdad now, because Mum and Jack got married. I always fancied being a bridesmaid. Sally's been a bridesmaid *three* times. She got to wear a pink silk dress with rosebuds, a deep blue dress with matching deep blue satin dance shoes, and an apricot dress with a pearl trim and a little string of real pearls around her neck. *And* she was a flower girl when she was very little, in a white dress with a coral satin sash. I didn't want Mum to get married, especially not to Jack, but I hoped at least I'd get to be a bridesmaid at last. But they didn't have a proper wedding at all.

'I don't think I'd fit into a white meringue gown,' Mum said, because she was already getting big with the baby.

She wore a pale grey dress with a red ribbon trim, and bright red shoes. Jack laughed and called her his scarlet woman. He just wore the suit he keeps for parents' evenings, and he got a stain on his new blue tie at the meal in the pub afterwards. They didn't *have* a bridesmaid as it was just a register-office wedding.

Mum said I could have a new dress all the same. We went all round Flowerfields shopping centre looking for one. We couldn't find any that were right. They were either much too little-girly, all frilly and flouncy, or much too cool and slinky. I quite wanted one of the cool, slinky dresses, but Mum said she wasn't having me looking like I was going out clubbing. So I ended up with this black and white polka-dot dress with a bow at the back, and black patent strappy shoes. I'd always longed for a black dress because I thought it would look so grown up – but I wasn't sure about black with white spots.

'Oh, look, it's a lovely little Dalmatian!' said Jack.

I nearly kicked him with my new black patent shoes. He gave me a present after the wedding: three little silver bangles. I loved the way they looked, so sleek and shiny. I loved the way they felt, sliding up and down my arm. I loved the way they sounded, *clink clink clink*. I haven't actually worn them since the wedding day. I don't want to, because Jack gave them to me.

It was a very *little* wedding. Mum's parents died before I was born so I don't have a granny or a grandad. I suppose I've got my *dad's* parents, but we don't ever see them. I haven't seen my dad for ages. He always sends me Christmas presents, though they're usually a bit young for me. He doesn't always remember my birthday.

Jack's parents came to the wedding. His mum was wearing a very tight shiny dress and talked all the time. His dad was in a wheelchair and didn't talk at all. I didn't like either of them much and I don't think they liked me.

'That little miss hasn't got much to say for herself, has she?' said Jack's mum. 'Looks a bit sulky, if you ask me.'

'Our Ella's a little star, and bright as a button,' said Jack.

I didn't want *him* to stick up for me. And I'm not *his* Ella. I'm just Mum's.

She invited her best friend, Liz, to the wedding, and some of the teachers from Garton Road. Jack had a couple of silly mates, but there were only thirteen of us at the wedding.

'Oh dear, unlucky thirteen,' said Jack's mum.

'Hang on, there's *fourteen* of us counting the baby,' said Mum, patting her tummy.

They went away for a honeymoon weekend to London.

'That's not fair, Mum,' I said. 'I want to go to London too. You've been promising for ages we could go to the Aquarium and the Natural History Museum and on the London Eye.'

'Yes, I know, darling, but we're not *going* to those places. This is just a tiny little honeymoon. We're going to stay overnight in a hotel and maybe go out for a meal, that's all. I promise we'll go to all your special places another time, in the holidays.'

They might not have gone to the Aquarium or the Natural History Museum, but they *did* go on the London Eye – I saw their photos. It was so mean of them to go without me. *I* wanted to go up on the giant wheel and see out all over London and pretend I was flying. Sally's been on the London Eye and she says it's brilliant.

I had to stay at Liz's flat. She's OK, but she doesn't really know much about children. She made us spag bol *and* pancakes for tea, which was double-yummy, and then she opened this big box of chocolates and said I could eat as many as I wanted. So I did, and then I felt really, really sick in the night.

I couldn't sleep properly anyway, because we'd watched this horribly scary DVD about people in a haunted house. I told her I'd watched it heaps of times already and she believed me. I wanted to show off to Sally that I'd seen a real 18 movie – but I so wished I hadn't when I went to bed on Liz's sofa. Every time I closed my eyes I felt I was in that haunted house and the ghosts were about to get me.

Liz slept ever so late on Sunday morning. I didn't like to switch on the television in case it woke her up. I'd brought a Tracy Beaker book with me, but I only had twenty pages to go and I finished it too quickly. *Tracy* wouldn't stand for her mum getting married. I had a good look through the big fat paperbacks on Liz's bookshelf, but they all seemed to be about stupid women wanting to meet men. I didn't want to read about *that*. So I just lay there on the sofa for *hours*, missing Mum.

I cuddle up closer to her now, on the bed.

'We never got to go to the Aquarium and the Natural History Museum and the London Eye in the holidays, Mum. Can we go today?'

'There's not time now, love.'

'Next Saturday then?'

'I'm too tired for a long day out in London at the moment, sweetheart. I promise we'll go in a few weeks, when I've had the baby.'

'But then you'll have to push the baby buggy, and it'll keep crying, and needing to be fed and changed and all that stuff.'

'No, no, we'll leave the baby with its daddy for the day,' says Mum.

'Oh! OK then! So Jack's going to look after the baby too?'

'Of course he is. Even though he hasn't got a clue about babies. He doesn't even know which end the nappy goes on!'

'Really?'

'He'll find out soon enough. He's very keen. He bought a giant Lego set the other day. I'm sure he thinks the baby's going to be sitting up and making plastic planes and cars by the time it's six months old.'

'Jack is so silly,' I say happily. I'm starting to hope the baby *will* be a little boy. Then he can play with Jack all the time while Mum and I do stuff together.

I reach out and gently pat Mum's huge tummy. 'Hello, baby. Are you a boy or a girl?' I ask it.

I can feel it kicking as if it's trying to answer me.

'I might be a boy. I might be a girl. You'll just have to wait and see,' Mum says, in a teeny baby voice.

I laugh and Mum laughs, and her tummy wobbles as if the baby is clutching its sides and laughing too.

'Did I kick like that when I was in your tummy, Mum?' I ask.

'You kicked, but not like this baby. It seems so big and strong. Maybe we'll have to call him Samson if he's a boy,' Mum says. Her voice is a bit gaspy and she clutches her huge tummy.

'Oh, Mum, is it really kicking you so hard that it hurts?' I ask.

'No, it's not the kicking. My tummy just felt funny.'

'What kind of funny?'

'I'm not sure. It's OK again now. Let's cuddle up and have a little nap, eh?'

She can't curl around me because the big bump of the baby gets in the way. I curl around her instead.

'You're like a big mother whale,' I say, patting her.

'Thanks a bunch,' says Mum.

We settle down and I very nearly go to sleep, but then I notice Mum is breathing in that slow, funny way again.

'You're practising your breathing, Mum!' I say.

'I'm doing it for real, sweetheart. I think the baby's started to come,' says Mum.

I sit bolt upright, terrified. 'Oh, Mum! What shall I do? How will we get you to hospital? Jack's not here to drive you!'

'It's OK, don't panic! We don't have to do anything for ages and ages. You took a whole day to be born. I'm sure this baby will be the same. We'll have a cup of tea and then we'll sort out our suitcases. Mine's already packed with a new nightie and a set of baby clothes. We'll just have to get yours sorted, with your pyjamas and washing things and a book to read.'

'I'll need heaps of books. It's ever so boring at Aunty Liz's.'

'Well, it's very good of her to offer to have you. She's not really into children.'

I'm not sure *I* am either. I don't ever want to have a baby. Mum keeps saying she's fine, but every now and then she clutches her tummy, and she's started to close her eyes and groan.

For the first time ever, I'm glad when Jack gets home.

'Oh, Jack,' Mum says. She puts her arms round him and hugs him hard.

'Hello, my Super-Sue. This is a lovely welcome,' he says, kissing her.

He waggles his fingers at me. 'Have you two girls been having fun?' he asks.

'The baby's coming!' I say.

'What? Really? You should have phoned me,' he says. 'Oh my goodness, sit down, Sue. Or should you lie down? Or shall I take you straight to the hospital?' He's in a right state, as if he's terrified too.

'Stop flapping, Jack, I'm fine! Ella and I are all packed. I've phoned Liz and told her we'll drop Ella off on the way to the hospital. But we don't need to go for ages yet.' Mum breaks off, clutching her tummy and gasping.

Jack puts his arm round her, staring at her anxiously. She does her breathing, in and out, in and out.

When she straightens up at last, she goes, 'Phew!' and pulls a funny face.

'We're going to the hospital *right now*,' says Jack firmly. 'Come on, Ella!'

Chapter 2

It takes me ages to get to sleep at Liz's. I keep thinking of poor Mum in pain in the hospital, breathing in and out, in and out, in and out. I breathe along with her, keeping her company long distance.

I get up to go to the loo, and Liz calls out from her bedroom. 'Are you all right, Ella?'

'Yes. Maybe. No,' I say, and start to cry.

Liz gets up and comes to find me. She stands awkwardly in front of me. 'Oh dear. Are you crying?'

'No.'

'Silly question. And silly answer,' she says, and she puts her arms round me.

I howl all over Liz's silk pyjamas while she pats my back and strokes my hair.

'I want Mum,' I wail.

'I know. But she's otherwise engaged right now.'

'She will be all right, won't she, Liz?'

'Of course. Come on, Ella, she's not ill, she's simply having a baby. Millions and millions and millions of women have babies all over the world all the time.'

'Yes, but sometimes they get ill too. Sometimes they *die*,' I sob.

'Stop it now. Your mum will be absolutely fine. She's maybe even had the baby already.'

'No – Jack said he'd phone us.'

'But he wouldn't phone in the middle of the night, sweetie. Which it is. Now, let's find you some tissues, because you're using my PJs like a giant hankie.'

19

I mop myself up while Liz puts the kettle on.

'We'll have a cup of camomile tea. That will make us both sleepy,' she says.

Camomile tea is *disgusting*. I don't like to say anything because Liz is trying to be really kind to me – but she sees my face.

'Would you sooner have real tea? What do children like to drink? I know, hot chocolate!'

I don't really want hot chocolate either, but she makes it specially. I lick all the frothy cream off the top. Liz sips her camomile.

'Didn't Peter Rabbit drink camomile tea?' she asks. 'I've got the new baby a lovely little white sleepsuit with Peter Rabbit embroidered on the chest. There's a big fluffy white blanket to match. Shall I show you?'

She unwraps them. I hold the little white suit in my arms. It's as if I'm holding a very tiny floppy baby already. I start rocking it without really thinking.

'There! You'll be a lovely big sister,' says Liz.

'No, I won't,' I say. I drop the sleepsuit. 'I don't want anything to do with this baby. I don't *like* babies.'

'Well, I'm with you there, chum,' says Liz.

'I don't like Jack either,' I dare say.

'Mm. He's OK, I suppose. He's jolly and kind, and quite sweet in his own way.'

'No, he's not. He's stupid. And lazy. And he goes out drinking with his mates and comes home late. And he watches daft telly. And he eats smelly curries, and *he* smells too. I don't know what my mum sees in him,' I say.

'I'm not sure I do either. Though she obviously adores him. But he's definitely not *my* type,' says Liz.

'Who *is* your type, Liz?'

She stretches. 'Oh, someone tall and hunky and romantic and sophisticated and a little bit dangerous. James Bond will do for me. Only he's taking his time turning up in his fancy car and whisking me off to the Seychelles. Or Barbados. Or Mauritius. Or wherever he takes his lady friends on holiday. Definitely not camping in Wales.'

'We went camping in Wales at half-term last year.'

'Exactly,' says Liz, rolling her eyes. Then she shakes her head. 'I shouldn't be talking like this. Jack's your stepdad. He loves your mum dearly. And he loves you too, Ella.'

'No, he doesn't! He doesn't love me one bit. He just has to put up with me because I come as a package with Mum. He'd *much* sooner I didn't exist. And ditto me him.'

'Well, he does exist, sweetheart, and I'm sure he's trying to be a good dad to you – and now he'll be a good dad to the baby too.'

Liz leans over and pats me on the shoulder. 'Finished your hot chocolate? Come on, then, let's get you tucked up on the sofa again. And then, when you wake up in the morning, I'm sure the phone will be ringing and we'll find out all about the baby.'

I do exactly as I'm told – but when I wake up in the morning, the phone *isn't* ringing. I wonder if Liz is going to sleep half the morning the way she did before – but she gets up surprisingly early. She fixes us both breakfast and then we sit around, staring at the phone.

'Mum must have had the baby by now,' I say.

'Not necessarily. Sometimes it can take twenty-four hours. Even forty-eight,' says Liz, shuddering.

'Oh!'

'Maybe I shouldn't have told you that. Oh dear, I'm hopeless with little children.'

'I'm not *little*,' I say, though I'm starting to feel *very* little now. I so want Mum to be all right and give me a big cuddle.

I struggle with Liz's very splashy shower. I forget to put the dolphin curtain inside the bath and everywhere gets very wet. I'm scared Liz will tell me off but she doesn't even seem to notice.

Then my hair won't go right. I'm trying to grow out my fringe. Mum has a way of fluffing it up with a brush and getting it to look OK – but I don't know how to do the fluffing bit. My fringe hangs limply way past my eyebrows so I can hardly see.

I get dressed in my clean clothes and find my skirt's been crumpled up in a corner of my case and is all over creases. I wonder about asking Liz to iron it for me but decide it doesn't really matter.

Then we sit around again all morning. We watch a bit of television, and then Liz suggests I choose a DVD. She's got heaps of DVDs but they're mostly TV series like *Sex and the City*. I try one of these, but Liz jumps up and says maybe it's not suitable. We watch endless episodes of *Friends* instead. I wonder if my hair will ever go like Rachel's once the fringe has properly grown out. I usually like *Friends*, but now I can't seem to get into each story.

I ask Liz for some paper and I start drawing a picture of Mum and me. I draw me OK, but when I try to draw Mum pregnant, she looks all lopsided and silly. I scribble all over her quickly.

'Oh, that's a shame! It was a lovely picture! You're very good at drawing, Ella. How about drawing me?'

I have a go. Liz doesn't look so keen this time.

'Oh God, am I really that fat? You haven't drawn *me* pregnant, have you? That's it – it's time I took my diet seriously.'

She's bought us fish fingers for lunch. 'I know children love fish fingers,' she says proudly.

I did use to like them when I was little, but I've gone off them now. We have proper Sunday dinners at home. Mum cooks a chicken, and we have crispy roast potatoes and green beans and broccoli, and I eat it all up, even the broccoli.

Liz gives me five fish fingers and some baked beans and oven chips. She fixes herself one fish finger and a green salad. I try to eat all my meal to be polite, but I'm not feeling very hungry. Liz ends up eating most of mine.

'Maybe I'll try phoning Jack,' she says when she's washed the dishes.

His mobile's turned off.

'Then perhaps I'll try phoning the hospital,' she says.

'Yes, do. I tell you, Jack's probably forgotten to phone. He'll be off drinking the baby's health in the pub with all his mates,' I say.

'Ella, you sound like a very bitter little old wife,' says Liz. 'He *won't* have forgotten.'

She phones the hospital. It takes her ages and ages to get through to the ward – and then they won't tell her anything because she's not Mum's next of kin.

'*I'm* her next of kin. I'll talk to them,' I say, but

they won't talk to me either, because I'm a child.

'They've told me to phone your mum's husband, and I'm *trying* to, but he's not answering,' says Liz. 'Oh, well. We'll just have to wait.'

So we wait and wait and wait some more. Liz keeps yawning and stretching and cracking her knuckles.

'I usually go round the shops on Sundays. I wish we could go now – it would do us both good.'

'What, shopping?'

'Take our minds off things. But I'm not sure Jack's got my mobile number. Oh, I do so wish he'd just phone *now*.'

We stare at the cream phone on the small table in the corner of her living room. Liz picks up the receiver, just to check it's working. Then we wait some more.

Much later on we have tea: small sausages and spaghetti – toddler food. Then we watch television. Every time I go to the loo in Liz's shiny bathroom I sit with my head in my hands and have a little private sob because I'm starting to feel so scared.

It's getting almost to my bed time again. I'm sitting counting up to a thousand in my head, telling myself that if I can only get through each number in sequence without getting mixed up and making mistakes, then Mum will be all right. I get to three hundred and something when the doorbell rings. Liz and I jump and stare at the phone, both of us muddled. No, it's definitely the doorbell.

Liz runs to the door. Jack's standing there. His hair is sticking up in a silly way. His face is white and sweaty and he smells of his horrible beer.

'Jack! You were supposed to *phone!*' says Liz. She sniffs pointedly. 'Have you been off drinking while we've been chewing our fingernails? How is she? Is the baby here?' Her voice is getting high-pitched.

'I've had just one drink,' says Jack. He walks round Liz towards me. He's moving very carefully, as if he's on a tightrope.

'Jack? Is the baby all right?' Liz asks.

'The baby's fine,' says Jack. 'A little boy, six and a half pounds.'

He reaches out and takes my hand. He's horribly hot and clammy. I can't say a word. I want to run away. I know there's something terribly wrong.

'Ella, love . . .' Jack says. He sits down beside me on the sofa, so heavily that he nearly squashes me. He clears his throat. 'Ella,' he says again, 'I'm afraid your mum's not very well.'

The ceiling drops on me. The walls crush my sides. I can't speak. I can't even breathe.

'Oh my God,' Liz says. 'What happened? What went wrong? Oh, Jack, tell us!'

Jack swallows. He looks like he's making a big effort. He's looking at me. 'Mum got very tired having the baby. She's gone to sleep now, a very deep sleep, and she maybe won't wake up for quite a while,' he says, and his voice suddenly wobbles. He's trying very hard to control his face, but it's wobbling too, his lips trembling, his chin crumpling, his Adam's apple bobbing up and down.

I hear *She's gone to sleep*, and tears start slipping down my face. I think I know what Jack means.

'You mean she's *dead*?' Liz gasps.

'No, no. She had this condition, eclampsia. I'd never even heard of it. Apparently it's very rare. Anyway, everything started going wrong, and then she lost consciousness – and now she's in a coma,' Jack whispers – though I hear every word.

'Oh no, how terrible,' Liz says. She starts sobbing, sounding oddly like a little girl.

'Stop it, Liz. Not in front of Ella,' says Jack. He tries to give me a reassuring nod. 'The doctors say Mum might get better soon.'

Might get better!

I open my mouth, licking my lips, trying hard to make my voice work. 'I want to see her,' I say.

'Yes, of course you do. I'll take you to see Mum tomorrow – and your new baby brother,' says Jack.

'I want to see Mum *now*,' I say.

'No, darling, it's much too late. They won't let you in the ward now,' says Liz.

But Jack is still looking at me. 'All right, I'll take you now,' he says.

'You can't, Jack, it's way past visiting time – and it'll upset her terribly.'

'Of course it will. But she needs to see her mum right this minute,' says Jack. 'Come on, Ella, I'll drive you there.'

'Are you all right to drive?' Liz asks.

'I've had one drink, that's all.'

'No, I meant you're so upset yourself.'

'I'll be very careful. Do you want to come too?'

Liz hesitates. 'I'll wait here,' she says.

So I go in the car with Jack. I forget to put on my coat. It's not really cold in the car but I start shivering violently.

'Hang on,' says Jack. He stops the car, gets out and goes to search in the boot. He brings back a tartan rug. We three sat on it a few months ago when we had a picnic in the park. Jack wraps it round me and then carries on driving.

We don't talk on the way to the hospital. I keep thinking about Mum sleeping. I'm still scared it means she's dead. I've never seen a dead person but I imagine Mum chalk-white, with her eyes closed and her mouth gaping open.

We leave the car in the hospital car park. Jack helps me out, tying the rug round my shoulders.

'You're sure you want to see Mum?' he asks.

I nod, though I'm not so sure now. Jack takes my hand and leads me into the hospital and down a maze of corridors. There are red routes and green routes and yellow routes. We keep going down unmarked corridors and losing the right-coloured route. It's as if we're stuck in the middle of some grisly children's game. Then, at long last, we come to the right ward. Jack pulls me in, though my legs have gone wobbly.

'Excuse me, sir. It's way past visiting time. You can't come in here now,' says a nurse.

Jack pauses. He puts his hands on my shoulders. 'This little girl must see her mother. She's very ill. She needs to see her just for a few seconds,' he says in his best teacher voice.

He doesn't wait to argue it out, he just steers me onwards, to the end of the ward, to a special room. I bite on my knuckles, terrified. I don't know what Mum's going to look like. I want *my* mum, not some weird nightmare half-dead mother.

I peep round the door and see her. There's a

nurse beside her checking some sort of machine. Mum's lying on her back, oddly flat now, with tubes coming in and out of her. But she's still Mum, eyes closed, her hair tousled on the pillow, her hands lying gently curled on the covers.

'Mum – oh, Mum!' I say, running to her.

I kiss her soft pink cheek. 'Mum, it's me, Ella. Oh, Mum, wake up, please wake up.'

Mum seems to catch her breath. The nurse looks round. But Mum's eyes don't open.

'Mum!' I say, right in her ear.

It's like Sunday mornings before Jack, when I used to climb into Mum's bed and try to wake her up. She'd lie still, eyes closed, pretending. I'd have to tickle her under her chin to get her to open her eyes.

I try tickling her now, very, very gently, but her eyes stay shut. I smooth her hair off her forehead, combing it with my fingers, and then I take hold of her hand.

'That's right, Ella. I'm sure Mum knows you're here,' says Jack. 'Give her a goodnight kiss. I'll bring you back tomorrow.'

I kiss Mum again and then whisper in her ear. 'Keep breathing, Mum. In and out, in and out. Promise you'll keep breathing.'

Chapter 3

I don't go to school on Monday. Neither does Jack. We spend the whole day at the hospital. We sit in Mum's room on hard orange chairs, Jack on one side, me on the other. Jack talks to her a lot, whispering all sorts of mushy stuff. Sometimes he tries telling her jokes. The nurse laughs a couple of times, but Mum doesn't give the flicker of a smile. Her eyes are still closed. A lady doctor comes and lifts up her eyelids and peers into her eyes with a little light. I hate this in case she's hurting her, but Mum doesn't seem to mind. She lies still, fast, fast asleep.

'When will she wake up?' I ask the doctor.

'We don't know yet. We'll have to wait and see. She maybe knows you're here, so you keep chatting to her, you and Dad.'

He's not my dad, I say inside my head.

I wish Jack didn't have to be here too. I don't want to talk to Mum in front of him. I don't really know what to say. I just burble stupid stuff.

'Hello, Mum, it's me, Ella. I'm wearing my stripy top again. Aunty Liz washed it for me but I don't like the smell of her washing powder – it doesn't smell like us, and home.'

Mum doesn't smell right either. She doesn't smell *bad*, but her hair hasn't got the fresh coconut smell of her shampoo, and she isn't wearing her rosy perfume. She smells of hospital.

She's wearing the wrong things too – a silly white gown that ties at the back – and the sheets are white and too crisp. I'm sure she'd sooner have her own soft pink nightie and her own cosy duvet. No wonder she's got a little frown on her forehead.

I wait until Jack goes out of the room for a coffee. The nurse keeps coming in and out, but I pretend she's not there. I stretch forward until I'm talking in Mum's ear.

'Don't worry, Mum, you're breathing just fine. I don't think you're really asleep, you're just having a lovely long rest, aren't you? Remember when I was little and you used to read aloud to me, and you'd stroke the back of my hand? Look, I'll stroke yours now.' I stroke her hand and all the way up to her elbow and back. I will her fingers to move just a fraction. I keep thinking they're about to, but they stay lying still and limp.

I start crying, my head bent.

'Ella,' says Jack, coming back into the room.

He tries to put his arm round me but I jerk away. 'I know,' he says quietly.

He *doesn't* know. He's only known Mum just over a year. I've known her all my life.

'Come with me,' Jack says.

'I'm staying with Mum.'

'Just for a minute or two. I want to show you something,' he says.

'Go with your daddy, dear. I'll keep an eye on Mum,' says the nurse.

'He's *not* my dad.' This time I say it out loud.

The nurse looks startled.

'I'm her stepdad,' says Jack. 'Ella, please, come with me.'

So I have to follow him, back down the long ward, out into the corridor, down another – until I hear the sound of babies crying.

Oh. I'd forgotten all about the baby. Jack's trying to smile.

'I want you to meet your little brother,' he says.

He's not my brother, *just a half-brother*, I think, but I don't say it out loud because it sounds so mean. It's easy being mean to Jack, but this brother is only a little baby one day old.

We look through the window of the nursery and see the babies in their grey steel cots.

'He's that one, in the corner,' says Jack. His voice is wobbly again. 'Poor little chap, all on his own.'

A nurse bustles past. She looks at Jack. 'Mr Winters? You can go in and give your son a cuddle if you like.' She nods at me. 'And you, poppet.'

Jack washes his hands very thoroughly with the special disinfectant stuff on the wall. I rub it all over my hands too. Then we go into the nursery, both of us walking on tiptoe, though most of the babies are wide awake. Some are screaming their heads off. It's much louder now we're in the room.

We zigzag round the cots until we get to the one in the corner.

'Yes, that's him,' says Jack.

My eyes are still teary, so I give them a good rub and then look. He's crying too, but quietly, dolefully, as if he's really sad, not angry. He's not red in the face like the babies who are really bawling. He's pink, with little mottled patches on his cheeks and forehead. His eyes are screwed up and his mouth is open. His nose is just a tiny button. I thought he'd look like Jack, big and bluff, but he's little and delicate, with the softest fair wisps of hair. His tiny hands are up by his head, his fingers clenched into fists as if he's fighting.

'Hello, little chap,' Jack whispers.

He reaches down into the cot and lifts the baby up very, very carefully. His gown is caught up, so one of his comically tiny bare feet dangles down. Jack smooths his gown and holds the baby against his chest. He's holding him tightly, but I can see his hands are trembling.

'There you are, poor little boy,' he says.

He tries rocking him. The baby snuffles. 'You like that, don't you?' says Jack. He presses his cheek against the baby's head. 'My little boy.'

I swallow.

Jack looks at me. 'Do you want to hold him, Ella?'

I shake my head, but Jack holds him out all the same.

'Don't look so worried, it's easy. Just hold your arms out. There we go.'

He presses the baby against me so I have to wrap my arms round him. He's heavier than I thought, a warm, solid little weight.

'Support his head with your hand,' Jack whispers.

I cup my fingers around his head. His hair feels so soft and silky. His eyes open. He's looking up at me, still frowning and anxious, but he's not crying now.

I thought I'd hate him. He's the whole reason Mum and Jack set up home together. He made Mum ill when he was being born. It's all his fault. No, that's silly. He's just a little baby. He didn't do anything on purpose. He just grew and got born, and now he doesn't really want me, he doesn't want Jack, he wants his mum.

'Can we take him to Mum?' I ask Jack.

'They're going to try soon. When Mum's more . . . stable,' says Jack.

'He needs her,' I say.

'Yes, I know. We all need her,' says Jack. 'Right, let's pop him back in his cot now and go back to Mum. We'll tell her all about the baby.'

I try to get the baby back in his cot. Jack helps.

'Does he want to lie on his side or his back or his tummy?' he asks me.

We put him very carefully on his back because that's the way all the other babies are lying.

'I like sleeping on my side best,' I say.

'Me too. Your mum says if I sleep on my back, I snore,' says Jack.

As we trail back to Mum's special room, I play a game in my head: if I can gabble *I love Mum* a hundred times, then she'll have her eyes open when we see her. It's such a little thing to ask. I'm not saying she's got to sit up, or give me a big hug, or say my name. All she has to do is open her eyes so she can see I'm there. I picture it again and again: Mum's eyelids opening, her beautiful blue eyes looking at me as I chant my *I love Mum*s.

I'm only on eighty-two when we get back to her room, so I hang back, pressed against the wall, muttering like mad.

'Ella? It's all right. There's no need to be frightened. Come on, hold my hand,' Jack coaxes, misunderstanding.

I take no notice at all. I stare at the wall and mumble until I reach a hundred. I'm sure I've done it right. I haven't miscounted. But Mum is still lying there, eyes shut.

I go up to her and shake her shoulder. 'Mum? *Mum?* Oh, Mum, *please!*'

A new nurse frowns. 'Maybe you shouldn't bring

your daughter in – it's just upsetting her,' she says.

'I'm *not* his daughter!' I shout.

'Hey, hey! I don't care who you are, you're not allowed to throw a tantrum in my ward,' she says.

'Can you calm down please, Ella? You need to tell Mum about the baby. Describe him to her,' says Jack.

So I whisper in Mum's ear, telling her about the baby's tiny hands and his little button nose and his thistledown hair and his big blue eyes.

'He's got your lovely eyes, Mum. Why don't you open them, just for a second, to show you're still in there? Show me you're still Mum.'

Mum lies very still, though her chest goes gently up and down, up and down. Then Jack talks to her while I loll on the orange chair, stretching, crossing my legs, yawning, unable to get comfortable.

After a long while Jack realizes we've forgotten to eat.

'I'm not hungry,' I say.

'I'm not hungry either, but we'd still better go and have a snack,' he says.

I don't want to, but the nurse is looking at me, and I'm scared she'll push me out of her ward if I argue again. So I follow Jack, and we trudge up and down corridors again until we find a canteen. We stare at all the food on display. I can't imagine poking any of it in my mouth, let alone swallowing it.

'Let's have two plates of chips,' says Jack.

I'd never normally be allowed just a plate of chips for my lunch. I usually love chips, and these are good crispy golden ones, but I can only manage half my plateful. Jack eats mine too. We don't talk. We've run out of things to say.

Then we go back to Mum's room and sit and sit and sit while she sleeps. Eventually Liz comes, in her navy work suit. Mum's not meant to have visitors, only immediate family, but Jack explains they're best friends, more like sisters. She gasps when she sees Mum, and then starts crying.

'Oh, Sue. Oh my God, Sue,' she says, over and over.

She's brought flowers, but Mum can't look at them. She's brought fruit, but Mum can't eat proper food. She's brought make-up and a hairbrush, but Mum can't do her face or fix her hair.

'Sit beside her, Liz. Talk to her. I think she can hear us even if she can't respond,' says Jack.

But Liz shakes her head, her hand over her mouth. 'I can't. I can't bear to see her like this. Oh God, Jack, I'm sorry, I just can't,' she mumbles, and then she runs out of the room.

I hunch up small, horrified.

'Silly old Liz,' says Jack.

'She's awful,' I whisper. 'Mum's her best *friend*.'

'She's not awful, she's just upset.'

'She'll hurt Mum's feelings,' I say.

'I expect Mum understands. Mum's just grateful you're such a sensible girl. You talk to her now, Ella. Brush her hair with the new hairbrush – make her look pretty.'

I brush Mum's hair until it crackles with electricity and flies up all by itself. I wonder if I brushed Mum all over whether her body would start moving too. But I don't want to risk scratching her with the hard bristles. I try rubbing her fingers instead, again and again, but they don't even twitch.

'Take absolutely no notice of Liz, Mum,' I say in her ear. 'You don't need her. *I'll* be your best friend.'

The nurse pops her head round the door. 'We're settling our patients down for the night. Are you two staying?'

'No, we'd better be going now,' says Jack. 'Kiss Mum goodbye, Ella. Tell her we'll come and see her first thing tomorrow.'

We find Liz dithering in the corridor outside.

'Oh God, I'm so sorry, Jack. I just couldn't make myself stay in the room. I've never been any good in hospitals. I couldn't stand to see Sue looking so awful.'

'She's not awful. *You're* awful,' I say.

'Hey, hey, Ella, none of that,' says Jack. 'She's just exhausted, Liz, she doesn't mean it.'

'I do so mean it,' I mutter darkly.

'What do the doctors say? Why can't they *do* anything? If her brain is affected, can't they operate?' Liz says.

'Apparently not. They gave her a scan yesterday, but they don't think there's anything they can usefully do. We just have to let nature take its course and hope for the best.'

'*Is* there any hope?' Liz asks.

'Liz!' says Jack sharply, looking at me. 'There's always hope.'

We go back to Liz's house, Liz in her car, me with Jack.

'I'll order in pizzas – I'm too worked up to cook,' says Liz. She kneads her forehead. 'I've got such a headache, like a real migraine. I had a lousy day at work too – they're letting people go, I'm going to have to reapply for my own job, I don't know what I'm going to do . . .' She witters on.

I'm not listening. I don't think Jack is listening. We're sitting here in Liz's flat, but it's as if we're still in the hospital, one on either side of Mum.

Liz opens a bottle of wine and pours Jack a glass.

'I don't suppose you've got any beer, Liz?' he says.

'I'm not really a beer sort of girl,' says Liz.

'Oh well, I'm driving anyway.' Jack looks at me. 'I think it's time we went home, Ella.'

'Listen, you can always count on me as a babysitter whenever you need one,' says Liz.

'Oh, Liz! That would be marvellous,' says Jack. 'The baby's perfectly healthy. The hospital will only keep him in the nursery for a certain amount of time. I've been going round and round in my head trying to think how I can fit all the hospital visits around the baby's feeds.'

Liz is looking appalled. 'Oh God. I meant babysit *Ella*. Jack, I wouldn't have a *clue* what to do with a newborn baby. I mean, in a total emergency I'll keep an eye on him, but I can't do it regularly. I'm so sorry, but babies are just not my thing. You'll have to get a proper nanny.'

'I can't afford a nanny,' says Jack.

'Well, a childminder, someone properly trained. When he's older, toddling around, I'll maybe feel more confident.'

'Mum will look after him then. When she's woken up,' I say.

I so want Mum to look after *me*. I don't want to stay at Liz's, but I don't want to go home all alone with Jack either. However, I gather up my things and thank Liz for having me. She puts her arms round me and gives me a proper hug.

'Oh, Ella,' she says, starting to cry, 'you poor little love, how are you going to manage?'

'We'll manage fine,' says Jack.

We go out to the car and he drives us home.

'I'm sorry, Ella. I know you probably wanted to stay,' he says.

I sniff and say nothing.

'I can't believe she can be so selfish. She's your mum's best friend, for goodness' sake. Sue would do anything for her. When Liz's last boyfriend went off with someone else, Sue had her to stay and made a great fuss of her. Yet now Sue needs her, she's freaked out by the whole situation – OK, some people can't cope with hospitals, I know that, but I still did hope she'd help a bit with the baby until . . . well, until . . .'

'Until Mum's better,' I say.

'Yes. That's right.'

'She didn't even order in those pizzas,' I say.

'What? No, she didn't! Well, we'll go and get our own pizzas, OK?'

We stop at a pizza place. Jack says I can order

43

any combination of toppings, as many as I want, but I can't remember what I like any more.

'It's OK, I'll choose for you,' says Jack, though *he* doesn't know what I like. He doesn't even seem sure of what he wants himself.

When we get home, it's so silent and empty that it seems all wrong to take our pizzas into the still living room. It's as if we're eating our pizzas in a church. Jack sits on the sofa. There's a space next to him where Mum should be. My pizza sticks in my mouth. It tastes like its own cardboard box.

Jack puts on the television, the sound turned up extra loud. We both stare at the screen. At least it means we don't have to talk. I leave most of my pizza. Jack only manages half of his. He snaps open a can of beer, and then another. I sniff, because I know Mum doesn't like him drinking too much.

'Can I get you a drink, Ella?' Jack asks. 'I think we've got some Coke in the fridge. Or juice. What about juice? That's healthier. Or there's always milk.'

I shake my head at all his suggestions. I tuck my feet up in my armchair, wrapping my arms round myself.

'I think it's getting on for bed time,' Jack says after a while.

'Bed time?' he says.

I hunch up, still ignoring him.

'Ella?' says Jack. 'Come on, you've had a very long, exhausting day.'

I get out of my chair and march out of the room without looking at him.

'Night-night,' he calls. 'I'll come up when you're in bed.'

'You don't need to,' I say quickly. 'Goodnight.'

Mum always comes and tucks me up. She keeps me company when I'm cleaning my teeth and washing my face. When I'm in my pyjamas, I hop into bed and she sits beside me. Sometimes she reads to me, all these old-fashioned girly books she liked when she was young: *Ballet Shoes*, *A Little Princess* and *Little Women*. Sometimes she'll make up a story specially for me. She used to tell me a story about a superhero girl called Ella-Bella who can fly. I'm too old for little Ella-Bella stories now, but sometimes if I've got a bad cold or I'm feeling fed up, Mum will make up a brand-new Ella-Bella story for me. I would give anything to have her tell me an Ella-Bella story now.

I go to the bathroom, then get undressed and crawl into bed. I arrange my soft toys around me. I hug Harriet the Hippo to my chest, putting my hand inside her plush jaws. Baby Teddy cuddles up on the other side, his head flopping on my shoulder. They don't feel *right*. Mum always tucks them in beside me.

I'm fidgeting about, rearranging them for the fourth time, when Jack knocks and puts his head round the door. 'Shall I tuck you up?' he says.

'No! I *said*, you don't need to.'

'Ella—'

'I want to go to sleep. I'm tired,' I say.

'All right, sweetheart. Night-night then,' says Jack. 'If you wake up in the night, you can always come and knock on my door, OK? Try – try not to worry too much.'

I don't get to sleep until long after I hear Jack go to bed himself. Then I wake up about four o'clock, my heart thumping, so hot my pyjamas are sticking to me. I've had the most terrible nightmare. Mum's had the baby, and then she's got desperately ill, and now she's lying in a coma in hospital. I'm still so scared even though it's just a dream, so I sit up and open my mouth to call for Mum . . .

No, wait. It isn't a dream at all. It's really happened. Mum isn't here. There's just Jack. I can hear muffled sounds coming from his bedroom. He's crying.

I pull the covers up over my head, clutch my old toys, and cry too.

Chapter 4

I don't go to school again on Tuesday. I think, just for a split second, *Oh, goody-goody*! Because we go swimming on Tuesday mornings, and I feel sick on the coach, and I hate all the noise in the baths, and I can't swim very well and so I don't get to splash in the top set with Sally. Then I feel dreadful because I'd sooner swim all day in a shark-infested pool and have Mum wide awake and completely well.

I don't know what clothes to put on. I don't know whether to dress up smartly or wear my old jeans. In the end I wear my black and white spotty bridesmaid's dress to please Mum, even though *I* think it looks awful, especially now, as I can't find any clean white socks and so I wear red ones which don't go with my shoes. I can't fix my hair either. It needs washing and it just hangs limply, especially my fringe. I'm nearly in tears as I tug at it. I so want to look lovely for Mum. I feel if I can only look like the perfect daughter, she'll open her eyes to take a proper proud look at me.

Jack isn't trying at all. He hasn't even *shaved* and he's tugged on the same shirt and jeans he had on yesterday. He looks awful, his hair sticking up, his eyes all red and bleary. I wrinkle my nose at the sight of him.

'What?' he says.

'Nothing.'

He sighs and rubs his hands over his face, then takes a deep breath. 'OK, what shall we have for breakfast? Toast? Cereal? Bacon and eggs?'

'I don't want anything.'

'You need something inside you, Ella. It's going to be a long day. Come on, don't be difficult. I'll make you anything. Pancakes?'

I stare at him as if he's mad. 'Let's just go to the hospital to see Mum,' I say.

'Bowl of cereal first, at the very least,' he says, but when he takes the carton of milk out of the fridge he peers at it doubtfully, and then sniffs it.

'Oh God,' he says, pouring it down the sink. 'I'll have to go shopping sometime.'

We have toast instead, nibbling in silence. Then the phone rings just as we're about to go. It's the head teacher at Garton Road, Mum and Jack's school.

'Look, I told you, I can't possibly come in, not when Sue's so seriously ill. What? Look, I can't help it if they've both got gastroenteritis. I couldn't give a stuff if the entire staff are throwing up all over the school. I can't come in and teach because Sue's in a coma, hanging onto life by a thread—' He sees me staring and says quickly, 'I've got to go now.'

Is Mum really hanging onto life by a thread? I imagine a long white thread tied round her ankle, tethering her to the bed, while she rises up and up and up . . .

'I didn't really mean that! I just needed to get

49

my point across,' Jack says. 'Come on, Ella.'

We drive to the hospital again and walk down the long corridors. I hope and hope and hope that Mum will be just a little bit better – but she's still lying there, eyes closed. I shout, *'Mum!'* right in her ear but she doesn't stir.

'No, no, dear, don't, you'll hurt Mummy,' says a new nurse crossly.

I shrink back, horrified.

'She was just trying to rouse her. She didn't mean any harm,' says Jack. 'She's very close to her mother.'

The new nurse sniffs. Her blonde hair is pulled very tightly into a bun, and the elasticated belt round her waist is at full stretch. She looks as if she could explode in all directions at any time.

'She shouldn't be in here then, it's too upsetting for a little girl,' she snaps. 'Small children aren't supposed to be running about these wards.'

Yet later they bring a very, very small child to Mum: the baby. The young lady doctor with long dark hair carries him into the room.

'Hello, remember me? I'm Dr Wilmot,' she says. 'I thought it would be good for Susan to have her baby with her for a while – and good for him too.' She rocks him gently, stroking his little wisps of hair.

'I keep forgetting he's so tiny,' Jack says, his face screwing up. 'It must be awful for him. All the other babies have their mothers.'

'He's still got a mother. I think he needs a little cuddle with her right now,' says Dr Wilmot. 'You hold him for me for a moment.'

She hands the baby to Jack and then bends over Mum and starts untying her nightie. I draw in my breath.

'I think Mum would like to cuddle up really close with the baby,' Dr Wilmot says to me. 'I'm sure she used to cuddle you like this when you were tiny.'

She takes the baby from Jack, unwraps his shawl and takes off his little nightgown too, so he's just in his nappy. He cries a bit, waving his legs about. They're so *small*, but he's quite strong, kicking his funny little feet. It's just the way he kicked when he was inside Mum's tummy. He's not really a little stranger – we've known him for months and months. We just couldn't see him.

Dr Wilmot lays him down very gently on Mum's bare chest, his head between her breasts. He gives a little snuffle, almost like a sigh, and then lies still, nestling in.

'There! He's a happy little chap now,' Dr Wilmot whispers, but she's looking at Mum. We're *all* looking at Mum. I clench my fists, praying for a miracle. She'll open her eyes and clasp the baby close . . . Her eyes stay shut. Her arms are still. She doesn't move at all, apart from breathing in and out, her chest rising and falling underneath the baby. He stays curled up there, his eyes shut too.

I wish Jack and Dr Wilmot and the grumpy nurse could vanish. I want to climb up on Mum's bed and curl up with them too.

Dr Wilmot puts her arm around me. I lean against her, sucking my thumb.

'Has he got a name yet, your little brother?' she asks.

'We thought we might call him Georgie – or Harry – or maybe Will,' says Jack. 'Something quite plain and simple.'

'No! He's going to be called Samson,' I say. 'Mum said.'

They stare at me.

'*Samson?*' Jack echoes, looking astonished. 'Your mum didn't say anything about calling him Samson!'

'She did, when he was kicking inside her. She said he was big and strong, like Samson.'

'Oh, I see! Like the strong Samson in the Bible. But she was joking, Ella,' says Jack.

'No, she wasn't! I was there, you weren't. She wants him to be Samson, Jack, truly.'

'Well, let's think about it. We don't have to name the baby just yet.'

'But he can still be Samson, can't he?'

'Perhaps he could have Samson as a middle name?' Dr Wilmot suggests.

'Mum chose Samson for his first name, she really did, honestly. Mum and I think it's a brilliant name,' I say. 'Samson. That's his name.'

'But it's not up to you, missy,' says the grumpy nurse. 'It's Mummy and Daddy who choose their baby's name. And your mummy can't say what she wants at the moment so Daddy has to choose, not you.'

It feels as if she's kicking me in the stomach. I can't even argue. Jack's not my daddy and I can tell everyone that – but he *is* the baby's dad, that's a fact.

I swallow and don't say anything.

The grumpy nurse nods as if to say, *That's settled her hash*.

Jack's looking at me too. He waits until the nurse is out of the room and Dr Wilmot is carrying Samson-Georgie-Harry-Will back to the nursery for a change and a feed.

'Hey, Ella?'

I still don't say anything. I sit beside Mum, tying up her nightie, smoothing her hair.

'How about Sam? It's like it's short for Samson. Will that do?'

I nod very slowly, though I still don't look at him. I'm angry with him now because he's trying to be kind. I don't *want* him to be nice to me. We're supposed to be deadly enemies. It's horrible having to spend so much time with him. Minute after minute, hour after hour, throughout the whole day.

'You don't have to sit here all the time,' says Dr Wilmot when she comes back. 'Why don't you take Ella for a bit of a walk, stretch her legs. There's a park at the end of the road.'

We both twitch.

'We'd sooner stay here,' says Jack.

Dr Wilmot pauses. 'Look, as far as I can see, Sue's stable now. She's deeply unconscious but she's breathing by herself, which is great. She'll be fine. We're all keeping an eye on her.'

I know what she means. She's saying, *Don't worry, Mum won't die if you go off to the park.* That's why we're here all the time. We're so scared she's going to die, every second is precious.

'Do you want to come and find this park, Ella?' says Jack.

I shake my head. He doesn't try to persuade me. We sit it out. Some of the teachers from Garton Road come after school. They're not allowed to see

54

Mum but they stand in the corridor with Jack. They all hug him, even the men. One of the women starts crying. They've brought all sorts of presents – flowers and baby things and bottles of wine. Mum can't drink *wine*. I suppose they're presents for Jack.

It's not fair – Jack can see all his stupid old teacher friends but I can't see *my* best friend, Sally. I feel a huge pang. I suddenly miss Sally so much. I only saw her on Friday but already it seems like years ago.

When Jack and I go home eventually, I say I want to ring Sally.

'Isn't it a bit late? Won't she have gone to bed by now?'

I think he's maybe right, but I take no notice. 'Sally stays up *ever* so late, ten, eleven o'clock, even later,' I lie.

'Well, finish your sweet and sour pork first,' says Jack. 'It'll be horrid if you let it get cold.'

I think it's horrid anyway. We got the Chinese takeaway on the way home. It's supposed to be a treat.

'Please let me phone Sally now,' I whine.

Jack sighs and says OK, if I really want to. He keeps giving in to me now Mum's ill. It feels so weird. He used to be strict, always ticking me off and bossing me about, telling Mum she let me get away with murder – and then, when I sulked, he'd crack silly jokes and expect me to laugh along with him. It would be bad enough having Jack for a teacher. It's absolutely awful to have him as a step-dad.

I hate it when he's mean to me, but I think I hate it even more when he's kind. It makes me feel as if I've been turned inside out. I need to be twice as mean back to him to try to make it seem normal.

He's giving me this understanding, encouraging smile as he sits there on the sofa. I don't give him even the merest glimmer of a smile back. I shut the living-room door on him, making it plain I want a bit of privacy.

I dial Sally's number on the phone in the hall and then stand waiting, heart thumping.

It's Sally's mum. I find my eyes filling with tears. Sally's soft blonde mum who puts yoghurt raisins in her packed lunches and gives her choco-late cookies when she comes home from school, and still reads her bedtime stories – Sally's mum, who's almost as lovely as my mum.

'Hello? Is anyone there?' she says.

'It's me, Ella,' I whisper.

'Oh goodness, Ella! You're phoning very late,

sweetheart. Sally's already upstairs in bed. Has Mum had the baby yet?'

'Mm.'

'Oh, wonderful! Is it a little girl or a little boy?'

'A boy.'

'What's he going to be called?'

'Samson.'

'Oh, that's a very special name. So, is Mum back from the hospital yet?'

I swallow painfully. 'Not yet. *Please* may I speak to Sally, Mrs Edwards?'

'Well, I'll go and see if she's still awake. Won't be a moment, pet.'

I wait, rubbing my eyes, standing on one foot and then the other. 'Please please please let Sally come to the phone,' I whisper, over and over.

'Hello?' she says sleepily.

And then I don't know what to say to her.

'Hello? Ella, are you still there? What are you playing at?'

'I'm here. Hello, Sally,' I say in a tiny voice.

'What? I can hardly hear you! Why haven't you been at school? I've phoned you twice but you weren't there. It's been horrid without you. I haven't had anyone to go round with at play time. I ended up playing Piggy-in-the-Middle with Dory and Martha. Dory's OK, she's quite good fun.

Remember when she brought that mouse to school in her pocket? But I can't stick Martha – she's always showing off. Ella? Are you ill?'

'No,' I say, though I realize I've been feeling ill for days. My head hurts and I feel sick and my tummy's tight all the time.

I can hear Sally's mother talking in the background.

'Oh, Mum says your mum's had her baby!'

'Yes.'

'You lucky thing! I'd give anything for a baby brother or sister. I think babies are so cute.'

'You've got Benjy.'

'Yuck, he doesn't count, and he's not a baby, he's more like an *animal*. Is your baby a boy too? Watch out he doesn't grow up like our Benjy, he's enough to drive you mental. Did I tell you he broke my pen the other day? You know, my real fountain pen. He *stabbed* me with it and bent the nib in two.' She pauses. 'Ella? What's your baby like then? Are you allowed to feed it and dress it and all that?'

'Well, I suppose so. When he comes home.'

'Is he still in hospital then?'

I hear Mrs Edwards muttering again.

'Is he . . . all right?' says Sally.

'Yes. Yes, he is. He's fine,' I say. I feel the tears spilling down my cheeks. 'It's my mum.'

'What do you mean, your mum?'

'She isn't all right. She's had something go wrong inside her head. She's gone to sleep and she won't wake up,' I whisper.

'You mean she's *dead*?' says Sally.

Her mother exclaims and snatches the phone. 'Oh, Ella, sweetheart, how *awful!*' she says, sounding truly shocked.

'Mum's not dead, but – but she's in this coma thing.' I'm crying so hard now I can barely talk.

'Let me speak to your dad, dear,' says Mrs Edwards.

'He's not my dad, he's my stepdad,' I gabble, and then go running for Jack.

He stays on the phone to Mrs Edwards for ages. It's not fair. I wanted to have a proper talk with Sally. I wanted her to tell me how sorry she was and how she'd give anything to make it up to me. I needed her to tell me she'd be my best friend for ever, no matter what. I wanted her to say all those things but she didn't get a chance – and then Jack hangs up the phone before I even get to say goodbye to her.

'I didn't get to talk to her *properly*,' I sob.

'I know. But it's getting really late now. And I think you should go to school tomorrow, so you can see her there and catch up with everything,' says

59

Jack. He flops down wearily on the sofa and opens a can of beer. He's hardly touched his Chinese either.

'I can't go to *school*, not when Mum's ill,' I say, outraged.

'Ella, it looks like Mum might be ill for a long time,' says Jack. 'You can't stay off school week after week. And neither can I. I've got to go back soon too.'

'Are you going to Garton Road tomorrow then?'

'No, I've got things to do.' He kicks the tray of lukewarm Chinese with his foot. 'I've got to go and do some shopping for a start.'

'You're going *shopping*?'

'We've got to start eating some decent food – we can't live on takeaways. And I've got to see if I can find someone to look after the baby.'

'But the nurses look after him in the hospital.'

'Yes, but he can't stay there, not indefinitely. He's got to come home with us, so we need a nursery or a childminder or someone to look after him during the day while I'm teaching. Mum was going to look after him herself for six months so we hadn't got anyone lined up yet.' He looks at me, rubbing his eyes. 'We'll have to find someone to look after you too whenever I have to work late. There's so much to organize. I can't get my head round any of it just at the moment. Anyway, off you hop to bed. And tomorrow morning I'll drive you to school, and then come and pick you up afterwards and take you to see Mum then.'

'No! I need to be *with* Mum.'

'Well, you can't,' Jack snaps. 'Will you just stop arguing! I'm trying my hardest to do what's best for you. It doesn't help if you argue back all the time.'

'I don't always argue.'

'There you go! For pity's sake, Ella. Couldn't you try to be reasonable and do as you're told just for a few days, while Mum's so ill?'

'Mum's ill because of you! If you hadn't come along, she wouldn't have had the baby, and so she wouldn't have got ill!' I shout. 'It's all your fault, Jack.'

He stares at me, shaking his head. 'Ella, it's not anybody's fault. We weren't to know Mum would have this reaction. She was absolutely fine when she had you.'

'Yes, we were all fine then, Mum and my real dad and me.'

'I know you find it hard that I'm your stepdad—'

'I wish you weren't!'

'I wish I wasn't too!' he shouts.

I run out of the room and up the stairs. There!

I *knew* he didn't like me. He's as good as said so. I don't know why it's making me cry so much. It just feels so *lonely*. I haven't got anyone else but Mum. Jack wishes I wasn't here. Liz doesn't want me around. Sally doesn't understand.

I lie down on my bed and cry and cry. I keep waiting for the footsteps on the stairs – but Jack doesn't come. So at long last I wash my sodden face and get into my pyjamas and crawl into bed.

I lie under the covers, arms wrapped tightly round myself. I haven't got a proper mum any more, I haven't got a dad . . . Well, I *do* have a dad. A real one, not a stepdad.

I screw up my face in the dark, trying to conjure up my dad. I last saw him two years ago – maybe three. He came to take me out on my birthday. Mum and I couldn't believe it when we opened the door.

'Surprise!' he said.

It was *such* a surprise we just gaped at him. For a second or two I didn't even guess that he was my dad. I thought he was someone else's dad, or maybe one of Mum's teacher friends, or a seldom-noticed neighbour. Then of course I realized. This was *my* dad, and he had his arms open wide and he was hugging me. I felt hot with embarrassment, my face crammed against his stripy shirt.

'My lovely little Ella,' he said.

I was only small then but I knew he was expecting some kind of loving reaction. I thought of Mum's favourite old DVD, *The Railway Children.*

'Daddy, oh, Daddy,' I said in a choked voice.

He said he wanted to take me out and buy me the best birthday present in the world, whatever I wanted.

'Come on, sweetheart, get your coat. We're off to the shops,' he said, spinning me round.

'Well, that's a lovely idea, and of course Ella is thrilled, but in half an hour's time nine little girls are arriving for her birthday lunch,' Mum said. 'I think maybe you'll have to go *after* the party.'

Dad looked fed up at first, and we both wondered if he was going to walk out then and there. But he stayed for the afternoon. He was actually the life and soul of the party. He played all the games with us, and jumped about when we danced, and conducted everyone when they sang 'Happy Birthday'. He played his own grizzly-bear game with us, giving every single one of my friends a bear ride on his back. They all squealed with joy and said, 'Oh, Ella, you're so *lucky*, you've got such a funny dad.'

Then they all went home, and Dad was as good as his word.

'Right, Ella, serious shopping time,' he said.

He didn't ask Mum to come with us. I feel so dreadful remembering. I just left her tidying up after the party. Dad and I went to a big shopping centre and he bought me a new sky-blue dress (to match my eyes, he said). He gave me a giant teddy bear with a blue ribbon round its neck, though I didn't really *want* it because it had such beady eyes. But I thanked Dad very, very much all the same, and made a great show of hugging the huge bear, though it made my arms ache. Dad must have detected my lack of enthusiasm.

'We're not done yet,' he said. 'One more present to make it the best birthday ever. What would you really, really like?'

I thought hard. Martha at school had just had her ears pierced and we had all tutted and squealed enviously over her little gold studs.

'Please can I have my ears pierced?' I asked Dad.

I expected him to laugh at me and say, no way, not until I was a teenager. But he just shrugged and said, 'That's fine with me, darling. Let's go and find a jeweller's.'

I jumped up and down with joy, but when I was actually sitting down in the back of the jewellery shop, I wasn't so sure it was a good idea. I felt a bit faint and funny when they did my ears, and cried a little, but Dad gave me a cuddle and said I was his big brave girl. He said my new earrings looked beautiful.

When we got home hours later, Mum flew at me and hugged me tight as if she thought she'd lost me for ever. Then she saw my ears. She got really, really mad.

'How *dare* you have her ears pierced!' she screamed at Dad.

'She wanted them pierced, she practically begged me,' he said.

'Of course she begged! Every little girl wants her ears pierced. But Ella's my daughter and I didn't want her little ears stuck all over with horrible studs!'

'She's my daughter *too* and I don't think it matters a damn. I just want to make her happy,' Dad shouted back.

They had a horrible row then. I crept into the kitchen, dragging my big bear along with me, and nibbled miserably at birthday-cake icing. Then Dad came in and said goodbye to me. He said I was his birthday princess and I wasn't to listen to silly old Mummy, the earrings looked beautiful. He promised he'd come and see me again very soon – maybe the very next Saturday.

I wore my new blue dress every Saturday for the

next six months, even in winter, but he never came back. He's always sent Christmas presents though. He's sent me several pairs of earrings, but actually they're no use to me now. Mum made me take the first little studs out the very same day and the holes closed up.

I was cross with her for a while. I thought Dad didn't come to see me because she shouted at him. Then I got cross with Dad instead because he broke his promise to me. But I stopped minding ages ago. I gave the teddy to my school's jumble sale, but the blue dress is still hanging in the back of my wardrobe.

I get out of bed and search for it now. It's weird thinking I was once that small. I can barely get my arms in the sleeves and the dress wouldn't even cover my bottom. I thought I'd grown out of needing my dad the way I'd grown out of my dress, but now I want him so badly I start trembling.

I put on my dressing gown and go downstairs. Jack is sprawling on the sofa in the living room, empty cans of beer littering the carpet. The room smells horrible. Jack has his hands over his face.

'You're drunk!' I say accusingly.

'No, I'm not,' he mumbles. 'I've just had a beer.'

'You've had lots and lots of beers!'

'Well, I *need* lots and lots of beers,' Jack says.

'What is it now, Ella? I thought you'd gone to bed.'

'I want my dad.'

'What?'

'I want my *dad*,' I repeat.

'Well, what do you want *me* to do? I can't conjure him up right this second. According to your mum you haven't seen him for donkey's years.'

'I need to see him now,' I say, clenching my fists.

'All right. I'll try to find out where he is. I'll get your mum's address book, OK? I'll contact him tomorrow.'

'No, you won't.'

'Yes I will, I promise. Now, go to *bed*!'

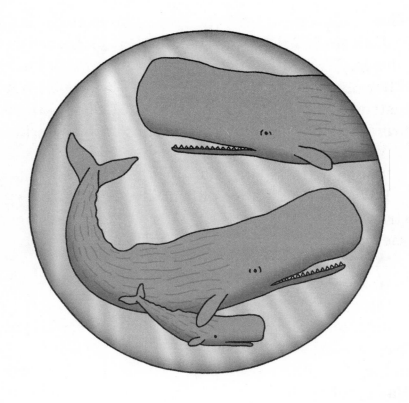

Chapter 5

Jack gets ready to take me to school on Wednesday. He hasn't done any washing so we have to fish my grubby school blouse out of the laundry basket. I'm running out of socks and knickers too.

I struggle with my bunches myself. I don't know

what to do with my fringe. I want Mum so.

Jack makes us both toast, which we crunch in silence. We've barely said a single word to each other this morning. He drives me to school, but instead of stopping in the road to let me out he drives right in through the gates to the car park.

'What are you doing?'

'I'm going to talk to your head teacher.'

I feel a sudden clutch of fear. Mrs Raynor is very strict and shouts a lot. I once dared shout back and she got *furious*.

'Are you going to tell on me?' I whisper.

'Tell on you?' Jack says, looking puzzled.

'That I shouted at you.'

Jack blinks at me, and then gives a silly laugh. 'No, of course not. I'd have to tell on myself too. I did my fair share of shouting. I'm going to tell Mrs Raynor about Mum – explain that things might be difficult for you for a while.'

'I don't want you to talk about Mum to *Mrs Raynor*,' I say, shocked.

'I think it's the best thing to do. We'll tell your form teacher too. What's she called?'

'Miss Anderson.'

'She's OK, isn't she?'

'Yes, I like her lots, she's ever so kind.'

'Great. Well, you sit outside Mrs Raynor's door

while I have a little chat, and then I'll take you to your classroom.'

'You don't have to take me! I'll look like a *baby*,' I say – but I actually *feel* like a baby.

It suddenly seems so loud and noisy in school. Some boys run down the corridor, and one knocks me with his school bag. I don't think he did it on purpose and it didn't really hurt, but I have to screw up my face to stop myself crying.

I sit on the chair outside Mrs Raynor's room while Jack is in there. Everyone going past stares at me as if I've done something really bad. I wait, kicking my legs against the wall. Jack's inside for an *age*. Mrs Raynor's usually so busy you're in and out in a flash. I try hard to catch what they're saying but I can't hear a word. When the door opens, there's Jack, red in the face, eyes all teary – and Mrs Raynor's got her arm round him! She gives him a pat on the shoulder and then turns to me. She reaches out and pats me too.

'I'm so sorry about your mother, Ella. It must be dreadful for you. I do hope she recovers soon,' she says.

I can't *believe* she's being so nice. Then she comes *with* us to Miss Anderson's class. Everyone stares at us, sitting up straight. Even Miss Anderson flushes pink.

'Hello, everyone,' says Mrs Raynor. 'I'd like you all to be especially kind to Ella. Her mother's very ill in hospital.'

She pushes me gently towards my desk beside Sally and I sit down, burning. Sally reaches out and squeezes my hand. Dory mouths, *Poor you!* Even Martha nods at me sympathetically. Joseph, the boy behind me, gently pats me on the back. Mrs Raynor whispers to Miss Anderson. Jack catches my eye and waves goodbye to me.

'Is that your dad?' Dory asks.

'No! He's my stepdad,' I say wearily.

Sally sighs and squeezes my hand again. After Mrs Raynor goes out, Miss Anderson comes up to my desk and squats down beside me so that her face is very close to mine.

'Chin up, Ella,' she says softly. 'You're a good brave girl to decide to come to school.'

I didn't do the deciding at all, but I smile in a good brave way.

'Don't worry if you find it hard to concentrate in lessons.' Miss Anderson is so close I'm breathing in her rosy soap smell, and her long hair lightly brushes the backs of my hands.

'You tell me if you want anything,' she says, getting to her feet.

I really want a cuddle with Miss Anderson

because she's so soft and warm and gentle, but I'm not an infant, so I nod and smile instead.

The first lesson is maths and we're doing division. I'm a bit rubbish at maths, *especially* division. I write down all the numbers but they stay squiggles on the page. I mutter my way through my times tables, but I can't remember my seven times, so I have no idea how many times they'll go into twenty-eight. Sally obligingly writes '4' as an answer, so I copy her. I draw four stick people in the margin – a lady, a man, a girl and a blobby little baby. Then I draw a safe line all round the lady, and sun rays. I put the girl inside the safe line too, joining them together. I give the lady big, wide-open eyes with long lashes.

Miss Anderson walks past and peers at my notebook. 'It's a maths lesson, Ella, not art,' she says quietly, but she doesn't tell me off!

Sally has worked her way through a whole page of long division now, but I can't be bothered to copy her any more. I sit and sigh and yawn because this division is a very l-o-n-g lesson, but at last it's over and play time.

I usually just hang out with Sally: we swap snacks and play drawing games and giggle together. Jack forgot to give me a little box of juice and my mini pack of raisins, but it doesn't matter.

Sally hands me half her Twix bar, Dory gives me a handful of crisps, Martha offers me a bite of her apple, Joseph gives me a carrot stick, and I get sweets and orange slices and peanuts and a quarter of a Marmite sandwich from people who aren't even my friends.

I stand in a great cluster of children, Sally's arm round me because she's my best friend.

'Tell us about your mum then, Ella!'

So I tell them about the hospital with the special room, and the nurses and the doctors and Mum's tubes and her closed eyes. My heart's thumping as I speak because I feel this might be a bad thing to do. It's as if I'm taking them all into hospital with me to gawp at Mum, to peer in her face and poke her still body. I try to stop, but my mouth keeps on saying stuff. I start crying, but no one sneers and calls me a baby. They pat me and hug me and offer me paper hankies.

I'm treated in this special way all day long. I can't help wallowing in the attention. When one of the dinner ladies at lunch time tells me to hurry up because I can't choose whether I want spaghetti or fish and chips, a whole chorus of voices defends me.

'You mustn't pick on Ella, miss!'

'Ella's mum's dangerously ill in hospital.'

'Ella can't think straight because she's so worried about her mum.'

'We've all got to be kind to Ella, miss.'

The dinner lady looks really sorry and upset, and gives me spaghetti *and* fish and chips. I only pick at them, still not really hungry, but I feel proud she let me have a heaped plate.

I think about Mum, who hasn't eaten for days and days. They drip liquid food into her tubes. She can't even suck from a bottle like Samson.

I don't like to think of him all lonely in the nursery with no mummy to cuddle him. It's horrible for me but perhaps it's even worse for him. I wonder if he'll think of her soft chest and cry to be lying there again. Maybe he'll struggle up in his cot, slide down to the floor and toddle along on his bandy little legs, looking for her, wailing, 'Mama, mama, mama.'

I wonder when babies can really walk, really talk. I wonder what he'll be *like*, this little brother of mine. Will he stay fair like me and keep his blue eyes? Will he like all the things *I* used to like? Will he love spaghetti, especially if he can suck each strand up into his mouth? Will he like those big fat wax crayons? Will he cut pictures out of magazines with little plastic scissors? Will he watch *Charlie and Lola* on the television? Will he love Thomas the Tank Engine? Will he like to cuddle up in bed with a teddy guarding him on either side?

I think of this future fantasy brother and I want to rush to the hospital to start looking after him right this minute.

But he's Jack's little boy, not Dad's. I imagine a little Jack, showing off, telling silly jokes, picking his nose, doing daft monkey imitations. No, I don't want a baby brother like that. He'd be far worse than Sally's brother, Benjy.

I leave nearly all my spaghetti and fish and chips. I want to go off somewhere secret with Sally, but half the class are still hanging around with us. Dory and Martha even trail with us to the toilets. I sit in the cubicle and have a little private cry. I try to do it very quietly, but I must have made a sniffing sound because Sally's hand comes under the partition from next door. I bend down and cling to her hand for comfort.

Then the bell goes and I've still got the rest of afternoon school to get through. It's science, and Miss Anderson starts talking about food chains.

'From the tiniest shrimp to the biggest whale, all living things play roles in the food chain,' she says.

I draw a tiny shrimp on the back of my rough-book. It's hunched up and wrinkled, a bit like

Samson. Then I draw an enormous mouth and huge teeth. It's open wide, ready to gobble up the shrimp. The rest of the class are writing but I keep on drawing great pointy teeth. Then Sally gives me a nudge. Miss Anderson is walking towards me. I freeze. She's already told me once.

She shakes her head. 'You're meant to be taking notes, Ella,' she says quietly. 'What's that you're drawing?'

'It's a tiny shrimp, Miss Anderson. And the biggest whale.' I give a little nod. 'I *was* listening.'

'Mm. All right, what kind of a whale is it?'

What kind?

'It's a very big one.'

'There are many different kinds of whales, Ella. Seventy-seven different kinds. There are eleven baleen whales. What are baleen plates, everyone? Come on, I've just told you. Joseph?'

'They're instead of teeth, Miss Anderson,' says Joseph. 'They're all frayed like old hair-brushes.'

Joseph nearly always knows the answers to everything. Some of the naughtiest boys groan and mimic his voice.

Miss Anderson frowns. 'Shh, now! Well done, Joseph.'

'And there are sixty-six toothed whales,' says

Joseph. Sometimes he forgets and gives answers without even being asked.

'So my whale's a toothed whale,' I say.

'Ah, he's certainly got lots of teeth,' says Miss Anderson. 'But as you say, he's very big, with a massive head. That means he's more likely to be a baleen whale. They like to scoop huge mouthfuls of food from the sea and strain it through their baleen.'

'I eat spaghetti like that, Miss Anderson,' says Toby, laughing.

He's the largest boy in our class. We're not allowed to call him fat, but he is.

'Now, Ella, I think you'd better settle down and copy from Sally's notes,' says Miss Anderson. 'Why weren't you taking your own notes, hm?'

'I like drawing whales, Miss Anderson.'

'Well, perhaps you can draw me one for home-work. You can borrow a book from the book box and copy a picture, making sure all the details are accurate.'

'Can I draw a whale for homework too, Miss Anderson?' asks Joseph.

'Of course you can, Joseph,' she says, smiling at him.

Miss Anderson tries hard not to have favourites, but we all know she'd choose Joseph if she had one.

When the bell goes, she beckons both of us to the book box. 'There we are. Choose a book each,' she says.

I flip through and pick out a little book on fish.

'Whales aren't actually *fish*, Ella, they're mammals,' says Joseph, very gently and tactfully. He holds out his own great huge whale book. 'You can have this one if you like. It's the best in the box.'

'Thank you, Joseph. But it's OK, I'll take this one.' I select a very thin book with big print.

'Are you sure? That one doesn't look as if it's got much information,' Joseph says earnestly.

'I just need a picture to copy, don't I?'

'I suppose.'

'Off you go then, little whalers,' says Miss Anderson. She gives me a gentle pat. 'Will you be going up to the hospital to see your mum today, Ella?'

I nod.

'Well, you give her a big hug then, won't you?' she says.

'Miss Anderson,' I say in a rush. 'Miss Anderson, you know Mum's in a coma? Well, will she ever wake up?'

I stare at her imploringly. She stops looking like a great big teacher who knows everything. She suddenly looks much smaller, and scared.

'I hope so, Ella,' she says. 'Lots of people recover from comas. You read about it all the time.'

'But lots of other people ... don't recover,' I whisper.

Miss Anderson doesn't answer. She looks very sad. Then I hear a sniff. It's not me, not Miss Anderson. It's Joseph!

We both peer at him, astonished.

'I'm sorry,' he says. 'It must be so awful for you, Ella.'

'It is,' I say.

I'm very touched that he's really crying for Mum and me. I've always quite liked Joseph because he's never rough and silly like most of the other boys and he often says interesting things. Now I decide I like him quite a lot. In fact, if he wasn't a boy I'd want him as my second-best friend, after Sally.

She comes running back into the classroom, with Dory and Martha following her.

'Sorry, Miss Anderson, but Ella's dad's out in the playground and he's getting worried because she hasn't come out of school yet.'

'My *dad*!' I say, and I rush off to find him, not even saying goodbye to Miss Anderson and Joseph. Sally and Dory and Martha come running after me.

'Dad!' I shout, bursting out the door. He's come for me! He's going to make everything all right! He'll stay this time – he'll look after me just like a real dad . . . But it *isn't* Dad. It's just Jack, standing there in his stupid old jacket, nibbling his thumb and looking anxious.

'He's not my *dad*,' I say, turning on Sally. 'Why did you say he was my dad? You know he's only my stepdad! That was so *mean*, Sally!'

'I'm sorry. Don't get mad at me. I *meant* your stepdad. I just didn't say the step bit. And anyway, how could it be your real dad? You haven't seen him for years and years, you know you haven't,' Sally says.

'Well, I'm seeing him any day now, you wait and see,' I say.

I run up to Jack. 'Did you phone my dad?'

'What?'

'My *dad*. You said you'd get in touch – but you didn't!' I say.

'Hey, hey, calm down. I found a number in your mum's address book. He didn't answer, but I left a message. Don't look at me like that, Ella. I promise I did.'

I don't think I believe him.

'What did you say?'

'I said Sue's very ill and it's obviously very

upsetting for you, and you need him,' Jack says.

'Oh.'

Sally and Dory and Martha walk past, staring. Sally knows Jack because she's been on a sleepover at our new house.

'We're so sorry about Ella's mum,' she says.

'Thank you, Sally,' Jack says.

Then Sally's mum gets out of her car and comes over, and she and Jack yatter away about Mum. Dory goes off to find her own mum, and Martha goes into the hall for after-school club. Then Joseph comes out, clutching his big whale book to his chest. He nods at me and I nod back.

'What are you nodding at him for?' Sally asks. 'I can't stick Joseph. He's such a swot.'

'Yes, I know he's a swot, but I like him,' I say.

'You're mad!' says Sally.

Sally's mum hears and gives her a little shake. 'Are you being nasty to Ella?' she says, sounding horrified.

'No, Mum!'

'I should hope not. Ella, I was wondering, would you like to come to tea today, while your dad – your stepdad – is so busy? In fact, would you like to stay the night, and then we could take you to school in the morning?'

I normally love going to tea at Sally's house. Her

mum always makes cakes for us – proper cakes from scratch, not out of a packet – and we get to help and scrape out the mixing bowl afterwards. I think raw cake-mix tastes even nicer than baked cakes. Sally has her own computer in her bedroom so we can play about on that, and she's got all these lovely long evening frocks in her dressing-up box so we can play we're grown-up ladies at a dance. Sometimes we play pretend games with Benjy – we're two explorers and he's our faithful dog, or we're two nurses and he's our sick patient, or we're two teachers and he's our very naughty pupil.

I so want to stay at Sally's – but then how can I visit Mum? And what about Dad – my real dad? If Jack's being truthful – and actually I know he doesn't usually lie about stuff like that – then Dad might ring tonight when he gets home from work. He might even drive to our house and take me back with him.

'I'm sorry, Mrs Edwards, but I can't. Not tonight,' I say.

'Oooh, Ella, please come!' says Sally.

'It's OK Ella. You go and have tea,' says Jack.

I shake my head. 'I want to see *Mum*,' I mumble.

'Well, perhaps you can come tomorrow then? Whenever you want to,' says Mrs Edwards.

'You're so kind,' says Jack. 'Right, Ella, we'll go to the hospital and see Mum.'

I wave goodbye to Sally and Mrs Edwards, and go to the car with Jack.

'Have you been to the hospital already today?' I ask.

'Yes.'

'And Mum's still the same?'

'Yes. I saw little Sam too. They let me give him his bottle.'

'Oh!'

'Maybe you'd like to give him a feed sometime?'

'Maybe.' I want to very much but I don't want to sound too eager.

'What's that book you've got?'

'It's about whales. I have to draw one for Miss Anderson.'

'What, like homework?'

'Yes, sort of.'

'I've probably got some spare paper in my brief-case. You can do your whale drawing while we're sitting with Mum. So, how did school go today?'

'It was OK.'

'Miss Anderson was understanding? She seems like a lovely teacher.'

'Yes, she is.'

'And the other children, they were OK too?'

'They were all very nice, even *Martha*, who's usually not very nice to anyone. And Joseph *cried*, just because he was sorry about my mum. Joseph isn't even one of my friends, and he's a *boy*.'

'Boys have feelings too, Ella, and they can sometimes be very kind,' says Jack. 'I'm a boy, and *I* try to be kind.'

I don't answer him. We don't say any more until we get to the hospital. My tummy starts turning over. I'm desperate to see Mum, of course I am, but when I do it's so sad and scary.

Jack holds out his hand but I don't want to take it. I march into the hospital and trudge down all the corridors, humming a little tune as if I haven't a care in the world – but I'm saying words to the tune inside my head: *Please let Mum be all right . . . Please let Mum be all right . . . Please let Mum be all right*, over and over again.

It's a terrible shock when we get to Mum's room because her bed is empty. There are no covers on it. All her cards are gone from her locker top.

I stop. Jack does too, his hand over his mouth.

'Oh God!' he whispers.

We stand there blinking, willing Mum to be back in her bed. It stays empty.

Then the grumpy nurse bustles past and sees our faces. 'It's all right,' she says quickly. 'We decided to move her this afternoon because she's so stable. We need this room for patients who need constant monitoring.'

'Then she's getting better?' I ask.

'Well . . .' The grumpy nurse hesitates, looking almost kind. 'She's not getting any worse.'

She takes us down further corridors, and there's Mum in a curtained-off bed by the nurses' station. She's there in her new place but she looks exactly the same, lying on her back, her mouth a little open, breathing in and out, in and out . . .

'Oh, Mum,' I say, and I rush to her side. She's still got all the tubes dangling in and out of her. I look at the nurse. 'It is all right to hug her, isn't it?'

'Yes, so long as you're gentle.'

So I lay my head on the pillow beside Mum and rub my cheek against hers. Jack's standing the other side of the bed, holding her hand.

'Oh, Sue,' he whispers.

The tea trolley comes rattling down the ward. The tea is just for the patients and Mum can't drink anything from a cup, but the lady in the yellow apron gives Jack a cup of tea. She gives me a biscuit. I try to eat it to be polite, but my mouth's so dry the crumbs stick in my throat and coat my tongue like grit.

When I start to get a crick in my neck, I

straighten up reluctantly. I sit in the hard orange visitor's chair and start to copy the whales from my book onto Jack's piece of paper.

I draw a killer whale first, doing a lot of shading so that it looks properly black and white. It looks more like a smiley penguin than a whale, so I draw its mouth open, with a row of vicious-looking teeth, and half a baby sea lion sticking out. I do a little speech bubble: 'I am a killer whale and I am killing.' Then I flick through the whole book to find a baleen whale. I draw a humpback, with long flippers and little bobbles on its head. The book says humpbacks are very acrobatic so I draw it leaping out of the water, going, 'Wheee! Look at me!'

'Let's have a look,' says Jack.

I flash the paper very quickly, so he can only see it for a second.

'Mm. You're good at drawing, Ella. But I'm not sure Miss Anderson would appreciate the speech bubbles,' says Jack. 'Isn't it meant to be a serious drawing, not a comic strip?'

'Miss Anderson always lets us do speech bubbles,' I say, which is a downright lie.

I start to worry abut them. I can't rub them out because I've drawn in black felt pen. I suppose I could ask Jack for another piece of paper and start all over again, but it would be such a nuisance. I flip through my whale book instead. There's a page headed 'Mothers and Babies', with a photo of a mother whale swimming very close beside her little baby. I run my fingers over them as if I'm stroking them. The book says that whales make very good mothers. They stroke and pat their babies and keep them by their side constantly.

I look at my poor mum. I think of the baby in the nursery.

'Shall we go and find Samson and bring him to Mum for a cuddle?' I say.

'Yes, that's a good idea. We'll go to the nursery right now,' says Jack.

'You go. I'll stay here with Mum,' I say, so I can have a proper private cuddle with her.

Jack goes off.

'Look, Mum,' I say, and I wave my drawing right in front of her face. 'I've drawn a picture of whales. Can you just open your eyes for a second and have a little look? You'd really like it, I know you would.'

Mum doesn't move.

'Well, never mind. I'll tell you about it, shall I? These are two different kinds of whales, did you know that, Mum? There are killer whales – they have teeth – and baleen whales – they have weird hairbrush thingies in their mouths and they filter their little shrimpy food through them. You might think whales are fish but they're mammals: they feed their babies milk, just like we do. Well, you can't feed Samson yourself yet, but it's all right, Jack will feed him for you, and I'm going to feed him too. And we'll bring him to you lots so you can have a cuddle. Well, I can lift your hand up and you can give him a stroke. That's what mother whales do, they stroke with their flippers. I *like* whales, Mum.'

Jack comes back into the room with Samson. He's crying, thrashing about miserably inside his shawl.

'Oh dear, oh dear, he's not a happy little lad just now,' says Jack.

'He needs his cuddle with Mum,' I say. 'He's been missing her.'

'I think you're right, Ella,' says Jack.

I undo the top of Mum's nightie, the way that Dr Wilmot did, and Jack unwraps Samson from his blanket and lies him very gently on his side, on Mum's chest. Samson starts, gives one tiny sobbing cry, and then relaxes. He gives little snuffles but he's stopped crying altogether.

Jack and I look at each other. Jack's got tears in his eyes.

'Works like magic!' he whispers.

So why why why won't the magic work for Mum, too?

Chapter 6

There's a message on the telephone when we get back.

It's Dad!

Well, I don't even know it's him at first – his voice doesn't sound the way I remembered – but it must be Dad because he's talking to me.

'Hello. This is a message for Ella. It's all right, darling. Don't worry. I'm sure Mummy will get better very soon. I'll take the day off work and come tomorrow.'

I stand transfixed. Then I play the message again – and again – and again.

'There,' says Jack. 'I told you I left a message for him.'

'Shh! Let me *listen*,' I hiss.

'You've heard it three times,' says Jack, and he goes off to the kitchen to fix us tea.

He spends ages fussing around. He's done a big shop today and he says he's going to cook a proper meal. I don't know why he's bothering. I'm not the slightest bit hungry. I just crouch in the hall listening to my dad, whispering along with his message because I've learned it by heart.

Jack comes back into the hall. 'Give it a rest now, Ella, eh? Would you like two sausages or three?'

'I don't want any sausages, thanks.'

'Don't be silly, of course you do. Sausages are your favourites,' Jack says. 'And I'm doing my special creamy mash. And we've got broccoli too – vitamin C, very important.'

'I hate broccoli.'

'Ella. Stop it. Look, come and give me a hand. I'll teach you how to cook sausages.'

'I *know* how to cook sausages.'

'Well, great, come and cook them.'

'I don't want to.'

'Oh, for God's sake!' Jack marches back into the kitchen and slams the door.

I stand there in the hall, my heart thudding. I feel just a little bit mean . . . but I decide it's not fair. I don't have to do what Jack says. He's not my dad. My *real* dad is talking on the telephone to me, and he's coming to see me specially tomorrow. He must really, really care about me to take the day off work. *And he says Mum's going to get better!*

'Mum's going to get better!' I say, and I whirl round and round the hall.

Maybe Dad will fall in love with Mum all over again when he sees her lying asleep in hospital. He'll be like a fairytale prince and waken her with a kiss. Then Mum and I can live with Dad like a proper family. We can send Jack packing. And Samson. Although he's Mum's. When he lies on her chest he looks like he really belongs to her.

I get worn out trying to work out how everyone can live happily, together and apart. Jack can just shove off all by himself. It's just tough luck that Samson's his little boy too. But I think of Jack's

91

face when he was watching Samson snuffling on Mum's chest. I feel cross. I don't don't don't want to feel sorry for Jack.

I can smell his sausages cooking. Perhaps I feel a little bit hungry after all. Maybe he's in such a sulk with me now that he won't let me have any.

But eventually he opens the kitchen door and calls, 'Supper's ready.'

I stand still, wondering what to do. I could be really fierce and yell back, 'I don't want any of your horrid old supper.' Then he might get really mad. He might even smack me. So I'd smack him back. Even though he's a lot bigger than me.

I could just ignore him altogether and slope off to my room. That would be mega-effective. He couldn't even tell me off for being cheeky because I wouldn't have said a word.

But I am actually quite hungry now, so I shuffle into the kitchen and sit down at the table. Jack has put two and a half sausages on my favourite plate, the orange one with the little gold elephants. There's a small mound of mash with a knob of butter on the top and four little sprigs of bright green broccoli. It all looks very nice — even the broccoli.

I don't say anything, but I pick up my knife and fork and start eating. Jack starts eating too.

I decide I will maybe just eat the half-sausage, but once I've started I feel ravenous and in ten minutes it's all gone, apart from one tiny sprig of broccoli, because I feel I have to leave something.

Jack looks at me. 'Was that good?' he asks in a neutral sort of voice.

'Yes,' I say. I wait. 'Thank you.'

Jack nods at me. 'You're very welcome, Ella.'

I stand up and start stacking the dishwasher.

'Oh, thanks, love,' he says.

'J-a-c-k?'

'Yep?'

'Can I phone my dad now?'

'Yes, I was going to suggest it. We need to fix up exactly when he's coming.'

He gives me the number. My fingers go a bit trembly as I'm dialling. Mum never gave me the number. We didn't ever phone Dad. I'm not really sure Mum would want me to. She always said we didn't need him. But we need him now, badly.

So I dial the number and wait. The phone rings, once, twice, three times, four, five. There's a click after the sixth ring and the answerphone message starts up.

'Hi there. Mike and Tina can't get to the phone right now. Can you leave a message and we'll get back to you as soon as possible.'

Mike and *Tina*? Who's she? My thoughts spin, trying to find a suitable explanation. Perhaps Dad has a dog called Tina. I make her up in my head: a cream Labrador, very sweet and gentle, with big brown eyes. Dad takes her for walks every morning and evening and feeds her special titbits, and she crouches at his feet all night. No, perhaps Tina is a cat, and she sits on Dad's lap when he watches television and purrs softly to herself. But it's no use. No matter how hard I try to imagine a Tina dog or a Tina cat, a new type of Tina keeps sidling into my mind. A girlfriend. She's curling up with Dad at night, she's sitting on his lap, she's whispering softly . . .

I put down the telephone.

Jack puts his hand on my shoulder. 'Didn't you want to leave a message?' he says gently.

I shrug his hand away. I don't want him feeling sorry for me. 'There's no point leaving a message. I'll be seeing him tomorrow,' I say.

I can't get to sleep for ages and ages. I hear Jack getting up at some point and making himself a cup of tea. I wonder about calling out to him to make me a drink too. I feel ever so thirsty – but I won't call out. I imagine what it must be like for Mum. She could be feeling terribly thirsty, terribly hungry, but she can't call out. She's lying there all alone in that strange hospital bed and she can't call for a cuddle . . .

I start crying again. After a minute or two Jack comes knocking at my bedroom door.

'Ella? Are you OK?'

What a stupid question! Of *course* I'm not OK. I burrow underneath my duvet, and sob there, where he can't hear me. He opens my door.

'I'm here if – if you need anything,' he whispers.

I don't answer and he goes away again. I fall asleep in a sodden heap under the covers. When I next surface it's morning.

Jack stares at me when I go down to the kitchen. I'm in my best black and white dress again, though it's a bit creased and crumpled now.

'Why aren't you in your uniform?'

'Because my dad's coming!'

'Yes, I know, but you've still got to go to school, silly.'

'No, I can't! Dad said he's taking the day off work. He'll be coming this morning!'

'Look, he knows you have to go to school. *I* can see him, we can come and meet you at school together.'

'No! No! If I'm not here he might go away again!'

'Hey, hey, calm down. Of course he wouldn't do that.'

'Yes, he might. He said last time he'd come back to see me really soon, maybe the next Saturday, and then he didn't come back – he didn't come back *ever*.'

'Well, what kind of a father is that?' Jack snaps.

I flinch as if he's slapped me.

Jack puts his hand over his mouth. 'I'm sorry. I didn't really mean that.'

'Yes, you did!'

'Look, tell you what. We'll phone your dad again, and see what time he reckons he'll be here.'

'All right, let *me* talk to him,' I say.

We only get the answerphone again. *Mike and Tina, Mike and Tina, Mike and Tina . . .*

'There, see! His answerphone's on. Which means he's left already. He could be here any minute!'

'He lives in Sussex – it'll take him hours to drive here.'

'I bet he got up first thing. I bet he's been driving for hours already.'

'Ella—'

'I'm not going to school, Jack. You can't make me.'

'But we've just got you settled back into going to school.'

'I'm not going, I'm not going, I'm not going!'

'All right! You're not going. I think we've

established that. Only *I* have to go out and do one thousand and one things. I've still got childminders to find and nurseries to see, I've got to meet this social worker, I need to buy all the food and stuff I forgot yesterday . . . How am I going to do all that?'

'You can do that when my dad's here.'

Jack sighs. 'You're so like your mum, Ella. She always has to have the last word too.'

Then he puts his cup of tea down, looking stricken. I sit silently at the table. Mum can't have the last word now. She can't say any words at all.

Jack pours me a bowl of cornflakes. We eat morosely. Then the phone goes and I rush to answer it – but it's just the Garton Road head teacher wanting to speak to Jack. He's on the phone for ages. I sit stirring my cornflakes aimlessly, watching them go soggy and sink to the bottom.

'Well, I need to go to my school *soon*, even if you don't,' Jack says, coming back into the kitchen. He yawns and stretches. 'I'm going to set my class a whole load of stuff to make it easier for the supply teacher. If you insist on staying home, you can do the work too.'

'That's not fair! You teach Year Six!'

'Well, you're bright, aren't you?' says Jack.

'I'll do my own schoolwork,' I say.

Jack clears the kitchen table and we sit at either end doing our work, Jack typing away on his laptop, me drawing. I draw lots more whales. I draw a blue whale that takes up the whole paper because it's the biggest whale ever. Its tongue weighs as much as an elephant! It eats four tons of food a day. I imagine four tons of little shrimpy things getting sucked into that great mouth every day. Blue whales live in little family groups, so I get more pieces of paper and draw a great big mother blue whale and then a baby blue whale that only takes up half the page.

I'm almost certain Dad will be here by the time I finish my family of blue whales. I run to the door several times, just checking that the bell's working. 'You did tell Dad we live in this house now, didn't you, Jack?'

'Yes, of course. I gave him the postcode so his satnav can take him straight to us,' says Jack, writing rapidly.

'Mm,' I say.

I flip to a new page about pilot whales. They look funny, with big bulging foreheads and wide mouths, showing their teeth. They act like they've got brilliant satellite navigation themselves. They can home in on big schools of fish many miles away.

It's an odd way to think of talking about fish. I imagine a fish school. I draw a little fish Sally dividing twenty shells by four. I draw Dory edging up to her, admiring Sally's shiny scales and pointy tail. I draw Martha doing a back flip, her fins raised, showing off like mad. I draw Joseph with his nose in a big book strewn with seaweed.

'What's a book with a fishy title?' I ask Jack.

'*Twenty Thousand Leagues under the Sea*,' says Jack.

There's no way I can print all that on the cover of one little book, so I make do with *Under the Sea*. Then I draw a Miss Anderson big haddock with a smiley mouth and curly hair and a coral necklace.

'What subject is that schoolwork?' Jack asks, still typing away.

'Science.'

'Well, that drawing doesn't look very scientifically accurate,' Jack says. 'What's it supposed to be?'

'A school of fish.'

'What? Oh, I get it.'

'And this pilot whale is homing in on them fast,' I say.

I give Sally and Joseph and Miss Anderson extra fins so they can flap them quickly and escape. It looks like Dory might be in trouble. And as for

Martha, flashing her fins and drawing attention to herself – she's going to disappear in one gollop.

I sit up and stretch. I can't believe that only twenty minutes have gone by. *Come on, Dad. Please please please come now.*

I sigh and yawn and rock my chair.

'Don't tip it like that – you'll go right over and bump your head,' says Jack.

'That's such a teacher thing to say.'

'Well, tough, I *am* a teacher. Now shh, Ella, I'm trying to work out this wretched lesson plan. Draw another whale.'

'I'm a little bit *tired* of whales,' I say. 'They'll have gone on to something else in science today.'

'Well, you could work on doing your own special whale project at home,' says Jack.

I think about it. I don't usually like any of Jack's suggestions simply because he's Jack – but I suddenly see a big glossy folder with MY WHALE PROJECT carefully printed in fancy lettering, with little whales spouting up and down the page. Joseph once did a special planets project and showed it to Miss Anderson, and she was positively ecstatic.

'Do you have a special folder, Jack? Preferably a blue one?' I ask.

'What do you think I am, your local branch of

Paperchase?' says Jack. 'But I expect I can buy one for you. If you're very good and don't disturb me now.'

I draw a grey whale with lots of scars on his poor head, scraping his way along the ocean floor, eating lots of little creatures. Then I copy out all the things the book says about grey whales and pilot whales and killer whales.

'I think projects are meant to be in your *own* words,' says Jack.

'I'm rearranging them, sort of,' I say.

'I'd soon sort you out if you were in my class.'

'I'm ever so glad I'm not,' I retort.

And then the doorbell goes, and I jump up so quickly I tear my grey whale almost in two and I don't care, I just have to get to the door and see . . . my dad. It is him! He's so *smart* too, wearing a proper grey suit, a beautiful blue shirt, and a pink and blue silk tie. Oh, he's got dressed up properly for *me*. It's as if a famous rock star is standing on the doorstep. He looks so strangely familiar and yet so different too, somehow taller, older, not really the way I've been picturing him at all.

'*Dad!*' I say.

'Hello, Ella!'

We stand there, stuck, freeze-framed with the strangeness of it all. Then he bends a little and opens his arms. I stumble forward awkwardly, feeling the blood thumping in my head, but when I feel his hands holding me, I suddenly cling to him and start crying.

We stand there on the doorstep, rocking to and fro. After a long while Jack comes to the door and invites Dad inside.

Jack puts on the kettle and Dad looks at my whale drawings.

'You did these all by yourself? My, but you're brilliant! Imagine you knowing all this stuff about whales!' says Dad. 'You're such a clever girl.' He's acting as if I'm about four.

'I just copied them,' I mumble.

'You're a real little artist! Isn't she brilliant, Jack?' says Dad.

I take him into my bedroom and pull out all my old drawing books and flip through them quickly. He admires each one, and stares around my room.

'This is a very pretty room, Ella. Purple and silver, eh? Very sophisticated.'

'They're my favourite colours.'

'I thought blue was your favourite colour.'

'That was *ages* ago,' I say.

'Where's your big teddy?' Dad asks, looking around.

Oh help. I can't tell Dad we gave him to a jumble sale.

'It was so sad. He got lost,' I say quickly.

'Lost? How could a great big bear that size get lost? He was bigger than you!'

'Yes, I know, but – but it was when we moved here. It was horrible. We couldn't find him any-where,' I fib. 'He was my all-time favourite cuddly toy, Dad, honest.'

'Well, don't worry, pet, we'll get you another,' says Dad. 'So, do you like it here?' He nods at the door. 'He's OK, is he, this Jack?' he whispers.

'I don't really like him. I don't know what Mum sees in him. Oh, Dad, Mum's so poorly. She's just lying there in hospital and she can't move, she can't speak, she can't even open her eyes. Dad, she will get better, won't she?'

'Yes, yes, of course she'll get better,' he says.

'You promise, you absolutely promise?'

'Of course. Don't worry so, Ella. They'll be looking after her in hospital, doing their very best for her.'

'Can we go and see her now?' I beg.

Dad looks startled. 'Well, I'm not sure that's appropriate. They won't want you to see your mummy if she's so poorly.'

'Yes, they will! I go to see her every day. Oh please, Dad, please, please!'

I'm desperate for him to come. Then the three of us will be together and Dad will make Mum better – he said he would, he *promised*.

'Well, Jack can take you later—'

'I don't want Jack! I want *you*, Dad!'

'Oh. Right.' His eyes get misty. 'I'll take you then.'

'Now? Please say now.'

'Yes, right you are. Now. This very minute.'

I'm worried Jack will come too, but when we tell him, he says he's got all these people to see.

'What do you want to do about lunch?' Jack says, looking at his watch.

'Oh, I'll take Ella out for lunch,' Dad says.

'Right. Thanks, Mike. I'll see you back here then. I'll give you a spare key so you can let yourselves in if I'm not back,' says Jack.

'That's good of you, Jack,' says Dad.

They're being very smiley-smiley and calling each other Mike and Jack, but I can tell they don't like each other.

Jack's hesitating. 'Obviously we've got all sorts of things to discuss. All sorts of stuff to consider. But – but you won't do anything rash, will you? I mean, I know you're Ella's dad, but I'm her stepdad and – well, we both want what's best for her, don't we? I mean, you wouldn't just

104

take off with her without discussing everything first?'

Jack drones on and on in his teacher's voice. Dad's not listening either. He squeezes my hand.

'Yeah, yeah, I take your point, Jack. Right, come on then, Ella.'

'Get your jacket, love,' says Jack, following us to the door. 'And you're walking funny in those patent shoes. Why don't you change into your school shoes? I'm sure they're much comfier.'

I don't want to wear my old jacket – one of the buttons has come off and the sleeves have gone all bobbly. It looks awful with my black and white dress. I have to take it because it's cold outside, but I'm *not* wearing my scuffed brown school shoes – they'd look *awful*. The black patent shoes are a little bit small for me now, but they look lovely. Dad's so smart. I want him to think I'm smart too.

Jack's picking up my shoes from where I kicked them off in the hall yesterday, but I take no notice.

'Bye, Jack,' I say, and rush out of the front door.

Chapter 7

I look around for Dad's car. Parked right behind Jack's ancient Ford Focus there's a shiny red Jag. My mouth opens. I look at Dad. He clicks his keys and it gives a little clunk as it unlocks.

'Oh, Dad, how *cool*!' I say.

Dad bows and opens the door. 'Care for a little spin, my lady?'

'You bet!'

'Right you are. Where do you want to go? We could go out into the countryside, if you like. I know, there's a special farm where you can stroke all the baby animals – would you like that?'

'I'd absolutely love it!'

'And we can have a spot of lunch in this gastro-pub—'

'Mum and Jack had their wedding reception in one of those pubs,' I say.

'Oh, very stylish,' says Dad, grinning. He starts the car.

'Do you know the way?'

'To this farm? Yes, I checked before I left home.'

'No, to the *hospital*! We're going there first, aren't we?'

'Well, yes. If you want. Though if your mum's unconscious—'

'Oh, Dad, she might be a little bit better today. And when we *both* talk to her, she'll be so surprised she might just open her eyes! *Do* you know the way?'

'I think so,' says Dad, sighing.

He drives through the town, going the long way round, past my school. I peer out hopefully, willing

Sally and Dory, and especially Martha, to glance out of our classroom window to see me driving past in such style. We even pass the end of our old road.

'Oh look, Lanford Road. I *wish* we still lived there,' I say.

I wait, hoping that Dad will say he wishes he still lived there too. He doesn't say a word. When we get to the hospital car park, he starts fussing.

'I'm sure visiting hours are in the afternoon.'

'Dr Wilmot says we can visit Mum any time, if we're family.'

'But I'm not family. Not any more.'

'Yes, you are! You're my dad. Of course you're family.'

Dad parks the car and we go into the main hospital entrance. He peers around, looking bewildered. 'Perhaps we'd better go to the reception desk.'

'No, I know the way.'

I take Dad's hand. It's surprisingly sweaty.

'It's all right, Dad,' I say. 'I know some people get all freaked out in hospitals. Aunty Liz *hated* coming.'

'Oh, Liz! I'd forgotten all about her,' says Dad. 'I don't think she liked me very much.'

'Well, I don't like *her* much,' I say.

I lead Dad down all the corridors. My own hand's starting to get sweaty now. My tummy's churning. I start whispering, 'Oh, Mum, oh, Mum, oh, Mum.'

'What's that you're saying?' Dad asks.

'Nothing.'

I say it silently instead. And then we're in the right ward, and there's Mum's bed, and Dr Wilmot is bending over her, listening to her chest with a stethoscope.

She smiles when she sees me. She's still smiling when she looks at Dad – and then blinks in surprise. 'Hello, Ella. And . . . ?'

'This is my dad, Dr Wilmot, my real dad.'

'Mike Lakeland,' says Dad, shaking her hand. 'I'm Ella's father. Sue and I used to be married.'

'But not any more? You're not still Sue's next of kin?'

'Oh no, no. That'll be her new chap, Jack. No, I'm just here because Ella wanted to see her mum.'

'Of course,' says Dr Wilmot. She takes hold of one of Mum's hands and strokes it lightly. 'You've got two visitors to see you, Sue.'

Mum doesn't stir. Dr Wilmot walks away, waving goodbye to me.

'Mum, Mum, it's *Dad*. He's come specially to see you,' I say, leaning down and rubbing my cheek against Mum's. I look up at Dad. 'Come and talk to her, Dad!'

Dad's looking so strange, standing stiffly, as if his smart suit is made of cardboard.

'Dad?'

He clears his throat. 'Hello, Sue,' he says, as if he's meeting a stranger. 'How are you doing?'

Mum breathes in and out, not taking any notice at all.

'Mum,' I say, giving her shoulder a little shake. 'Open your eyes, Mum. It's Dad.'

'Don't, Ella! You'll hurt her,' says Dad.

'I wouldn't hurt Mum!' I say. 'Oh, Dad, please, come and talk close up to her ear – and then try giving her a kiss.'

'A *kiss*?' says Dad.

'Like in the fairy stories,' I say, blushing because I know it sounds silly. But I don't care if I sound like a stupid baby, I have to try. Dad might just make Mum better – he *said* he would.

'Mum, Mum!'

'Ella, leave your mum alone. She can't hear you.'

'Yes, she *can*. Dr Wilmot says – all the nurses say too – patients in comas *can* hear you, and one day they'll wake up. Couldn't you just *try* kissing her, Dad?'

Dad steps forward, bends awkwardly and kisses the air above Mum's cheek. 'There.'

Mum doesn't stir.

'You didn't kiss her properly. You didn't even touch her.'

'Ella. You're being silly. Let's leave your poor mum in peace.'

Dad starts walking away.

'But we've only just got here!'

He carries on walking.

'Oh, Mum, I'm sorry,' I whisper into her ear. 'I'll see if I can make him come back. I love you so. You look lovely here, just like Sleeping Beauty.' I comb her hair with my fingers. I can smell soap and some sort of mouthwash: the nurses clean her gently every day. She doesn't look or smell scary at all, so why why why couldn't Dad kiss her properly?

I run after him. His face is very red.

'Dad?'

He's struggling. 'She was always so *lively*, full of fun, tossing her hair around—'

'We can go back and talk to her. Perhaps you can talk about the old days when we all lived together. I think she'd like that.'

'Ella, there's no point,' Dad says sharply.

'She will wake up soon, I know she will. You said she'll get better.'

'Yes, but I didn't realize. Come on.'

I stop suddenly, remembering. 'Do you want to see my little brother?'

'What? Oh, the baby!'

'I know the way to the nursery. Come and have a look.'

I take him along the corridors until we get to the nursery. A new nurse looks at us enquiringly.

'No visitors just now, not in here,' she says.

'Oh please, can't I just show my dad my little brother, Samson Winters?'

'Baby Winters? The one whose mother's . . . ? Oh. Well, just a peep.'

'It's all right, nurse, we'll leave the babies sleeping,' Dad says quickly.

'Well, we can see through the window. That's Samson there, in the corner. Oh, I think he's crying! He's missing Mum. We have to go to him.'

'He'll just be hungry. All babies cry, Ella.'

'Did I cry?'

'Lots.'

'Did I look like Samson when I was little?'

'All babies look the same. Small and wrinkly.'

'Did you ever feed me, Dad?'

'Yes, of course. Once or twice.'

'Jack feeds Samson sometimes. I can too, if I want.'

Dad sighs. 'You don't want to feed him *now*, do you? Come on, that nice nurse will look after him. Let's go and feed ourselves.'

We go back down the long corridors. I feel I've been trailing up and down them for ever.

'No, Ella,' says Dad as I try to turn down Mum's corridor. 'This is the way out.'

'But we're going back to Mum, aren't we?'

'No, we're going for our meal out in the country.'

'But we have to say goodbye to Mum!'

Dad sighs again. 'Ella, she can't hear us.'

'She *can*, I told you.'

'For goodness' sake, will you stop arguing!'

I don't say another word all the way out of the hospital and into the car. After five minutes' driving Dad says, 'Are you sulking?'

I shake my head, tears starting to spill out of my eyes.

'Yes, you are! Come on, cheer up. You can't expect to get your own way all the time,' Dad says, and he reaches over and pats my knee.

I sniff.

'You're not crying, are you?'

'I just – I so hoped – I thought you'd make Mum better. You *said*—' I howl.

'Ella, I hadn't realized just how ill your mum is.'

'But she is still going to get better, isn't she?'

'Well – I'm sure the doctors and nurses are doing all they can.'

Dad puts on the car radio, fiddling through the

stations until he finds some pop music. 'There! Shall we have a little sing-song?'

The last thing in the world I want to do is sing, but I'm scared Dad is starting to dislike me. I need to try to please him, so I sing, and he sings along too. He's got a lovely voice, he's singing really properly. Jack just mucks around and plays air guitar and acts like a fool when *he* sings. I look at my dad's profile as he drives. He's really good-looking. No wonder Mum fell in love with him. I wonder why they had to fall out of love.

'Dad, can I ask you something?'

'Mm?' he says cautiously.

'Why did you and Mum split up?'

'What has your mother told you?'

'Mum says you both decided to go your separate ways.'

'Well, that's exactly it.'

'But did you just stop loving each other?'

'I suppose so.'

'Did you stop loving me?'

'No!'

Then why did you go off and leave me? But I can't say it out loud. There's something else I can't say. The name Tina echoes in my head. *Tina-Tina-Tina*, like a terrible two-note song in my brain.

I'm starting to feel sick. I'm never very good at

long car journeys. I think with horror about having to beg Dad to stop the car. I imagine throwing up in the gutter, with Dad looking and hearing and smelling. I close my eyes and keep very, very still, willing my cornflakes to stay in my stomach.

'Look at the hills, Ella! Don't fall asleep on me!'

I peer blearily at the hills, holding my breath as we go up them and down them – and then at last, just as I think I really am going to have to tell Dad, he draws up at a pub called the Grey Goose. I stagger out and take deep breaths, feeling terribly wobbly.

'You OK?'

I give him a queasy smile and follow him into the pub. He must come here quite a lot because the man and lady behind the bar call him by his name, and then stare at me curiously.

'This is my daughter, Ella,' he says.

They look at me in surprise and make a fuss of me. I still feel so sick, I don't say much when they ask me questions.

'She's going through a traumatic time at the moment, poor kid. Her mother's very ill,' Dad says.

They fuss even more. The lady gives Dad a glass of red wine and me a pink sparkly drink with lots of cherries bobbing on the top. It tastes so sweet and fizzy that my stomach lurches and I have to rush to the toilet. I'm a little bit sick, and then sit shivering on the lavatory for a while, wondering what on earth I'm doing there. I don't want Dad. I don't want Jack. I just want *Mum*. I want her to open her eyes and see what's going on. I want her to pull out all her scary tubes. I want her to climb out of her bed and put on her own clothes. I want her to get in our old car and come and find me. I want her to put her arms round me and hold me tight and never let me go.

There's a tapping at my cubicle. 'Are you all right in there, dear?'

It's Margie, the lady behind the bar. Dad must have sent her. I dry my eyes quickly with loo paper and then emerge sheepishly.

'I'm fine, thank you.' What else can I say?

I wash my hands and splash my face with cold water and start to feel a little better. I still don't like the pink drink very much, and I don't like lunch either. I ask for sausages, but when they come they don't look like proper sausages at all, they're all coiled round and round like little snakes. I just nibble at one end and eat my mash, though that doesn't taste right either – it's got something weird and herby all the way through it.

'Eat up, Ella,' says Dad. 'Don't you like it?'

'It's lovely,' I fib. 'I'm just not very hungry, thank you.'

'Ah, bless,' says Margie. 'Don't you worry, pet. It's only natural you haven't got much appetite, given the circumstances.'

Dad eats up all his steak and offers me a few of his chips. 'Ah, typical woman, you're happy to eat off *my* plate,' he says. He swallows the last of his wine. 'Come on then, poppet, let's go and find those farm animals.'

'Oh, she'll *love* them, Mike.' Margie giggles. 'Fancy you being a dad!'

'Well, I've only been a part-time dad up till now,' he says, pulling a funny face at me.

Up till now. Oh, I so hope he decides to be a proper full-time dad now. It didn't work with Mum this time, but perhaps if Dad and I visit her regularly . . .

I reach out and hold Dad's hand. He pulls me close and gives me a hug.

'My little girl,' he says.

We walk out of the pub door together, bumping awkwardly in the porch. Dad blows me a little kiss.

'There! Did you like my friends?'

'Yes, Dad.' I pause, trying to think what to say. 'I like going out with you, Dad.'

'Well, that's good, then. Come on, we'll go up to the farm now.'

I'm not quite so keen on the farm. We have to

leave the car at the entrance and walk up a very long muddy track. It's hard work stepping this way and that, keeping my patent shoes clean. They're really hurting now, stabbing my toes at every step.

Dad pays for us to go round the farm to see all the animals. There's a lovely grey donkey and lots of sheep – and several goats, but I'm not so keen on getting in their pen. They have horns and spooky yellow eyes, and one tries to nibble the sleeve of my jacket. I get goat slobber all the way up to my elbow.

There are mostly very little kids going round with their mums or grannies, two-year-olds and three-year-olds, too young for school. I feel very big and self-conscious beside them. There's a little animal enclosure full of rabbits and guinea pigs, and they're very sweet. I squat down and stroke a fluffy little brown and white guinea pig. I can feel it quivering, but it doesn't try to jump away.

'Oh, I wish I had my own little guinea pig,' I say, sighing.

'Don't you have any pets?'

'Well, I had three stick insects at our old house, Sticky and Picky and Kicky, but to be absolutely honest I couldn't tell which was which – and then they died. Mum said I could have a proper pet when we moved to the new house with Jack, and

I *so* wanted a puppy, but she said it wouldn't be fair leaving it on its own all day. She said she'd maybe think again after the baby was born, but now . . .' My voice tails away.

'I'm sure you could have a little guinea pig,' says Dad. 'Tell you what, there's a notice over there: *Young guinea pigs for sale*. Would you really like one?'

'Oh, Dad, I'd absolutely *adore* one!'

'Then let's see if you can choose your perfect pet,' says Dad.

He talks to one of the farm women, and she takes us to an indoor room where there's a special cage of weeny little baby guinea pigs.

'Oh, they're so sweet! How am I ever going to choose?'

I very gently stroke each one. They give little squeaks, as if they're saying, *Pick me! No, pick me! Oh, pick* me*!*

I choose the littlest, who's a beautiful brown all over, with black beady eyes and a pink quivering nose.

'Can I really have one? Then can it be *this* one?' I say, holding him.

'Of course you can,' says Dad, smiling. 'Is it a little boy or a little girl?'

The farm lady picks it up and squints at its

underneath carefully. 'I think you've got a little boy here,' she says.

'Oh, I'm glad it's a boy!' I say.

'What are you going to call him?'

'I shall call him Butterscotch, because he's exactly that colour,' I say.

'And have you got a proper cage for him at home?'

I look at Dad. He sighs. 'Well, we'd better buy one.'

There are two different sorts: a very plain wire cage affair and an elaborate hutch with a special bed area.

'Which do you think he'd like best, Dad?' I say, dithering hopefully beside the big hutch.

'I dare say he'd better have the special one. It's a veritable Ritz for guinea pigs. Still, I don't see why little Butterscotch shouldn't live in style.'

I want to sit with Butterscotch on my lap in the car, but Dad says it isn't safe – and he doesn't want Butterscotch doing little poos and wees all over his upholstery. We put him into his very superior hutch, cushioning him with straw, and Dad wedges it on the back seat. My insides have started churning again. Dad's bought me Butterscotch *and* his special hutch so he can live in his luxurious new home. Am *I* going to live in style in *Dad's* luxurious home? I'm not quite sure where Dad lives. He had to drive a long way this morning. Will he be able to take me to see Mum every day?

'I can still see Mum, can't I?' I blurt out.

'What? Of course you can,' says Dad.

I breathe out. I curl up beside Butterscotch's cage and whisper little soothing words to him.

'What's that, Ella?' says Dad.

'I was just chatting to Butterscotch, Dad.'

'You're a funny little sausage.'

I think of the strange sausage I had in the gastro-pub. It's not such a good idea. I'm starting to feel sick again. I slump down, my chin on my chest, my eyes closed. It's very dark and swirly and scary inside my head. I wonder if this is what it feels like for Mum. I feel really bad for her. I'll try to be extra soothing next time I see her. I want to see her right this minute.

'Dad?'

'What?'

I swallow. 'Nothing.' I know it's no use asking him to take us back to the hospital today, not when we've already paid one visit.

Dad drives us straight back to the house. He knocks at the door, fingering the peeling part round the letter box. 'For heaven's sake, can't he give it a lick of paint?' he says.

'Jack's hopeless at stuff like that. The loo cistern kept dripping and he said he'd fix it, and he pulled the whole ballcock off and we had to get an emergency plumber who charged heaps, and Mum was very cross,' I say.

'No wonder,' says Dad. 'I don't think he can be in yet. Lucky he gave us the key.'

He lets us in and parks Butterscotch in his hutch in one corner of the living room. He peers at the books crammed on the shelves and spilling over in piles on the floor. 'I don't suppose he's a dab hand at erecting more bookshelves either,' he says.

He looks at the wedding photo on top of our television: Jack with his arm round Mum, Mum with her arm round me. He doesn't say anything, but he raises his eyebrows.

'I'm wearing the same dress, see,' I say. 'And the same shoes.' I unstrap them and rub my poor sore toes.

'Are those shoes too small for you?'

'A bit.'

Dad sighs. 'Doesn't anyone keep an eye on stuff like that? I mean, I send your mum lots of money for your keep – certainly more than enough for a new pair of shoes every few months!'

I don't want to listen in case he's getting at Mum. I look at Butterscotch instead. He's cowering uncertainly in a corner of his hutch.

'Can I get him out now, Dad?'

'Yes, I suppose so.'

I unhook the cage door, very carefully take hold of Butterscotch round his fat tummy and hook him out. He looks more uncertain than ever, and squeaks pathetically.

'I think he's hungry,' I say. 'What do guinea pigs like to eat?'

Dad shrugs. 'Special guinea-pig food, I suppose. It looks a bit like muesli.'

'We've got muesli! Mum has it for breakfast!' I stop and swallow. 'Shall I try giving Butterscotch some muesli, Dad?'

'Well, you could give it a go.'

Butterscotch doesn't seem very keen on muesli, but he nibbles on a few segments of orange and laps water out of his bowl.

'I'd like a drink too,' says Dad.

'I'll make you a cup of tea. I can make a good cup of tea, Mum taught me,' I say proudly.

'OK then. Though I was actually thinking about a *drink* drink,' says Dad.

'Oh, you could have one of Jack's beers. He has cans or bottles. They're in the fridge.'

'Good idea!' says Dad.

I fetch him a beer and find myself a can of Coke. I pour a packet of crisps into a bowl and find some salted peanuts too.

'You make a very efficient little bar girl, Ella. You could get a job at the Grey Goose any day.'

'Perhaps you'd like to leave me a tip, sir,' I say.

Dad laughs. I grin, so proud that I've made my dad laugh. We're still chuckling together when we hear the key in the door, and Jack comes in.

He walks into the living room. Dad takes a sip of his beer.

'I see you've made yourself at home,' says Jack. 'Good.' It doesn't sound as if he means good at all. Then he sees Butterscotch's hutch. 'What the hell's that?'

'It's my guinea pig's hutch,' I say. 'Look, Jack, isn't he *sweet*?'

I hold Butterscotch up. He squeaks and does a poo right in my lap. *I* squeak and Butterscotch wriggles free, frightened. He makes a mad dash for the dark under the table.

'Oh, for God's sake,' says Jack. 'Stop squawking and come and catch him, Ella.'

'But he's done a poo on me, look!'

'Just brush it off and wash your hands. It's not

the end of the world.' Jack crawls under the table himself. 'Come on, little fellow.'

He makes a lucky grab at him and puts him back in his hutch. Then he goes and gets himself a beer too.

'How come we have a guinea pig in the living room?' he asks.

'Ella fell in love with him,' says Dad.

'Well, I dare say, but it's not the most sensible idea, given the circumstances. Especially if she's going to be shuttling backwards and forwards between us.'

'What?' says Dad. 'She's not going to be shuttling.'

Jack stands still. 'Now, look, matey, I'm very glad you're here for her – the two of you are obviously getting on like a house on fire – but I'm not going to let you just walk off with her. She needs to see her mum and her little brother, and she's got her school here, and all her friends. I've been thinking – it would maybe work best if she stays here Monday to Friday and then goes to you at the weekends. How would that be?' Jack is looking at me.

Oh yes, oh yes, oh yes!

But Dad is frowning. 'Now hang on, I can't possibly have Ella every weekend!

It feels as if he's punched me in the stomach. I wrap my arms round myself, head bent.

'But I thought – on the phone you said . . .' Jack's voice tails away.

'Of course I care very much about Ella and this desperately sad situation. I want you both to know I'm always here for her. I dropped everything to be with her today. I was supposed to be meeting two really important clients but I cancelled straight away—'

'Oh, we wouldn't want to interfere with your work,' Jack says sarcastically.

'Well, it happens to be an important job – and one of the reasons Ella's child support is always paid promptly into her mother's bank account.'

'But that's the only regular commitment you're prepared to make – a financial one?' Jack says.

'I'm not saying that at all. I'd love to have Ella come and visit some time. Maybe we could even fix a little holiday next summer. We've had a lovely day together, haven't we, Ella?' he asks.

'Yes, Dad,' I mumble.

'And I promise I'll come and see you as often as I can, especially if . . . if the situation changes. But it just wouldn't work on a *regular* basis. I mean, I'm two hours' drive away.' Dad lowers his voice. 'And, well, I'm in a new relationship. It's early days yet, coming up to our one-year anniversary, and I can't quite see it working if there were three of us. We're not really ready for the happy family scene.'

I clutch myself harder.

'Sue and I haven't known each other much longer,' says Jack pointedly.

There's a little silence.

'Well, I'm very sorry. I know it's tough for you. I swear I'll bob up as frequently as I can. Anyway, I'd better be getting back now. You know how it is.'

'Yes, I know how it is,' says Jack.

I hear Dad walking across the room. His shadow hovers over me. He reaches out and tries to brush the fringe out of my eyes. 'Bye, darling. I'll come and see you very soon. You take care now.'

I swallow. I haven't got any voice left to reply.

Dad waits. 'Bye-bye, Butterscotch,' he says, poking his finger into the hutch. Butterscotch can't manage a squeak either.

'I'll see you out, then,' says Jack.

I stay where I am, my fists clenched. I hear them muttering at the door. Then it closes, and Jack comes back into the living room.

I wait for him to start criticizing my dad. I know he hates him. Maybe I hate him now. But he doesn't say anything. He drinks his beer straight down and then goes out into the kitchen. I hear the back door open and shut.

Has Jack walked out too? I kneel on the floor, eyes closed, wondering what on earth I'm going to do. Maybe I can live in a corner of Mum's hospital room? Oh, Mum! You're the only one who really wants me, and yet how on earth can you look after me now?

I'm being silly. Jack hasn't *really* gone. He'd never leave me on my own. Though he seemed really angry. Perhaps he's mad because he was hoping to get rid of me, and now he's lumbered. He's already had one drink. Maybe he's gone out to the pub to drink some more with his mates.

He'll be sitting back, drinking pint after pint, telling them all about his awful stepdaughter – such a sour and surly girl, a total mess, a good job her hair hides her ugly little face, what a pity she doesn't take after her poor mum . . .

The back door slams. I jump. So he's back. He comes into the living room holding a big bunch of green weeds like a bouquet.

'What's that?'

'Butterscotch's supper. Guinea pigs love dandelions – and luckily that's about the only thing we've got growing in the garden. These will keep him going until I can get to the pet shop tomorrow. Want to feed him?'

I poke a couple of dandelion leaves through the bars of Butterscotch's hutch. Jack's right. Guinea pigs clearly *love* dandelions. Butterscotch gives a delighted squeak and starts munching joyously.

'I think we'd better shift his hutch outside tomorrow. It takes up half the living room,' says Jack. 'And it might get a bit smelly in here too.'

'Jack – I didn't mean *us* to have the guinea pig and his hutch. I thought . . .'

'I know,' says Jack. He pauses. 'Your dad was upset. I think he really, really wanted you at the weekends. It's obviously his new girlfriend who's the spanner in the works.'

'Tina,' I say.

'Is that what she's called? Tina.' Jack sniffs. 'She won't be a patch on your mum.'

'I know,' I say. I wipe my eyes and stuff more dandelions into Butterscotch's cage. 'Jack, I know I've been to see Mum already today, but—'

'But you'd like to go again? So would I! Come on, then.'

I slip my feet into my comfy old school shoes, pull on my jacket, and we set off for the hospital together.

Chapter 8

I can't get up the next morning.

'Come on, Ella, breakfast,' Jack calls.

He comes knocking at my door. Then he walks into my room. He pats me on the shoulder. 'Ella?'

I keep my eyes closed and shake my head.

'Look, you might not want any breakfast, but your guinea pig does. He's squeaking away very hungrily.'

But I won't even wake up for Butterscotch. My head hurts and my tummy's churning. I can't bear the thought of staggering through another day without Mum.

I don't know what to do. I don't think she's ever ever ever going to get better. It doesn't make any difference what we do. I can't wake her up. Jack can't. She won't even put her arms around Samson. I so hoped Dad would make her better, he practically promised he would, but he was totally useless. And last night, when Jack and I were at the hospital, those nurses said . . .

I start crying again, thinking about it. Jack and I were sitting behind the curtain on either side of Mum, holding her hands. The nurses didn't have any idea we were there. They were walking along, sensible shoes squeaking on the polished floor, chatting about who they wanted to win on *The X Factor*.

'Come and help me turn Sue Winters,' said one.

'Poor soul,' said the other. 'I don't know why they're keeping up the pretence. I think it's cruel. It's obvious she's never ever going to recover.'

And then they drew the curtain and saw us

sitting there. They gasped, horrified, then started talking terribly quickly and earnestly about some other patient, obviously hoping we hadn't heard.

But of course we heard every awful word. Now those terrible words play backwards and forwards across my brain like a ping-pong ball: *Never ever, never ever, never ever.*

They're at it now, so I burrow further down under my duvet, the pillow right over my head. I'm not moving, no matter how hard Jack shakes me.

'All right, chum,' he says. 'Don't worry. I know how you're feeling. You can stay there.'

So I don't go to school. I huddle up in my bed, barely moving. I wonder if Mum feels like this. Maybe she *could* open her eyes and sit up and speak – but it's just too hard for her at the moment.

I have to get up around half past eleven because I need to go to the loo so badly. When I come out of the bathroom, Jack's there, waiting for me. He looks awful too, great bags under his eyes, his hair tousled, bristles on his cheeks and chin.

'Ready for breakfast now?'

I shrug. I'm sick of soggy cornflakes.

'I know. We'll have brunch. I'll make us bacon sandwiches – they never fail.'

'I'm not the slightest bit hungry,' I say – but the

132

smell of sizzling bacon as I wash and dress makes my nose twitch. I suddenly feel ravenous.

We eat two bacon sandwiches each.

'They're good, eh?' says Jack. 'Buttery golden toast, really crispy bacon – delicious!'

'Jack, do you think if someone cooked bacon sandwiches beside Mum she'd start to feel hungry and wake up?'

'Well, it's a good idea, but I'm not sure it would work.'

'Can we go and see her this afternoon?'

'I'd rather you went to school this afternoon – but OK, I haven't got enough energy to bully you. You'd better do a bit of schoolwork here at home. I don't want you falling behind. I could phone Miss Anderson and ask her to set you some work.'

'You don't need to, Jack. I'll work on my whale project.'

'Yes, that's coming along a treat – but you need to practise your literacy skills and do some extended writing.'

'No problem,' I say.

Jack is busy sending emails and making phone calls out in the hall. I write a story about a long-ago whaling ship going hunting for whales. I know there is a famous old classic book about a man hunting a great white whale called Moby Dick, so

I play around with that idea in my story. I decide my ship is run by fierce female pirates, scary women clenching cutlasses in their teeth. They're all hunting a big blue whale called Blue Jack. They spot him spouting, and the four bravest pirate whaling women cram into a little rowing boat, harpoons at the ready. They row madly after Blue Jack, and one of them wounds him with her harpoon. His faraway blue-whale friends all hear and come swimming up from the depths of the ocean. They gather together, and the biggest seizes the deadly harpoon and plucks it from Blue Jack's back. Then they all open their great mouths and swallow the four pirate whalers whole. They eat four tons of food a day, so a pirate woman is just a tiny little snack. They all leap up and splash so hard with their flukes that they make a tidal wave and the big pirate ship is bowled right over. It sinks with all its crew, down down down to the bottom of the ocean.

I get my felt tips and draw the wrecked ship and fifteen pirate ladies lying dead on the sandy bottom and fish swimming all around them. Then I draw four great big blue whales at the top of the picture. I make little porthole windows in their stomachs so we can see an eaten-up pirate lady inside each one.

Jack comes into the kitchen and glances at my picture. 'Good heavens! That's a scene of mighty carnage. It's a very good drawing – but I thought you were having a go at writing a story for me?'

'I've written it – look. This is its *illustration*.'

'Oh, I get you. Can I read it, then?'

He smiles as he reads, which is odd, because it's a scary and tragic story, not the slightest bit funny.

'It's very good. It's very imaginative and you've used lots of great descriptive words,' Jack says. 'I'd give that story full marks and a great big tick.'

'You can mark it for me with your red pen,' I say.

So Jack writes 10/10 – *A brilliant story, Ella. Well done!* And gives me an enormous big red tick.

'Shall I take it to show Mum?' I say. 'I mean, I know she can't see the picture but I could describe it to her.'

'And you could read her your story,' says Jack. 'Yes, great idea. Ready to go out? We've got some ladies to see before the hospital. I've been fixing up appointments.'

'Ladies?'

'Ladies who can look after little Sam while we're both out at school.'

'Is he coming out of hospital then?'

'Yes, he needs to start a bit of family life, poor

little chap. I can't stand the thought of him being stuck in the nursery all the time.'

'But what about Mum?'

'We'll bring him with us to visit her every day.

'So he'll be with us in the evenings and all through the night and in the early morning?'

'Yep. He's our baby, so he'll live with us.'

'Do you know how to look after babies, Jack?'

'How hard can it be? We'll feed him – and change him—'

'You can do the changing!'

'And give him a bath and put him to bed in his special cot. Plus give him lots and lots of cuddles. Here's the bargain, Ella. You don't have to change him, you don't have to bath him or feed him, not if you don't want to – but you must give him lots of cuddles. I'll cuddle him too, but I'm all hard and hairy. You're little and smooth and soft, like a mini version of your mum. You must cuddle him so he knows what it feels like to be loved by a mummy.'

'Yes, I'll cuddle him lots, I promise,' I say solemnly. 'I'm good at cuddling.'

I hook Butterscotch out of his cage and hold him tenderly to my chest. He squeaks and scrabbles for a few seconds, but then relaxes. I stroke him. His fur's so soft.

'Look, Jack?'

'Yes, you're great with him. And you'll be even greater with your little brother.'

We set off in the car to meet the childminders.

'You come in with me too, right?' says Jack. 'You imagine yourself a little baby and work out which one you'd sooner have looking after you. This first one, Mrs Chambers, is the one the social worker recommended. She certainly sounded very pleasant on the phone.'

Mrs Chambers lives in a neat black and white house with a very tidy garden.

'No dandelions for Butterscotch here!' says Jack, and he knocks on the door.

Mrs Chambers opens it immediately, a dazzling smile on her face. She's wearing a bright white overall to match her startling teeth.

'Mr Winters! Do come in. And is this your daughter?'

'I'm his *step*daughter,' I say quickly.

We're shown through the pale cream hallway into the children's playroom. A little boy is sitting on the floor playing with building blocks on a rug. A toddler girl is staggering around the room, pushing a dog on wheels.

'Here's my little family,' says Mrs Chambers. 'This is young Sean – you're building a tower block, aren't you, sweetie? And this is little Molly taking Doggy for a walk.'

Sean and Molly stare at us solemnly. Molly sneezes and Mrs Chambers rushes forward with a tissue to wipe her dribbly nose.

'That's better, dear,' she says brightly. She throws the tissue away in a bin and then goes into the kitchen. We hear her washing her hands thoroughly. I can't help thinking that if little Sean or Molly needs a nappy-change, Mrs Chambers will give herself a surgical scrub, Dettol up to her armpits.

She makes Jack and me a cup of tea. I try to sit up straight and not slurp. I hope for chocolate biscuits but Mrs Chambers says she doesn't want to spoil our lunch. She shows us she's cooking a very healthy fish pie for little Sean and Molly.

'I don't believe in that tinned rubbish for small children. *I* don't want to eat out of a tin and so I'm not going to serve it to my charges,' she says proudly. 'You don't need to have any worries about little Sam, Mr Winters. I'll feed him the very best formula milk and get him onto solids in a matter of months. I'll give him tip-top care.'

'I know she'll look after Sam splendidly,' Jack says as we walk down the path to the car. 'Like I said, she's the one the social worker recommended.'

He looks at me anxiously. 'What do you think, Ella?'

'I think she's too . . . clean and smiley and sensible. She's like a lady in an advert. She doesn't seem real.'

'That's true. What if our Sam takes after me and is a scruffy little tyke? Maybe she's not the right one for us. We want someone a bit more laid-back for our little boy.'

Mrs Brown is so laid back she barely moves. Once she's shown us inside her flat, she lounges on her sofa, her great mound of tummy straining against her tracksuit bottoms. I'm not sure if she's having a baby herself or if she's just got very fat. She's just minding one child, a little boy strapped into a baby chair, sucking on a crust of bread as he watches television. He's certainly scruffy: he's got jam all round his mouth and his nose is running and there are stains all down his jumper, but he looks happy enough. He kicks his legs and grins at Jack when he squats beside him to say hello. I keep my distance, breathing shallowly. I'm pretty sure his nappy needs changing.

Jack tries to tell Mrs Brown all about Sam, and she smiles and nods.

'Don't worry, I'm sure he'll be fine with me. All my babies are very happy. You're a happy boy, aren't you, ducks?' she says, giving the baby in the chair a little nudge. He giggles at her and dribbles all down his chin.

'I'm sure Sam would be very happy with her too,' says Jack when we get back in the car, 'but I'm not too sure about it. I wouldn't want him stuck in front of a television all day long. I don't know, maybe I'm just being too picky. I keep thinking of your Mum, Ella, and what a lovely job she'd make of bringing up our boy. All these other women just seem *wrong*.'

'No one could ever be as good as Mum,' I agree.

We don't say any more as we drive to the last lady on the list, Mrs Smallwood. We don't speak because we're both trying not to cry.

Mrs Smallwood lives in a little old house at the very end of her street. It's covered in ivy, with a wild, untidy garden, though there are lots of rose bushes, some still in bloom. Mrs Smallwood herself is little and quite old. She's got a soft grey perm curling all over her head like dandelion fluff. She smiles as she opens her door. A delicious warm savoury smell escapes.

'Mrs Smallwood?' says Jack.

She laughs. 'Nobody calls me that, dear. I'm Aunty Mavis to one and all. So you're the poor gentleman with the sick wife? And who are you, darling?' she says, rubbing my cheeks with her fingers.

'I'm Ella. I'm his stepdaughter. It's my mum who's sick.'

'You poor little lamb. Well, come in, come in!'

We go into her house. The hall is choc-a-block with toys: a push-along cart, a spinning top, a toddler trike, beach balls and a family of floppy teddies. In an alcove there's a cardboard box with a rug and a cushion in it, a saucepan and several spoons, and some old dresses and shoes trail down the stairs.

'We've been playing house and cooking and dressing up,' says Aunty Mavis. 'Come and say hello to my girls.'

She opens the kitchen door. There are two smiley-faced little girls sitting at the table with big bibs tied round their necks. Their cardie sleeves are rolled up as they stab at their food with plastic forks. The girls are comically identical, with big blue eyes, pink cheeks, and tiny bunches tied with cherry bobbles.

'This is Lily, and this is Meggie. Say hello, girls,' says Aunty Mavis. She's reaching for two more plates and getting a half-served shepherd's pie out of her oven.

'We're having our din-dins,' says Lily, or maybe Meggie.

'We eat it all up and then we get pudding,' says Meggie, or perhaps Lily.

'Well, your din-din looks very yummy,' says Jack. 'I'm so sorry to call at such a stupidly inconvenient time, Aunty Mavis.'

'You're not sorry at all, you're practically licking your lips, hoping I'll offer you a plateful. Here we are, I've made heaps. Sit yourselves down, both of you. Now, tell me all about this little baby of yours. I don't generally take on kiddies so young, but your little lad sounds like a special case.'

'He's called Sam,' says Jack, looking joyfully at his plate of shepherd's pie.

'Samson.'

'Very distinctive,' says Aunty Mavis. 'Would you like to help yourself to carrots and peas, Ella? Show these two girlies what a sensible grown-up girl you are. I have a terrible job getting them to gobble up their veggies. Don't I, you hopeless pair!'

She tickles Lily and Meggie under their chins and they giggle and squirm. 'Would you like a little baby boy to come and play with us, girls?' she asks.

'Is he a nice little baby?' asks Lily (or Meggie).

'Is he a smiley baby?' says Meggie (or Lily).

'He's a sad little baby at the moment,' says Jack solemnly. 'Because his mummy can't look after him right now.'

'So we'll all look after him instead – his daddy and Ella and Lily and Meggie and me,' says Aunty Mavis. She looks at Jack. 'Yes?'

Jack looks at me. We both smile and nod. We don't need to consult each other. Aunty Mavis is perfect.

Jack and I go straight to the hospital to see Mum. He sits on one side of her, I sit on the other. We both hold a hand.

'OK, Sue, we've found a lovely childminder for little Sam,' says Jack.

'She's called Aunty Mavis, Mum, and she's ever so kind.'

'She makes the best shepherd's pie I've ever tasted. Well, apart from yours, of course,' says Jack.

Mum's never made a shepherd's pie in her life, she just heated up pies from the supermarket, but I suppose Jack's trying to be tactful.

'Aunty Mavis will look after Samson, Mum – but not as well as you would,' I say, because I can be tactful too.

Mum doesn't say anything – she doesn't open her eyes, she doesn't squeeze our hands – but we feel better for telling her.

'Would you like to give Sam a cuddle right now, Sue?' Jack asks. 'We'll go and fetch him.'

We go to the nursery together. Sam is in the corner, wailing dismally.

'It's all right, my little boy. Daddy's here,' says Jack, picking him up. 'Oh dear, your nappy's a bit soggy. I think we'd better change you. Now, where do those nurses keep the clean nappies?'

'Jack! I'm sure we're not allowed to change him,' I say anxiously. 'Wait till the nurse comes back.'

'It's not like it's a complicated surgical procedure, Ella,' says Jack, peering in different cupboards. 'Ah, here we are, clean nappies. We'll have you dry and comfy in two ticks, little Sam.'

Jack lies the baby down on a table and unpops his sleepsuit. I see Samson's alarming pink boy bits and back away.

'Want to give me a hand, Ella?' asks Jack.

'No thanks!'

'This is just wee, so it's fine. I believe it can get a *lot* muckier,' says Jack, dabbing at Samson's bottom with a babywipe. 'There! You like having a little kick about, don't you, son?'

Samson gurgles and waggles his funny little feet in the air.

Jack closes the nappy with its sticky tabs and grabs each little leg to stuff back into the sleepsuit. 'I told you – piece of cake!' he says, poppering up Samson's legs.

He lifts him up. One leg is all puckered up. Jack tries to straighten it out but it won't go.

144

'You've done the poppers up wrong, silly,' I say. 'Here, let me.'

I sort them out in a jiffy.

'OK. Let's make a bargain. I'll do the undressing and deal with the nappies – and you do the dressing. After all, you must have had lots of practice with your dollies,' says Jack.

'As if I still play with *dolls*!' I say witheringly – though I still do in secret. I wouldn't ever tell anyone, not even Sally. She'd laugh at me and call me a baby.

I wonder what she's doing now. Has afternoon school ended yet? I hope it hasn't been too lonely for her all day. I hate it when Sally's off school with a cold or a tummy bug, because there's no one to whisper to in class and no one to play with at break times.

'Jack, can I ask Sally round to ours for tea?' I ask.

'Oh, Ella, I'm finding it hard enough to feed you and me – and now there's the wretched guinea pig too. Tell you what, let's give little Sam *his* tea now. Don't fuss, I know exactly how to do it.'

He gives me Samson to hold while he goes into the kitchen at the side to hunt for baby bottles. Sam quivers at the change of arms. His little face puckers up.

'Don't cry, Samson! It's OK. I'm Ella, your sister, remember?'

I jiggle him in my arms. He gives a tiny whimper. It's not a full-blown cry, but he looks doubtful.

'Are you hungry? Your dad's just fetching you a bottle and we'll give you a lovely drink – and *then* we're taking you for another cuddle with Mummy. She's the best mum in the world but she's very sick at the moment, so she can't look after you properly. But your dad will take care of you. And Aunty Mavis. And I can look after you too, if you'd like that.'

Samson looks thoughtful.

'Shall I take that as a yes, then? I've got a new little guinea pig at home – he's called Butterscotch. I think you'd like him. When you get older, I'll let you hold him, so long as you're very gentle. And I've got some old teddies – you can play with them if you like. You can't really borrow my felt-tip pens for ages and ages because you'll muck up all the points and maybe poke your eye out – but I'll draw for you if you like. I'm getting very good at drawing whales. Would you like me to do you your own whale picture, Samson?'

Samson seems quite keen because he nuzzles against me, his little mouth opening and shutting, as if he's whispering me a little message.

Jack comes back into the nursery with a baby bottle full of milk. 'Here we go. Now, you sit on that chair, Ella, with Sam on your lap. Rest his head on your left arm. That's it. OK – feeding time!'

When Samson and I are settled, Jack gives me the bottle.

'How do I do it, Jack?' I ask, a bit panicked now. I don't want to pour it down his throat and choke him.

'He'll do it for himself, you'll see. Just gently put the teat against his lips and he'll start sucking. Hold the bottle up nicely so he won't be taking in too much air – but halfway through he'll still need to be sat up and burped.'

'Goodness,' I say, giggling.

I nudge the teat against Samson's lips and his mouth clamps on it eagerly. He starts sucking for all he's worth, an expression of intense concentration on his face. His blue eyes look up at me. I feel a weird squeezing pain in my tummy. I think I'm starting to love him, when I didn't think I'd even *like* him very much.

'There now, little Samson,' I whisper.

'Ah!' says Jack. 'Oh, Ella, if only your mum could see the two of you together.'

That does it. He starts crying. I start crying. Samson loses his grip on the bottle and he starts crying too.

'Goodness, we'll be flooding the nursery at this rate,' Jack says, scrabbling through his pockets for a hankie. He mops at my eyes and wipes his own. I nudge the teat back into Samson's mouth and he gives a little snuffle and starts sucking again.

'There now,' says Jack.

'Is he ready for burping yet?'

'Give him another few minutes.'

So I wait – and then gently detach the bottle from his lips and sit him up.

'Rub his back quite firmly – there's a knack to it – though I'm not quite sure what it *is*.'

Samson makes a happy little noise.

'Oh! *You've* got the knack, Ella, obviously,' says Jack.

I carry on feeding him. One of the nurses comes in and smiles at Samson and me.

'You make a good little mother,' she says, and I feel so proud.

Jack lets me carry Samson all the way to Mum's room. He starts to feel surprisingly heavy but I hold him proudly, carefully supporting his noddy little head.

'Sue, darling, look, here's Ella and little Sam. She's just given him his bottle. They look a picture together,' Jack says to Mum. He strokes her face. 'Don't you want to wake up and see them, sweetheart?'

Mum doesn't move. Jack helps me lay Samson on her chest, and I squeeze onto the edge of the bed, my head on Mum's pillow.

'I fed Samson, Mum, and he burped specially for me. Jack says I've got the knack.'

'She certainly has,' says Jack. 'We're going to manage all right, Sue. Ella and I will look after Sam in the evenings and at weekends, and Aunty Mavis will be in charge while we're both at school. We'll be fine. You mustn't worry about a thing.'

Mum still looks a bit worried. There are little frown lines between her eyebrows. I rub them gently, trying to smooth them away.

'We can only manage for a little while, Mum,' I say firmly. 'Just until you get better. You really need to wake up as soon as you possibly can. Touch Samson – can you feel his little hands? He's trying to hold onto you. He needs you so.'

Mum gives a little sigh.

'She heard me!' I gasp. 'Oh, Jack, she really heard me!'

'I hope so, Ella. But maybe – maybe she was just breathing out.'

'She *heard* – and she sighed, because she so wants to look after Samson herself,' I insist. 'Isn't that right, Mum? Sigh again, go on, to show Jack.'

Mum's very quiet now. She clearly can't be

bothered to convince Jack. But *I* know. And Samson does too.

I want to take him home with us right now but Jack says he's got to be checked over by the paediatrician first. So we kiss Mum goodbye and take Samson back to the nursery. He's as good as gold until we put him in his cot, and then he starts squirming and spluttering, revving up for a good cry.

'See, he doesn't want us to go,' I say. I hang over the cot and kiss his hot little forehead. 'Don't cry, little Samson, we're coming back tomorrow.'

'Hey! Leave that baby alone!' a new nurse cries, running over to us. 'Whatever are you doing?'

'He's my brother!' I say. 'I'm not hurting him, I'm just giving him a kiss.'

'Breathing all your germs right in his face! And why are you here unsupervised? We only allow mothers into the nursery.'

'Are you an agency nurse? I think you'll find there's a detailed explanation in our baby's notes. His mother's very ill in Portland Ward,' says Jack.

'But she's getting just a tiny bit better,' I say.

Chapter 9

The phone rings while Jack is making the supper. I run to answer it, my heart pounding. Perhaps it's the hospital: 'Come at once, your mother's woken up and aching to see her baby, it's a total miracle!'

No, it's only Mrs Edwards, Sally's mother.

'How are you, Ella? Sally says you haven't been in school and I was very worried in case – in case your mum's taken a turn for the worse.' She's whispering the last bit in a holy voice.

'She's taken a turn for the better,' I say firmly.

'Really! Oh, thank God! So is she talking now? Can she sit up? Walk at all?'

I'm silent for a moment, wishing.

'Ella?'

'She's not quite walking and talking *yet* – but I'm sure it will be any day now,' I say. 'Can I talk to Sally?'

'Yes, of course, dear.'

I hear a lot of whispering and then Sally comes to the phone.

'Hi, Ella! So your mum's getting better?' she says.

'Well. Sort of. It's kind of gradual.'

'So are you coming back to school next week?'

'Yes, I'm sorry, I've mostly been at the hospital. Have I missed much?'

'Well, Miss Anderson's got us all started on a Tudor project, working in pairs.'

'Oh, Sally, I'm *so* sorry. So have you had to work all by yourself?'

'No, it's OK, Miss Anderson said I could be in a threesome with Dory and Martha.'

'Oh, you poor *thing* – how *awful* to be stuck with Martha. She's so mean and bossy.'

'Yes, she is a bit – but Dory's OK. She's very nice, actually. She only lives round the corner, in the bungalows – remember those little ones we always called "the Doll's Houses"?'

'Of *course* I remember. Look, I only moved away a few months ago.'

'It seems *ages*. Anyway, I was round at Dory's and she's got two rabbits and the lady one's going to have babies and Dory says I can have one!'

'You went to tea with Dory!'

'No, no, I just nipped in on our way home from school. Her mum's got this catalogue – she was showing it to my mum, yawn yawn – so Dory took me out to her back garden and I saw her rabbits. They are sooo fluffy and lovely, and they've got the cutest long floppy ears.'

'I've got a guinea pig,' I interrupt.

'No you haven't!'

'I have so, my dad bought it for me. Not Jack, my real dad. He came and took me out to this dead-posh pub and then we went round to a farm and—'

'Pubs aren't dead posh.'

'*This* one is. And *anyway*, my guinea pig's a lovely golden brown and he's got a little pink twitchy nose and I've called him Butterscotch. Isn't that a good name?'

'I don't really like Butterscotch, it always makes me feel a bit sick.'

'No, but the *name* is perfect, because he's butterscotch-brown, see.'

'Has he got cute floppy ears?'

'Of course he hasn't, he's a guinea pig, not a rabbit. He's got little tufty ears.'

'I think I like rabbits best,' says Sally.

I feel so irritated with her I'm nearly crying. I swallow hard. 'Why not come round now and see Butterscotch?' I say, trying not to let my voice go wobbly.

'I can't – it's much too late and I've had my tea and that.'

'Well, what about tomorrow?'

'Mm? I think we're going round to my gran's.'

I swallow. She's making excuses. She's *Sally*, we've been best friends for years, we *always* see each other. When I lived just round the corner, we played together after school nearly every day. All right, it's more difficult now because she has to get her mum to drive her round, or I have to get *my* mum to . . . How can I forget, even for a moment?

'Ella, are you crying?' Sally asks.

I sniff.

'You *are*. Is it because of your mum? But I thought you said she's getting better?'

'She *is*. Look, I have to go now, I have to feed Butterscotch,' I say, and I slam down the phone.

I stand there in the hall, leaning my forehead against the wall.

'Ella?' Jack comes out of the kitchen, a tea towel round his waist. 'Supper's nearly ready – sausages and mash. Want to lend a hand with the mashing?'

'No.'

'What is it? Were you talking to your friend Sally?'

'She's not acting like she's my friend. She's going off with this other girl, I just know she is, and it's not *fair*, and it's all *your* fault,' I sob.

'Sorry? How come it's *my* fault?'

'If you hadn't met Mum and made us move, I'd still be living practically next door to Sally and she'd still be playing with me, not with that stupid Dory.'

'That's ridiculous. If Sally's a *real* friend, she'll stay friends no matter where you live. And she doesn't sound too kind a friend if she's hanging out with some other kid exactly when you need her most. I'd say good riddance to Sally – find *another* friend.'

'Don't you *dare* say horrid things about Sally,

155

you don't even know her! You don't know *anything*! You're not like a real dad, you're *nothing*!' I shout.

Jack stares at me. 'For God's sake, Ella, what's brought this on? I thought we were starting to get along at last,' he says, sounding hurt.

I want to hurt him *more*, because I'm hurting so much. 'I don't *ever* want to get along with you! I can't stand you. I wish wish wish my mum had never met you. It's all *your* fault she's ill!' I scream.

I want him to shout back. I want to have a real fight. But he's just standing there, still wearing that silly tea towel.

'Don't you think I worry about that?' he says.

There's a smell of burning coming from the kitchen.

Jack sighs. 'The sausages,' he says, and goes to rescue them.

I go into the living room and kneel beside Butterscotch's cage. I reach in and stroke him. 'It's not fair, he's so mean to me,' I mutter – though I know that I'm the mean one now.

I think of Sally and Dory together and the tears start spurting down my cheeks.

'I think guinea pigs are much much much sweeter than rabbits,' I say. 'I especially like your cute little ears, Butterscotch.'

Butterscotch squeaks eagerly, but I think he's

just hoping for more dandelions. I hear Jack clattering about in the kitchen, and then the clink of dishes as he serves up. He doesn't call me. I don't come. I stay sitting beside Butterscotch, crying. I feel as if no one in the whole world likes me, only my mum, and she can't tell me she loves me any more. She can't even cuddle me or give me a kiss.

Jack comes strolling back into the living room. 'Well, are you going to come and eat or not?'

'Not.'

'Suit yourself,' he says, and marches back.

It doesn't really suit me. My tummy feels painfully empty. Even if the sausages are burned, they still smell so good they're making my mouth water. But I don't want to go into that kitchen and face Jack. I might have to say sorry to him.

The phone rings and I run to it, suddenly sure it's Sally again, all set to tell me she wants to come round after all, she's dying to see Butterscotch, and she doesn't know what she was doing wanting to play with that stupid boring old Dory.

It's not Sally at all, it's Aunty Liz.

'Just checking you're in, darling, and not at the hospital. I'm coming round.'

She rings off before I can say any more. Jack looks out into the hall. We look at each other. Neither of us says anything.

'Was that for you?' he says eventually.

'It was Aunty Liz.'

'Oh, her. About time,' Jack says, chewing on a sausage. 'I thought she'd vanished off the face of this earth – when her best friend's in dire straits in hospital. So, what was she saying?'

'She's coming round.'

'What, here? When?'

'Now.'

'Oh God. Look at the place! I don't want her round here, especially now. I'll phone her back and tell her not to bother.'

He tries, but there's no answer. 'She must have set off already. *Hell!* Come on, get your supper or it's going in the bin.'

'I don't want it. The sausages are burned anyway,' I say.

'Go without then,' says Jack. 'See if I care. But you can scurry round and clear up a bit. The place is a tip and I don't want Liz Posh-Knickers looking down her nose at us.'

I can't help sniggering at the Posh-Knickers part. I leave Jack rushing round the kitchen juggling dirty saucepans while I go into the living room. Butterscotch's cage looms large, with bits of his bedding and wilting dandelions scattered on the carpet. There are trays of dirty plates, and

Jack's manky old trainers, and some of my school books, and crumpled carrier bags all over the place – and there are piles of dirty washing trailing down the stairs: the laundry basket on the landing got tipped over and neither of us have ever stopped to pick everything up. Jack's horrible socks and jockey shorts are there. Yuck! I'm not picking *them* up! I give them a kick – and Jack sees me because the kitchen door is open.

'Hey! Stop it! You're making it worse. Now listen to me.' Jack comes stamping up the stairs, red in the face. His arms go out, and I'm scared he's going to hit me – but he just takes hold of my shoulders. I try to wriggle free but he hangs onto me. 'Look, we're in this together, whether we like it or not. I can't *make* you do stuff, Ella. You're too old and I'm too tired. We're both worn out with worrying. We're both sick to the back teeth of each other – but do you think we could somehow put on a united front for Liz? She's your mum's *friend*.'

'All right. Just don't keep *on*. Especially about Mum,' I say.

I pull away and start gathering up all the horrid washing. I trail the full hamper downstairs to put it in the washing machine, but when I open it up there's a horrible sour smell and a lot of soggy clothes.

'Oh God, I forgot to take the last lot out,' Jack says. 'I'll have to wash it all over again.'

He switches the machine on again, sighing, and then notices the thick grease on the top of the cooker. He's just started attacking it (with the tea towel – we can't find any other cloths) when the doorbell goes.

'She's not here *already*?' he groans.

She is. Liz walks in briskly in her navy work suit and high heels. She has large shopping bags in either hand. She goes into the living room, sees the cage, and screams.

'Oh my God, you've got an *enormous* rodent in there!'

'It's not a *rodent*, Aunty Liz, it's my guinea pig, Butterscotch. Dad bought him for me. Shall I get him out so you can stroke him?'

'Don't you dare!' Liz looks at Jack. 'Are you *mad*?'

'He's nothing to do with me – though I suspect I'll be the poor fool lumbered with cleaning out his cage,' Jack says.

'My *real* dad gave me Butterscotch,' I say. 'He's really very sweet, Aunty Liz. You can't be frightened of a guinea pig!'

'Oh yes I can!'

'But that's silly!'

'Not as silly as being frightened of hospitals,' says Jack.

Liz winces. 'All right. I asked for that. I agree, I'm a hopeless coward – and I feel very bad about it. How is she? Is there any improvement at all?'

Jack shakes his head.

'Yes there *is*. Mum practically spoke to me!' I insist.

Liz looks at Jack. He looks at me.

'I'm not sure she did, Ella. I know she gave a little sigh, but I don't think it really meant anything.'

'It *did*.'

'Well, maybe you're right,' Jack says. 'Would you like a drink, Liz?'

'Yes please, I'm dying for one.'

'I *think* we've got a bottle of white wine in the fridge – hang on a minute.'

He comes back into the living room with a glass of wine for Liz, a can of Coke for me and a beer for himself.

'About all I *have* got in the fridge now. I'll have to do a big shop some time. I *must* get that poor little blighter some proper pet food.'

'Well, I can't help you with that – but I can help with *your* food,' says Liz. '*I've* just done my big shop in Marks. I thought you might be struggling in the catering department, so I've got you some ready meals. Pop these in the freezer, Ella.'

'Oh, wow!' I say, delving into the bag. There are *heaps* of meals – all ultra-yummy posh things – and there's even packets of ready-prepared vegetables and a big dish of mashed potato.

'I make a mean mashed potato myself, I'll have you know,' says Jack. 'But it's very kind and thoughtful of you, Liz. Er – how much do I owe you?'

'Nothing, idiot. It's the very least I can do. And there's a few bits in the other bag, Ella. I thought you could do with some more socks and stuff so you don't have to fuss with the washing machine every day.'

She's bought me new socks and knickers and new pyjamas, white with little red hearts all over them. She's even bought Jack some black socks and black boxers!

Then there's a little white tissue-wrapped parcel.

'I know Sue's got heaps of stuff for the baby – but I wanted to buy him one more little present,' says Liz. 'Open it up for him, Ella.'

It's a very small stripy blue and white sleep suit – with a little spouting whale embroidered on the front.

'Oh *cool*, it's a whale!' I squint at it. 'I think it's a humpback, and they're my favourites. Humpbacks can sing.'

'Well, hopefully it can sing little Sam to sleep,' says Aunty Liz.

There's one last thing at the bottom of the bag, something wrapped in pink tissue and tied with a black ribbon.

'You'd better open it, Jack,' says Aunty Liz.

Jack pulls the ribbon and parts the tissue. A beautiful black filmy nightie tied with pink ribbons slithers through his hands. 'Oh thanks, Liz – but it's not quite my style,' he jokes, but his voice wobbles.

'It's not for you, you clown. I bought it for Sue. I know it's not really her style either, she's more a checked-nightshirt girl – but she *did* tell me she rather fancied a ridiculous glamour nightie for her honeymoon. I thought she might like to wear it once in a while in hospital. I mean, that gown she had on was hideous. This might make her feel more of a woman. I know it's a daft idea when she's still in a coma—'

'I think it's a lovely idea. You're a darling, Liz,' says Jack, and he gives her a hug. His eyes are watering.

'Oh God, don't start crying, you'll set me off,' says Liz.

163

They take long sips of their drinks. Jack finishes his beer quickly.

'I think I might have another,' he says. 'More wine?'

'I'd better not, I've got my car. But you go for it. And listen, Jack – every now and then feel free to bring Ella round to my place and you can go out with all your boozy mates and get hammered. I know you like to.'

'Oh dear. Sue obviously had a good moan to you about my drinking habits!'

'Of course she did. That's what best friends are for – isn't that right, Ella?'

I shrug. I'm not sure I've got a proper best friend any more.

As Aunty Liz goes she gives me a special hug. 'Listen, babe, you phone me any time you want, OK? And come and stay whether Jack wants to go out or not. Just don't pack the rodent in your overnight bag.'

I cling to her, breathing in her lovely warm powdery smell. I so so so badly want to cuddle Mum like this. Liz kisses my forehead quickly and then she goes, waving her hand.

I wave back until long after she's gone. Jack slowly closes the door.

'Well, good old Liz,' he says softly. He pats me on

the shoulder very lightly and tentatively. 'Can you come and help me pack all the food away in the freezer?'

I follow him and start on the food bag. I'm better at squeezing the packets in neatly side by side than he is.

'I think I'll leave it to you,' says Jack, raising his beer bottle to me.

'Are you getting drunk?' I ask.

'No. I'd probably *like* to – but not when I'm looking after you.'

'I don't need you to look after me. I can look after myself,' I say, fitting the last packet in and shutting the fridge door.

'Well, how about we try looking after each other?' says Jack. 'And we'll *both* look after the baby.'

I think about it. 'OK,' I say in a very little voice. I pause. 'Jack, did you really throw my supper in the bin?'

'Oh dear, you must be starving. No, I didn't bin it. I hoped you'd weaken and eat it after all – but it'll be cold now.'

He gets a covered plate from the kitchen worktop. There's my sausage and mash. I poke a finger into the mash. He's right, it is stone cold.

'I'll pop one of Liz's meals in the microwave,' Jack says.

'No, it's OK. I can still eat the sausages,' I say. 'They taste fine when they're cold.'

'Even when they're burned?'

'I actually like them like this, really dark and crispy.'

'Tell you what – I'll do something with the mash. I'll make you potato cakes,' says Jack.

He makes my mound of mashed potato into several round patties, browns a little chopped onion in the frying pan, and then pops the potato cakes in to sizzle. He dishes them up for me with the sausages and some baked beans.

'There we are, mademoiselle, the Monsieur Jacques speciality of the house,' he says, serving it with a flourish. 'Mm, it smells good. Can I have one of the potato cakes just to check they're up to standard?'

We munch together at the kitchen table. I offer Jack one of my sausages and a spoonful of beans so that we're sharing properly.

'Did you enjoy that?' he says when I put my knife and fork down.

'Yes.' I look at him. 'Thank you.'

'You're very welcome.'

'You're quite a good cook.'

'Which is just as well, seeing as now I've got four mouths to feed.'

'Four?'

'Mine. Yours. The guinea pig's. And little Sam's.'

Chapter 10

We take Samson home from hospital. We go to the nursery and dress him up in his little spouting-whale suit. He stops looking like a hospital baby and turns into a real little brother. He opens his eyes wide, flings his arms out and kicks his legs to show he likes his new outfit. Then I wrap him up like a precious present in his new white shawl. Mum knitted it specially for him. Her needles clicked away for months as she watched television. She started off trying to do a very complicated pattern but kept going wrong, and one night she pulled all the stitches off in a fury and threw the knitting across the living room. She left it there for a couple of days, but then started all over again with a much easier plain and purl pattern. She tried to get me interested in knitting too, but my hands got all sweaty and my stitches were so tight I couldn't move them along the needle. I managed about ten centimetres of a very tiny scarf before I gave up altogether. It wouldn't even fit round baby Samson's little neck.

Jack carries Samson to Mum. There's a nurse there, wiping Mum's face and smoothing her hair. She's plump and smiley and she calls me soppy names like Sugarlump and Buttercup. I ought to like her but I don't.

'Here's our little Sam, Sue. We've wrapped him up in your beautiful shawl,' Jack says, laying Samson down in the crook of Mum's arm.

'I'm going to do knitting again, Mum. I could make you a scarf for when you get better,' I say.

The nurse moves Mum's head in my direction.

'Thank you, darling,' she says in a silly voice.

She's pretending to *be* Mum. I go stiff with horror. It's like she's doing a growly voice for a teddy bear. Mum isn't a toy – she's a real live person even if she can't talk at the moment.

'Shall we give Sue her wash and brush-up for you, Nurse?' Jack says.

Thank goodness she takes the hint and goes. Jack lays his head on the pillow and kisses Mum's forehead.

'Oh God, Sue, I'm sorry. I can't bear it that you have to stay in here. We're taking Sam home – and as soon as it's possible we're taking you home too.'

'That's right, Mum. And next time that horrid nurse tries to make you talk in a silly voice, you tell her to bog off,' I say.

'That's my girl, Ella,' says Jack.

Samson gives a little cry as if he's joining in too. I pick him up and hold him while Jack very gently sponges Mum's face and combs her hair.

'There now, there's my beautiful girl, all clean and fresh and pretty,' he says.

Mum doesn't really look beautiful at the moment. Her face is all slack and she's got the wrong sort of expression. Her mouth's slightly open but she doesn't look as if she's smiling, she looks as if she's groaning, though no sound is coming out. I do so hope she's not groaning inside her head.

'Mum, Aunty Liz came round and she's bought us heaps of food and stuff, and guess what, she's bought you the most lovely film-star black nightie. Shall we bring it next time, Jack, and dress Mum up in it?'

'I'm not sure I want your mum looking so gorgeous when I'm not here to keep an eye on her,' says Jack.

'Aunty Liz bought Samson this sleepsuit too – doesn't he look sweet in it? Mum, look at Samson. I'll hold him right in front of you and you just take one quick peek, yeah?'

I hold him out but Mum's eyes don't flicker.

'He's got this dear little humpback whale embroidered on the front. Humpbacks are baleen whales, Mum, remember? He's spouting through his blowhole – they actually have two blowholes side by side. He's jumping right up out of the water because he's just like an acrobat. He leaps up and down and flips over just for fun.'

My arms are aching and I have to put Samson down again, on Mum's chest. I want her to sigh once more, just a little tiny sigh to show she knows we're here – but she just breathes steadily in and out, in and out, in and out.

I put my face on the pillow again and try to breathe along with her, keeping time. Mum's breaths are very slow so it's quite hard. I think of all the whales swimming purposefully under the sea and then coming up for air.

'Come up for air, Mum,' I whisper, but her eyes are still closed as she swims in her sleep.

Samson is getting fretful lying on his back. I try to turn him round but he doesn't feel secure without arms wrapped round him. He starts wailing in earnest.

'Shall I take him?' I ask Jack.

'Just leave him crying a minute or two,' he says.

I know why. He's hoping Samson's crying will wake Mum. We stare at her as our baby wriggles and screams. My own arms ache to pick him up and comfort him. How can Mum bear it? She *must* be able to hear him.

Other people hear him too. The same silly plump nurse comes bustling back.

'Oh dear, this poor little chap needs a cuddle,' she says. She plucks Samson from Mum's chest. Maybe if she'd left him just a few seconds longer, Mum would have sighed again, or twitched. A tear might have rolled down her cheek . . .

'You should have *left* him,' I say.

'I beg your pardon, Sugarlump?' says the nurse.

'He was bawling his head off, poor little chap.'

'Yes, thank you, Nurse. I'll take him now,' says Jack. 'We're going to take him home.'

'Have you seen Sister?'

'Yes, I've seen Sister. Little Sam's been checked over by the paediatrician, all the paperwork's been completed. I've seen the social worker, I've been declared a fit father, I've got a suitable childminder – so we're all set,' says Jack, taking Samson from the nurse. 'Say goodbye to Mum, Ella,'

'We're taking Samson home now, Mum, but we'll bring him back soon,' I promise.

'We'll do our best for him, babe,' Jack whispers.

Then we walk out of the room, Jack and Samson and me. I hear noises behind us, and my head whips round in case it's Mum sitting up, swinging her legs out of bed, hurrying after us. But it's just the nurse pulling back the covers and rinsing the cloth in the basin, ready to wash Mum all over again, clearly not trusting us to have done it properly.

'I can't stick that nurse,' I mutter.

'Neither can I,' says Jack. 'Poor, poor Sue. She must be hating it so.' His voice cracks.

'You can't cry, not when you're carrying Samson,' I say.

Jack sniffs. 'OK, Miss Bossy-Boots. I'm not crying, see.'

We take Samson down all the long corridors. Visitors smile at us, and one lady stops Jack and coos at Samson.

'Oh, the little lamb! Are you taking him home?' she asks.

'Yes, we are.'

'So where's his mum?' she asks.

Jack takes a deep breath. 'She's still here in the hospital,' he says.

The lady looks worried. 'She's all right, isn't she?'

'She – she's just resting for a while,' says Jack.

We walk on to the main entrance and then step out into the sunshine. Samson stirs in his blanket, screwing up his little blue eyes. He starts whimpering.

'It's all right, Samson, this is outdoors and it's lovely, so much better than that horrid old hospital,' I say, rubbing his cheek with my finger.

Jack's already fitted a special baby seat into the back of his car. Samson doesn't like the idea of being strapped into it and cries hard.

'It looks so uncomfy for him. Can't I just hold him in my arms?' I say.

'It wouldn't be safe enough. I'm not risking any more accidents in this family,' says Jack. 'He'll stop crying when I get the car going.'

He's right. Samson stops screaming and starts nodding sleepily. I reach out and hold his hand, whispering to him, 'We're going home, Samson, you and me and Jack.'

It doesn't really feel like home when we get inside. It's cold and empty, and it smells of cooking fat and Butterscotch's cage. Jack carries Samson upstairs. Mum started turning the little box room into a special nursery for him. She turned up her nose at baby pastels and fluffy bunnies and cute kittens. She painted it white, with a slightly wonky frieze of jungle animals running all round the top. She'd found an old chest of drawers in an Oxfam shop and scrubbed it down and painted it a dark jungle green, with orange and scarlet and purple flowers twining round the handles. She was going to paint my old cot and a wardrobe to match, but ran out of time. She hadn't yet found another home for all our suitcases and old clothes and posters, and Jack's drum kit, and a big pile of cardboard boxes we'd never unpacked since we moved in.

Jack and I stand in the doorway, considering. Samson is a very small baby but there doesn't seem any way we can squash him in.

'I know, Samson can come in my room,' I say.

'That's sweet of you, Ella, but I don't want him

waking you up in the night, it's not fair. We'll put his cot in my room, OK?' says Jack.

It's easier said than done. We can't manoeuvre the cot out of the door because there's too much stuff wedging it in. Jack eventually collapses the cot and takes it out bit by bit while I joggle Samson up and down in my arms. He's crying quite hard now, bewildered.

Jack tries to put the cot back up again in his bedroom but he can't get the pieces to fit together. Samson is screaming now, clearly starving. Jack curses and goes to make up his bottle. He settles me in an armchair and gives me Samson to feed, then goes back to the cot. I hear him clanging and cursing above us. Samson tries hard to concentrate on his meal, but maybe it doesn't taste quite the same as the hospital milk. He starts fussing and whimpering, and when I sit him up and pat his back gently to burp him, he's suddenly sick all over his spouting whale. It's only milky stuff but it smells horrid.

'Jack! *Jack!*'

'What?'

'Come quick!'

There's a sudden crash and a very rude word. Jack comes rushing downstairs into the living room.

'What is it? What's happened. What's up with him?' he gabbles.

'He's been sick, look!'

'Oh, Ella, I thought it was something serious! I had the cot all set up at long last, just the final screw – and now I've dropped it and it's all in bits again. For goodness' sake, what are you playing at?'

'But he's been *sick*. I don't know what to do.'

'Mop him up, for God's sake.'

'Well, what with?'

'I thought you were meant to be *bright*. Use any-thing for now, any old towel. I'll buy baby wipes tomorrow. Then see if he wants to finish his bottle. I expect he just drank the first part too quickly.'

'You don't think he's ill or anything?'

'Give me strength! Ella, all babies are sick.'

'Since when are you the world expert on babies?'

'Hey, hey, less of the cheek. Now I'm going back to fix that wretched cot.'

I stick my tongue out at his back.

'I saw that,' says Jack.

'How?'

'I'm a teacher. I've got eyes in the back of my head,' he says, going up the stairs.

I hear him in the airing cupboard.

'Here, clean towel,' he says, throwing it down the stairs.

I lug Samson out into the hall and sit on the bottom step with him, gently mopping his front.

'Poor stinky little boy. There, that's better, isn't it? You don't really want the rest of your bottle, do you?'

When I'm sick I couldn't possibly eat anything afterwards. I especially couldn't gollop down a long drink of tepid milk. But Samson's lips clamp down on the teat of his bottle and he drinks with desperate intent.

'Slowly now, or you'll be sick all over again,' I say.

Samson takes no notice and drinks until he's drained his bottle. I sit him up and pat him very gingerly indeed, but he's not sick this time. He does something else instead. He grunts, his face going very red. It's very clear what he's doing.

'Oh dear, now you're stinky all over again,' I say, sighing.

I listen for sounds of progress upstairs but Jack's still cursing and muttering.

'He'll be finished soon – and then he can change you and pop you into bed in your new cot,' I say to Samson.

He's *very* stinky now and squirming uncomfortably. I think how *I* would feel in his situation. 'Shall I try and change you?' I ask.

178

I fetch the big pack of nappies in a carrier bag and go to the loo to get a handful of toilet paper. It'll only take a moment to whip the dirty nappy off, wipe his bottom and put the new nappy on. I'll do it all by myself and show Jack just how capable I am. Tomorrow I'll tell Mum that she doesn't have to worry about Samson in the slightest – I can feed him *and* change him, easy-peasy.

I lay him down gently on the carpet and start unbuttoning his sleepsuit, and then his nappy, and oh – oh – oh, I can't possibly . . .

'Jack! *Jack!*'

There's another crash, another curse. He comes pounding down the stairs.

What *now*?' he bellows – and then he sees. 'Oh Lordy!'

'I thought I'd change him, but I didn't know it would be so *much* – and he keeps wriggling – and I just *can't!*' I say, starting to cry.

'Hey, hey, it's OK. Oh God, I can't either. No, wait, come on. I'm the dad. I have to cope. Deep breath. *Not* a good idea in the circumstances! Sam, lie *still*, little chap, it's going all over everywhere.' Jack tries to hold his little waving legs and then starts wiping – and wiping and wiping.

'Perhaps we'd better give him a bath to get him really clean,' he says. 'Did your mum buy him a special baby bath? We can't just pop him in the proper bath, I couldn't hold him properly and he might bang his head.'

I go and search the crowded box room but can't find a bath anywhere. We end up commandeering the washing-up bowl. I fill it up with hot water, but Jack thinks it might be *too* hot. He tells me to test it using my elbow, which is totally weird. When I think it's exactly right, I haul it onto the draining board, and then Jack very slowly lowers Samson into the water. He keeps his hand cupping his head so he can't possibly go under. Samson's arms wave in the air, startled at the feel of the water.

'Oh, maybe it's still too hot!'

'No, no, it's fine now, he just needs to get used to it.'

'Doesn't he look cute in the washing-up bowl!'

'Yes, he's our little saucepan, aren't you, Sam,' says Jack, gently tickling his tummy.

Samson wriggles and kicks.

'Oh look, he's trying to swim! Jack, can we take him swimming when he's a bit older? I wish I'd learned properly when I was little. They do special mother-and-baby classes down at the pool.' My voice wobbles. I think of Mum in her lovely red swimming costume, holding little Samson and bouncing him around in the shallow end. Then I think of Mum now, lying flat on her back, motionless.

'I know,' Jack says softly, reading my mind. We both sniffle as we watch Samson, and then snuggle him up in yet another clean towel.

'Remind me to put the washing machine on,' says Jack. 'In fact, I think it's going to be on permanently now. God knows what the electricity bills are going to be like. *All* the bills – and Aunty Mavis too. It's not so bad now, while your mum's getting maternity pay. I just don't know what we'll do when it stops.'

'Mum will be better then,' I say firmly.

Jack takes a deep breath. 'Yes. You're right, Ella. We'll think positive.'

He picks Samson up. 'Are you clean as clean now, little saucepan?' He leans forward and blows a raspberry on his tummy, and then I wrap the towel round him.

We take him into the living room so we can sit on the carpet and dress him more comfortably in front of the radiator.

Jack puts the sweetest little T-shirt on Samson, totally doll-size. 'Shall we leave him kicking on his blanket without a nappy? It'll be nice for him to have a little freedom,' he says. 'I'll take a photo of him, and then we can show your mum. We'll keep a little record. He's had his first feed at home, his first nappy change, his first bath, and now his first little kick.'

Jack goes to find his camera, fusses around, choosing all kinds of angles, and eventually focuses, bending right over the baby. Samson focuses too. A sudden spurt of wee arches up and splashes all over Jack's chest.

I shriek with laughter. 'I'd love a photo of that!'

'It's not funny! Now *I'm* going to have to change,' says Jack, but he starts spluttering with laughter too.

When he's finally erected the cot, we can put Samson to bed. Butterscotch starts squeaking and I feed him in a matter of seconds. Guinea pigs are a *lot* easier to cope with than babies.

Samson starts a crying fit in the evening and won't settle, even after he's been changed and had another bottle. Jack and I take turns walking him up and down while he wails. We can't watch television properly, we can't even enjoy our own meal, though it's one of Liz's specials.

'What's *up* with you, little man?' says Jack anxiously. 'Here, Ella, hold him while I look it up on the internet.'

He finds a whole host of tips about crying babies, but none of them are much use. We've already fed Samson and changed him and cuddled him. He doesn't seem to be in any pain, just very unhappy.

'Lots of these so-called experts suggest putting the baby in his cot and leaving him to settle by himself,' says Jack. 'Shall we try that?'

So we take him upstairs and tuck him up in his cot and kiss him goodnight. Samson cries. We switch off the light and leave the room. Samson cries harder. We sit tensely out on the landing. Samson cries and cries and cries.

'Oh dear, this is awful,' Jack mutters. 'He never cried like this in the hospital. If only he could talk and tell us what's up.'

'I think he's missing Mum,' I say.

'You're probably right, but there's nothing we can do about it. He's stuck with us right now.'

We sit there for half an hour. Samson cries steadily. It's as if he's crying inside me. My head aches and my tummy's tight and I can't get comfortable. Jack's twitching and sighing and fidgeting too.

'I can't bear this,' he says. 'We *can't* leave him in there, all lonely and frightened.'

He goes back into the bedroom and lifts Samson out of his cot. Samson gulps and cries, his voice heart-breakingly hoarse.

'Poor little chap, he's all hot and damp,' says Jack, wrapping him in his blanket. 'There now, little Sam, Daddy's here.'

Samson snuffles and snorts and carries on crying, but less frantically now. We take him downstairs again.

'We're like the Grand Old Duke of York,' says Jack. He starts singing, *'The Grand Old Duke of York, he had ten thousand men, he marched them up to the top of the hill and he marched them down again. And when they were up they were up, and when they were down they were down, and when they were only halfway up they were neither up nor down.'*

He goes up a few stairs while he sings *'when they were up'* and down a few stairs for *'when they were down'*, and marches on the middle steps for the *'halfway-up'* part. Samson stops crying altogether, fascinated.

'There you are, Jack! You've just got to run up and down stairs all night long – that'll keep him happy!'

'I'm out of puff already!' Jack pants.

'You'll lose your beer belly.'

'I haven't *got* one, you cheeky girl! Oh Lord, I'm going to have to stop this lark in a minute.'

'I'll take him.'

'No, no, you might trip. You go and pop the kettle on, there's a good girl.'

We have a cup of tea. Samson cries some more so we give him another bottle. Jack feeds him this time, trying to make him slow down a little. Then he sings him more nursery rhymes – 'Rock-a-bye Baby' and 'Twinkle, Twinkle, Little Star'. Samson closes his eyes and goes to s-l-e-e-p. We carry him upstairs very slowly and then slide him gently into his cot. His starfish hands go up and his eyes open and we hold our breath, waiting for the crying to start – but he closes his eyes again and goes fast asleep.

'Phew!' Jack whispers as we tiptoe out of the room. 'Ella, I'm totally knackered. I'm going to bed too. What about you?'

'It's not my bed time yet!'

'Why don't you get into bed and read your whale book?'

'OK.'

'Just put your light out when you start to feel sleepy.'

'Mm.'

'Shall I come in and tuck you up?'

'No, it's OK,' I say quickly. But then I raise my hand and give him a funny little wave. 'Night-night, Jack.'

'Night-night, Ella.'

I sit up in bed with Harriet the hippo on one side of me, Baby Teddy on the other, and read about humpback whales. I like them most because they can sing. The book says it's only the males who sing, but I wonder if the females and the calves have their own songs too, but they just whisper them softly into the waves. I wonder what whale song sounds like. The book says the songs are complicated and melodious and are used in courtship. They sing for ten or twenty minutes at a time – but one male sang for *twenty-two hours* non stop.

I try singing 'Rock-a-bye Baby' over and over again, but I just get bored after four or five verses. But that's a lullaby, not a real love song. I think of Mum. I would sing to her for twenty-two hours if it would only make her better.

I lie back on my pillow and whisper my love song for Mum over and over again until I fall asleep.

Chapter 11

'Go away! I'm tired!' I mumble.

'What do you think *I* am?' Jack says, pulling at my duvet. 'I was up half the night with Sam. He didn't sleep for more than two consecutive hours. I'm absolutely exhausted. I've got a splitting headache. In fact I ache all over. Entire-body ache, that's what I'm suffering from.'

'So go back to bed and leave me alone,' I say, trying to burrow back under the covers.

Jack won't let me. 'You've got to get up *now*, Ella. You've got to go to school today.'

'I don't want to!'

'*I* don't want to go to school, but I've got to go and teach or I'll lose my job. *You've* got to go to school or I'll get prosecuted. And Sam's got to go to Aunty Mavis because he needs someone to look after him. He's not too happy about it either – he's bawling his head off, can't you hear him? You go and use the bathroom while I fix his bottle and make us breakfast. We're running late.'

I peer at my old Tinkerbell alarm clock. I used to believe she flew around my bedroom every night, sprinkling stardust and waving her little wand. I wish she'd wave it now and make Jack disappear.

'We are so *not* running late,' I say, shaking my alarm clock. 'I never get up this early.'

'Well, you'll have to get used to it. I've got to drop Sam off, drive you all the way to school, then drive back through the rush-hour traffic to be at Garton Road by quarter to nine. So *get cracking*!'

I slide slowly out of bed. I ache too from lumbering Sam around all day yesterday. It's not fair.

When Mum and I lived at our old house, I didn't get up till eight o'clock. And Mum never shouted at me. She often used to bring me breakfast in bed. Sometimes she'd get back into bed with me and we'd play silly games together. We'd pretend we were celebrities and make out we had extensions and great big boob jobs, and we'd plan shopping trips and talk about our new outfits. I *love* playing pretend games like that with Mum. I try sometimes with Sally, but she always gets the giggles and says I'm weird.

I think about Sally now. I feel a bit worried about seeing her at school. Sort of shy and scared. Now, that *is* weird, because Sally's been my best friend for years. I *think* she still is. She rang last night. Well, her mum rang first to ask Jack about my mum – and then she said Sally wanted to talk to me. I felt absolutely weak with relief.

We chatted for about ten minutes. We didn't discuss guinea pigs or rabbits. We didn't mention Dory and Martha. Sally told me all about her Saturday morning dancing class and how she's going to be a snowflake in the Christmas ballet, and then she talked about her favourites on *The X Factor*. I couldn't really say much because I don't go to ballet and we were too busy with Sam to watch much television. I *did* start to tell her about my whale project, and she said I was daft because they'd finished food chains now. Then we had one of those uncomfortable pauses. I couldn't think of anything else to say and neither could she, so we just blurted out goodbye.

I wish I could ask Mum if she thinks this means Sally's still really my best friend. She wasn't horrible to me – she said again that she was really sorry about my mum – but she didn't muck around and joke and act in our old casual Sally-and-Ella-best-friends-for-ever way.

It's so awful not having Mum around. Everything's *wrong*. There's hardly any toothpaste left in the bathroom so I have to squeeze and squeeze the tube. My flannel smells disgusting because I left it rolled up in a soggy bundle. My hair is beyond terrible. I tried to wash it in the bath yesterday but I don't think I got all the shampoo out properly, and now it hangs lankly in my eyes. I try to scrape it back into a ponytail but it won't go high or bouncy enough, it just draggles in a surly clump past my shoulders. Jack's done the washing so I've got a clean school blouse, but he didn't hang it up straight away so it's creased all over – and now I find the hem of my school skirt is starting to come down. Before, I'd always just go, 'M-u-m!' and she'd come and sigh, and teases me for being a helpless baby, but she always put it *right*. Now poor Mum is the helpless baby, having to let the nurses wash her and feed her and change her, and she can't even cry or kick her legs like little Samson.

He's certainly crying now as Jack struggles to change him downstairs. Then it's suddenly quiet so he must be feeding. I put my whale project and borrowed book in my school bag and stomp downstairs.

'There's a good girl,' Jack says. 'Get yourself some cornflakes, eh?'

'Why does it always have to be boring old cornflakes? I like Coco Pops,' I grumble.

'Right. Reach into the cupboard, find the cocoa powder, and douse your bowl liberally,' says Jack.

I'm not sure if he's serious. 'Will it taste good?' I ask.

'There's only one way to find out.'

I decide not to risk it. I sit down and sourly spoon plain cornflakes into my mouth. Jack sits Samson up to burp him.

'Oh, Ella, what a boring breakfast! Don't you fancy marmalade pops? Or what about *Marmite* pops?'

'You think you're so funny,' I say.

'Well, you've got to laugh – or you burst out

crying,' says Jack. 'Now, young man, are you going to burp so you can finish your bottle? Come on – one, two, three—'

Samson opens his mouth and gives a comically loud burp. Jack laughs delightedly. I can't help giggling too.

'There! One week old and he's doing exactly as he's told – *unlike* his big crosspatch sister. Ella, any chance of you making me a cup of tea while I finish feeding him?'

'No chance at all,' I say, getting out my whale project and flipping through it, hoping it will really impress Miss Anderson. I wait for Jack to nag and get sarcastic and start shouting – but he just sits there, feeding Samson. 'Oh, all *right*,' I say, and get up to boil the kettle.

I make myself a mug of tea too. Jack and I sip while Samson sucks. Jack holds his cup at arm's length and arches away from Samson every time he drinks so that he can't possibly spill any tea on him. I wonder if my dad was as thoughtful when he fed me when *I* was a baby. I start making up this little fantasy of lovely, handsome, beaming Dad holding me tenderly in his arms – and then I remember I've only just seen my dad. I think of his striped shirt and his silk tie and his smart suit. Perhaps he never ever fed me in case I made him messy. Perhaps I was so slurpy and sicky that he decided to walk out on us. How could he have left Mum to cope all by herself? How could he have left me? I can't stick Jack, he's just my stepdad, but I know one thing: he'd never walk out on little Samson, not ever.

I try telling him about the Sally situation when we're in the car driving to Aunty Mavis's house.

'Do you think she's still my best friend, Jack?'

'Well, of course she is.'

'But she wouldn't come round and she didn't sound right on the phone.'

'She *did* phone you.'

'I said she didn't *sound* right. You're not listening!'

'I'm *trying* to concentrate on the traffic – but I am listening too. I don't know what you're going on about. Sally's your best friend, full stop.'

'I think she likes Dory best now,' I say in a tiny voice.

'Well, can't you all be best friends together?' says Jack.

'Oh, Jack, you don't *understand*.'

'You sound just like your mother. And all the little girls in my class who come and tell me their sad stories – so-and-so keeps whispering about them, and so-and-so didn't choose them for a work project – and you're right, I *don't* understand. I don't see why women have to *analyse* everything to the nth degree. It's much simpler if you're a bloke. Everyone's your mate until they bash you, and then you bash them back, and then they're your mate again, no fussing.'

'Men!' I say witheringly.

Samson kicks his legs beside me. I take hold of one tiny foot.

'Are you going to be as hopeless, Samson? I don't think so. I'm going to teach you to be a *lovely* boy,' I say.

'That's what my mum thought about me. Oh God. My mum and dad. They were supposed to be coming on a visit when the baby was born,' says Jack.

'Oh no,' I say, and then I clap my hand over my mouth because it sounds so rude.

'It's OK. That's my reaction too. And it's mad – they live so far away they'll have to stay overnight, and I don't know where on earth they'll sleep, because my dad can't get upstairs, and it's hard enough getting us three fed, let alone entertaining two more . . .'

Jack carries on, and now I'm the one not listening properly. I worry on about Sally. I'm still holding Samson's foot.

'Will *you* be my new best friend, Samson?' I whisper.

He gives a little gurgle, as if he's saying yes. I start to worry about him going to Aunty Mavis, because he's got used to *us* so quickly. Perhaps he'll start screaming at the sight of Aunty Mavis, desperate for us to stay. But when she comes to her front door, holding out her arms, Samson seems happy enough to be picked up and cuddled.

'Where's this lovely boy then? Ah, *here* he is,' she says, folding back his shawl and giving his forehead a little kiss. The twins hop on either side, vying with each other to see the baby.

'Don't you worry about a thing. Little Sam will be fine with me,' Aunty Mavis says. 'Won't you, my pet?'

Samson certainly seems totally happy in her arms. Jack and I look at him.

'Bye, little boy,' says Jack, giving his chin a tickle.

'Bye-bye, Samson,' I say, and I blow him a kiss.

We both still stand there a bit anxiously.

'He'll be totally tickety-boo, I promise,' Aunty Mavis says, laughing at us. 'Off you go!'

So we slope back to the car and drive off. It feels so strange to be without Samson. We've only had him home for a weekend, and yet it feels as if he's been part of our lives for ever. I feel such a pang for Mum. She carried Samson around inside her for nine whole months – and now he's been taken away from her.

'We can take Samson to see Mum today after school, can't we, Jack?'

'Yes, of course.'

I hunch down in my seat, trying to distract myself by thinking about whales. My book says they sing in strange groans and moans. I try groaning softly to myself.

'Are you all right, Ella?' Jack asks.

'Yep.'

I try a few moans this time.

'Have you got a tummy ache?'

'No, I'm fine.'

'Then why are you making that weird noise?'

'It's whale-speak.'

'Oh. Right. You're a weird kid, Ella.'

'Sally sometimes says I'm weird.'

'Well, she's right.'

I hunch up a little more.

'You're not still worrying about this best friends business, are you?'

I swallow. 'No,' I lie.

'Sally will be fine, you'll see,' says Jack.

He parks the car outside school and insists on

196

coming into the playground with me, as if I'm one of the infants. I look around the playground. I see Sally straight away. She's standing in a little huddle with Dory and Martha. My breakfast corn-flakes churn in my stomach. But then Sally sees me and comes running over.

'Hi, Ella!' she says, and she gives me a big hug.

Jack grins at me triumphantly. 'There you are, Ella,' he says. 'OK, have a good day. I'll pick you up as soon as I can. I'm afraid you might have a bit of a wait. You'll be all right? You won't go off with any strange men?'

'As if,' I say, and I flash him a quick smile and then saunter off with Sally. I *think* it's OK.

Sally keeps her arm round me, talking all the time. 'How's your mum, Ella?'

'She's . . . about the same.'

'Is she very, very ill?'

I don't know what to say, so I just nod.

'You poor thing. I don't know what I'd do if *my* mum got that ill,' says Sally. 'And what about the baby?'

'He's lovely,' I say. 'I feed him and wind him, and sometimes I even change him – but not when he has a really dirty nappy. I leave that for Jack! You should have seen the way Samson peed all over Jack's chest, it was sooo funny!'

Sally laughs, and we both make silly peeing noises and gestures, and get the giggles, hanging onto each other. But Dory comes running over, sticking her nose in. Martha follows.

'Hello, Ella. What are you two laughing at?' Dory asks.

'I wouldn't be killing myself laughing if *my* mother was dangerously ill in hospital,' says Martha.

'She's not *dangerously* ill. That means she might . . .' I can't say the word. 'It's not dangerous,' I repeat. 'Dr Wilmot says she's in a stable condition.'

'So what's the matter with her?' Martha asks.

'She's in a coma.'

'What does that mean?'

'She's just asleep.'

'Asleep, like . . .' Martha shuts her eyes and makes silly snorty snoring sounds.

'No, nothing like that! Stop it! Don't you dare make fun of my mum,' I shout.

Miss Anderson comes hurrying across the playground out of nowhere. 'Hello, Ella. Welcome back to school! Martha, what are you doing?'

'Nothing, Miss Anderson,' says Martha, opening her eyes wide to act all innocence.

Miss Anderson looks at me.

'She was being horrid about my mum!' I say furiously, blinking back my tears.

I realize this is a *big* mistake as soon as I say it. You never ever tell tales to a teacher at our school, no matter what.

'Martha, I'm thoroughly ashamed of you! I can't believe you could be so unkind when Ella is worried and upset about her mother,' says Miss Anderson. 'I think you'd better go into school right this minute and sit by yourself in the classroom. Off you go.'

Martha glares at me in an *I'm-going-to-get-you* way and slopes off. Miss Anderson gives me a pat on the shoulder and then hurries off to separate two boys who have started wrestling. Sally and Dory are looking at me reproachfully.

'*What?*' I say. 'Martha *was* being horrid about my mum, you heard her.'

'She was just being silly about snoring,' says Sally. 'I know she upset you, Ella, but she wasn't really being *horrid*.'

'Oh yes she was,' says Dory surprisingly. 'Martha's very good at knowing *exactly* how to upset people on purpose. She's the world champion.'

'I thought you were her friend,' I say.

'Yes, but I wish I wasn't sometimes, because she

can be so mean. I wish I could be friends with you two instead.'

I want to be kind to Dory. She's a smiley girl with shiny black hair cut in a very tidy fringe (I still don't know what to do about mine!) and she can be good fun at times. I loved it when she brought her pet mouse to school. In fact the only thing *really* wrong with her is that she's always been best friends with Martha. So now she doesn't *want* to be friends with her, maybe we could all be best friends together, the three of us. Jack seems to think it would work — though he doesn't always know everything.

'I'd *love* it if you were our friend, Dory,' says Sally. She's looking at me imploringly.

I take a deep breath. 'Yeah, that would be great,' I say.

'Oh, fantabulistic!' Sally says, and she gives Dory a big hug.

Dory gives her a big hug back. Neither of them gives *me* a hug. Well, Sally *did* hug me when I came into the playground. We can't play huggy-bears all the time. It will be all right, all right, all right.

It's definitely all *wrong* with Martha. She glares at all of us when we go into class after the bell's gone. Her glare assumes ferocious werewolf proportions when she looks at me. I don't care. She was mocking Mum. I hate Martha.

She tries to talk to Dory, but Dory edges her chair away from Martha's desk, nearer to us. Sally writes Dory a little note. Dory writes one back to her.

'What's she saying?' I whisper to Sally.

'Oh, just that she's glad she's our best friend now,' says Sally. She doesn't show me. She crumples up the note and pops it in her desk drawer.

'She's just a *friend* friend, not a best friend,' I mutter.

'Whatever,' says Sally.

There's a gentle tap on my back. I turn round. It's Joseph.

'How's your mum, Ella?'

'Oh, sort of the same, thanks,' I say.

'She's still in a coma?'

'Mm. But it doesn't mean she can't get better,' I say.

'I know. I looked it up on my computer. I printed some stuff out for you. Here.'

He hands me a sheaf of papers. They're features from newspapers: MIRACLE MOM WAKES WEEKS AFTER MONTH IN COMA; COMA BOY OPENS HIS EYES AND SMILES WHEN POP IDOL VISITS; COMA BRIDE WHISPERS 'I LOVE YOU.'

My eyes fill with tears. 'Thank you so much, Joseph.'

'There was lots of serious medical stuff too, but I thought you'd like these true-life stories best.'

'I do, I do!'

'Ella, Joseph! Come *on* now, we're meant to be concentrating on weighing and measuring,' says Miss Anderson. 'In fact, you can help us, Ella. You have a new baby brother. Do you know how much he weighed when he was born?'

'He weighed six pounds eight ounces, Miss Anderson. But he probably weighs a lot more now because he's had lots of feeds.'

'Ah, you probably have to measure his baby milk too. How much are you feeding him at the moment?'

'Four ounces at a time, Miss Anderson. He absolutely gobbles it down. He makes really loud sucking sounds, he's so funny,' I say eagerly. 'Like this!' I demonstrate.

'Ah!' says Miss Anderson, smiling.

'Oh, per-lease!' Martha hisses. 'They're acting like this is little baby Jesus! All babies suck. And Ella sucks too. It's not fair – *she* doesn't get told off for making stupid sucking sounds and yet *I* get sent into school just for snoring.'

'Are you addressing me personally, Martha, or

making general comments like a Greek chorus?' says Miss Anderson. 'Perhaps you'd like to contribute properly. I think you've got a little sister, haven't you? Can you remember how much she weighed when she was born?'

'She's not my real sister, she's only a *half*-sister, and I haven't got a clue what she weighed and I couldn't care less,' Martha says.

I stare at Martha while Miss Anderson tuts and tells her off for being cheeky. I never knew Martha had a half-sister. So she's probably got a stepdad too. I still can't stand her, but perhaps I'm slightly more interested in her now.

I'm *not* especially interested in our weighing lesson now we've stopped talking about Samson. I wonder how much baby whales weigh. Their mothers feed them lots of milk, just like human babies. The calves are very weak at first, so they sometimes rest their flippers on their mother's body to help them swim along. They stay with their mothers for two or three years. The mothers teach them how to hunt and how to talk to all the other whales. I doodle a mother and baby whale on the back of my rough book.

Miss Anderson walks past and raises her eyebrows.

'I'm just trying to work out how much a baby

whale would weigh,' I say quickly. 'They're a quarter the size of an adult, so it's a sum I should be able to work out easy-peasy.'

'Oh, very good, Ella.'

'I started a special whale project when I was at home,' I say. 'Shall I show you?'

'Yes, I'd love to see it. Maybe after school? I'm glad you like doing special projects, Ella. You can make a start on your Tudor project today.'

But this is where everything starts to go wrong. Sally has started doing her Tudor project with Dory and Martha. They've chosen Tudor costume.

'But surely you can start another project with me now?' I say to Sally.

'Well, I really *want* to do Tudor costume. We've done pages and pages on it already,' she says. 'Tell you what, Ella, you can do some drawing for us.'

'Oh, great, then I can draw all those fancy sticky-out dresses,' I say.

'Over my dead body,' says Martha. '*You're* not part of our project.'

'But Sally and I always do our projects together,' I say. 'We're best friends.'

'And Dory's our friend too,' Sally reminds me.

Martha looks furious. 'Dory's *my* best friend,' she says. 'Aren't you, Dory?'

Dory doesn't look like she wants to be Martha's

best friend in the slightest, but she doesn't dare say so.

'So it's me and Dory and Sally. So you shove off, tell-tale,' says Martha.

She pushes me hard, so that my chair scrapes the floor. Miss Anderson looks up enquiringly.

'See if *I* care,' I mutter. 'I'm not the slightest bit interested in doing your silly costume project anyway.'

'What's going on?' Miss Anderson calls. 'What's the matter, Ella?'

I badly want to tell her – but I can't tell tales on Martha *again*, especially not in front of the whole class. So I just shrug a little and mumble, 'Nothing, Miss Anderson.'

'Are you four going to do your project together?' she asks.

'No, we're doing Tudor costume and Ella says she's not interested,' says Martha.

She's such a mean pig. And now *she's* telling tales, sort of.

'Oh well, perhaps you'd better have a delve through the Tudor book box and see if there's any-thing you *are* interested in, Ella,' says Miss Anderson.

She's not really telling me off at all, but I feel myself blushing. Martha is sniggering delightedly.

It's not *fair*. I don't want to do a Tudor project by myself. I flick through a book listlessly. I don't know what to pick. Unless . . . could I do a project on Tudor whales? They must have *had* whales in Tudor times. Whales go right back to ancient days in the Bible, because there was that whale that swallowed Jonah. (Oh, how I wish a whale would swallow Martha!) I could do a project on Tudor sailors and ships, and how they sailed all over the seas discovering new countries – but perhaps those same sailors stuck harpoons into whales and killed them and chopped them up into little pieces and boiled their blubber into oil.

I think of all those old whales swimming along so happily, kings of the sea, with only the odd giant squid to worry about. Then suddenly cruel men start killing them, thousands and thousands and thousands of whales for century after century after century, until some sorts of whale are almost extinct. No wonder the poor creatures moan and groan.

I droop down onto my desk, laying my head on the book. Then someone taps me timidly on the back. It's Joseph again.

'I'm doing a Tudor food project with Toby,' he says. 'Would you like to join up with us?'

Toby's certainly very interested in food. I don't really want to join up with them – girls never do projects with boys – and I don't think drawing a side of beef or a leg of lamb will be particularly inspiring, but I smile because Joseph's being very kind.

'Thank you, Joseph. Yes please, I'd like to join up with you,' I say. My voice is a bit croaky because I've been trying not to cry. I look at Toby anxiously in case he objects, but he grins at me cheerfully enough. Toby is always nice to everyone, even when he gets teased. If only Joseph and Toby were girls they'd be wonderful best friends.

I move my chair up beside them and peer at their project. They've done *pages* and *pages*, mostly in Joseph's scratchy handwriting. It starts sloping when he gets really enthusiastic, so half the lines tilt downwards dramatically and the bottom line gets squashed completely. They haven't left any room for drawing whatsoever.

I get a fresh piece of paper.

'What do Tudor tables look like then? I'll draw a big banquet,' I say.

It's quite good fun drawing in different platters of food at their suggestion. Toby gets a bit carried away, suggesting all *his* favourite foods – pizza and spaghetti bolognese.

'That's *Italian* food. These are *Tudors*, not the Medicis,' says Joseph, sighing. 'They were like

Italian royalty. Our English King Henry the Eighth would have liked roast beef and goose and swan—'

'*Swan?*'

'I think it was only for special occasions,' says Joseph. 'Like wedding feasts.'

'Well, he had a lot of those,' I say. 'He had six wives, didn't he?'

I draw fat King Henry with his fork stuck into a great platter of swan. Then I sketch three wives on either side of him, all with crowns on their heads.

'That's so good, Ella. You're ace at drawing,' says Toby.

'I agree, but it's not actually historically *accurate*, because you wouldn't have had them all sitting there together. In fact half of them would be dead.'

'It's OK,' I say, whipping out my eraser and rubbing out two of their heads. 'They're the ghosts of Anne Boleyn and Catherine Howard, without their heads – and I'll make Jane Seymour look very poorly because she died after having her baby—' I stop. There's a short agonized silence. Then Joseph reaches out and squeezes my hand.

'Your mum isn't going to die, Ella. She could get completely better,' he says. 'You read all those printouts I did for you.'

'And tell you what, we go to church every Sunday and there's a bit in the service where you pray for sick people. I'll ask everyone to say a special prayer for your mum,' says Toby.

'Thank you,' I mumble. My voice has gone croaky again.

They are being so sweet to me, yet I'd give anything not to be sitting here with them working on this pointless project. I don't even want to be sitting beside Sally. I just want to be at the hospital, murmuring into Mum's ear and making sure she's still alive.

Chapter 12

School seems to have lasted six years today. I can't *wait* for it to be home time. When the bell goes at last, Sally gives me a big hug.

'I hope your mum's a little bit better when you see her tonight,' she says kindly – but then she hurries off with Dory. She hasn't *said*, but I think she's going to play round at Dory's house.

Martha stomps off to after-school club, glowering. Toby rushes off, simply thinking of his tea, but Joseph hangs back.

'Are you going to show Miss Anderson your whale project?' he asks.

'Yes, if she'd really like to see it.'

Miss Anderson is busy talking to one of the other teachers, but she mouths at me, *Be with you in a minute.*

'Well, *I'd* like to see it too. If that's OK,' says Joseph.

So I get it out of my school bag and show him. He makes appreciative little grunts and murmurs. He especially likes the drawings.

'I'd love to do a proper whale project too, but I could never make it *look* good like yours. My writing's all wonky and I'm rubbish at drawing.'

'I'll always draw something for you, Joseph. I *like* drawing,' I say. 'It's all the word bit that gets me down sometimes. Especially the long foreign words.'

'I like the Latin bits the *best*!' says Joseph. 'I like saying all the names over and over until I know them by heart.'

'Maybe I'll try to learn some of them too,' I say.

'I know *cetaceans* already. *Cetaceans.* So I can speak Latin now.'

'Actually, I think that's from a Greek word, *ketos*, meaning sea monster. It said so in my book.'

'Oh, Joseph! How on earth did you get to be so brainy?'

'I'm just good at remembering,' he says modestly.

Then Toby charges back into the classroom, out of breath. 'Joseph! Your mum's getting all fidgety. She said she told you to run out of school early because you're visiting your gran.'

'Oh! I forgot!' Joseph meets my eye and chuckles. 'See! I'm not always good at remembering,' he says. 'Bye, Ella.'

'Bye, Joseph, bye, Toby,' I say.

The other teacher goes at last and Miss Anderson smiles at me.

'Right, Ella! Now I'd like to see this special whale project. Though won't your dad – your step-dad – be wondering where you've got to?'

'He said he's going to be a bit late fetching me,' I say. 'Here's my project, Miss Anderson. See, I've done heaps, and I'll probably do some more tonight.'

'Oh, Ella! You *have* worked hard! It looks lovely.' She flicks over the pages, looking really interested.

'And do I gather that you might be collaborating with Joseph?'

Teachers have the most amazing flappy ears that can hear everything.

'He's *such* a nice boy,' says Miss Anderson. 'He's been really worried about you, Ella. Well, we all have. How *are* things with your mum?'

I shrug. 'About the same.'

'Oh well . . .' Miss Anderson pats my arm sympathetically. 'There now. Off you go. And try not to get too upset about Martha. She's got her own troubles, you know.'

Huh! I'd like to know what troubles *Martha's* got. Miss Anderson can be pretty stupid sometimes.

I trail outside to the playground. It's practically empty now, just two little kids and me. They've rolled up a jumper and are kicking it around like a football. It's pretty muddy already. They're going to be for it when their mums come.

One mum turns up and doesn't fuss too much because it's not *her* kid's jumper. The other mum is taking ages. So is Jack. Where has he *got* to, for goodness' sake? It's not *that* far to drive from Garton Road.

I sigh. The little kid sighs.

'Want to play footie?' he asks.

'OK. But you're going to get into trouble for getting your jumper all dirty.'

Correction. *I'm* the one who gets into trouble when his mum comes puffing into the playground at last, pushing two howling babies in a double buggy. I just happen to be the one kicking the jumper back to her boy when she spots it.

'Oi! What in heaven's name are you *doing*, kicking our Davy's jumper about like that? Look at the state of it! You should know better!'

I wait for the little kid to explain. He doesn't say a word, just sticks his thumb in his mouth and looks sheepish. The mum rants on at me.

'What would *your* mother say if you kicked *your* good jumper all over the ground?' she yells.

I burst into tears because my mum can't say anything now. The kid's mum looks alarmed.

'Come on, there's no need to blub like a baby. My two are already making enough noise to wake the dead. Don't cry now – I dare say you won't do it again. Here.' She fishes in her pocket, finds a crumpled tissue and dabs at my eyes. 'There now. So where's your mum got to then?'

'She's in hospital,' I sniffle.

'Oh dear. Now you're making me feel dreadful. You have got someone coming for you though?'

'Yes, my stepdad.'

'That's all right then. Well, I'd better get my little lot home for their tea.'

I wave goodbye to them and carry on snuffling into my tissue. I want *my* tea. I'm starving. And little Butterscotch will want his tea too. He must have felt really lonely all day today with no one to talk to him. And how about Samson? He'll be fretting at Aunty Mavis's house, wondering when on earth we're coming to collect him. And then there's darling *Mum*. Maybe inside her head she's wondering where on earth we are and worrying that we've stopped caring about her. *Oh, Mum, I'm never ever going to stop caring. I'm going to visit you every day of my life, I promise. Come on, Jack, what are you playing at? Whatever time is it?*

I hear a distant clock strike four. It's getting really late now. Jack said he'd be a *bit* late but I'm sure he didn't mean as late as this. I start trudging up and down the playground. It's so mean of him to keep me waiting like this, when he *knows* I'll worry.

I count up to a hundred, two hundred, three hundred, straining my eyes to see his old black car, but it doesn't come, it doesn't come, it doesn't come.

I'm starting to cry now, like a baby. I want Mum so. We're supposed to go to the school office and tell someone if no one comes to collect us – but I don't like the secretary, she's always cross. I want Miss Anderson – but the classroom's empty. I run down the corridor and a cleaning lady looks up and says, 'What are you doing here, eh? Have you been kept in for being a bad girl?'

I shake my head and run back down the corridors. My whole *life* seems to be spent going down corridors now. I wonder if I'll ever get to the end of them. It's twenty past four now: Jack's nearly a whole hour late. I can't believe he can be so mean. Perhaps he's gone off with his teacher mates and forgotten all about me? No, he wouldn't forget me – he certainly wouldn't forget little Samson. What if something's happened to Jack? Maybe he's had an accident in the car. He was very tired because he was up a lot with Samson in the night – and he's had a whole day teaching. Maybe he got so tired he fell asleep at the wheel and crashed the car? Maybe *Jack's* in the hospital now?

So what am I going to do? Who will look after me now? Dad doesn't want me, Liz doesn't want me. I haven't got anyone – anyone at all.

I run out into the playground, crying – and see Jack running all round the tarmac, shouting, 'Ella, Ella, *Ella!*' Then he sees me and I see him, and just for a moment we both freeze, eyes wide, staring at each other. Then I run towards him, and part of me is ready to throw my arms round his neck and cling to him – but I'm mad at him too for making me feel like this.

'You mean pig!' I yell at him. 'I've been waiting ages and ages and *ages*!' I pummel him hard on the chest.

'Hey! Stop that! You're hurting me! For God's sake, I got here as quickly as I possibly could. I've been looking for *you* for the last ten minutes. Where the hell have you been? I thought you were going to be waiting in the playground. When I couldn't see you anywhere, I didn't know what to do. I didn't know whether you'd gone off with that little friend of yours—'

'She's gone off with this other girl – I *said* she would,' I say. Sally's still sort of my best friend, I know that, but I want to make Jack feel sorry for me.

He doesn't seem one bit sorry.

'Oh, for heaven's sake, is that all you've got to worry about?' he says, seizing hold of me and dragging me towards the gate. 'Look, I was late because some poor kid in my class came running back into school with blood pouring down his face because some thugs had stolen his pocket money, knocked him over and kicked his head in just for the fun of it. You don't know how lucky you are, Ella. I'm sick of you whingeing and whining because you and your silly little friends keep falling out. Grow up, can't you? Now, come on, get in the car. We've got to collect Sam and we're very late and I don't want Mavis to get fed up with us.'

I stamp into the car. 'I hate you,' I mutter.

'I heard that. And as if I care,' says Jack, driving off.

We don't say another word to each other on the journey. We get to Aunty Mavis's house. Jack takes a deep breath and knocks. Aunty Mavis comes to the door, a twin on either side of her.

'I'm so sorry we're so late,' Jack says. 'There was an unfortunate accident at my school—'

'Never you mind, dear. Little Sam's having a lovely nap. He's been *such* a good boy, hasn't he, girls?'

They chirrup about him excitedly.

'Tell you what, why don't you come in and have a cup of tea? You both look like you need a bit of a sit-down.'

'Well, that's very kind of you, but we're really in a bit of a mad rush. We have to get to the hospital,' says Jack.

'Ten minutes won't make too much difference. And I've made one of my lardy cakes. They're very good, though I say so myself.'

So we go into Aunty Mavis's warm, cosy living room and sip tea and eat her lovely gooey curranty cake. Jack and I still don't say a word to each other. He talks to Aunty Mavis and I play a daft game of Hunt the Teddy with the twins. I make the teddy peep out at them and wave his paw. They both scream with laughter, as if I'm the funniest comedian in the entire universe. It's quite a good feeling. I wonder if I'll be able to make Samson laugh like this when he's a bit bigger.

Samson himself is stretched out in his baby chair, legs dangling, fast asleep. When the twins squeal extra loudly, his arms shoot up and his hands open wide into starfish – but then he settles down again, not even giving a whimper. He doesn't even wake up when we carry him to the car and get him strapped into place.

Then we drive to the hospital – and all the warmth of Aunty Mavis's home drains out of us. Samson wakes up and starts crying as we start the long trek down the corridors. At long last we get near Mum. I hang back, eyes shut, willing it to be different this time. Mum will sit up and smile and open her arms wide – and I'll leap up on the bed and hug her to bits, and all this long, lonely nightmare will be over. But when I go up to her bed, she doesn't sit up, she just lies there. She isn't smiling, she's looking so sad and odd and awful. She doesn't open her arms wide. They stay limp by her side, her hands at odd angles, so that she looks like a broken doll.

'Hello, darling,' Jack says. 'I've brought our little boy to see you. Here he is.' He arranges Samson on Mum's chest. We wait for him to quieten but he wails dismally.

'Come on, Sue. Give him a little cuddle,' says Jack.

Mum doesn't move. Samson cries harder. A nurse comes in to see what's going on. She's young and rosy-cheeked, with black curly hair.

'Oh dear,' she says. She looks at Samson, she looks at Mum, she looks at Jack and me.

'He usually calms down when I lay him on my wife,' Jack says. He sighs. 'But it's not working today.'

He picks Samson up and gives him to me. 'You give Sam a cuddle, Ella.'

Then he moves close to the nurse as she takes Mum's temperature and blood pressure. 'Is there any improvement at all?' he whispers.

'She's in a very stable condition at the moment, Mr Winters.'

'Yes, but that's a totally meaningless statement. Of course she's stable, she's in a coma.'

'She's doing well, considering. There's no sign of any infections, her lungs aren't congested, we're giving her physio on her hands and feet to keep them in a good position—'

'But she's not showing any signs of recovery whatsoever, is she?'

'Well . . .' The nurse is starting to sound a bit panicky now.

'Do you think Sue will ever get properly better?' Jack whispers. His voice is very low but I hear every word, even though Samson is howling.

'I couldn't possibly say, Mr Winters.'

'Yes, you can. You must have nursed patients before in this sort of state. How many of them recover?'

'Some do, Jack. I've got some printouts from newspapers. *Lots* of coma patients recover,' I say.

'Shh, Ella. Why don't you take Sam for a little walk along the corridor?' he says. He takes hold of the nurse by the arm. 'I just want you to tell me the truth. I'm going crazy here. I see you and your colleagues giving me pitying looks, like you think it's all hopeless. I just want to know the odds. I'm not going to give up, I'm not going to do anything dramatic, I just need to *know*.'

'You can always make an appointment to see Dr Clegg – he's your wife's neurologist.'

'Yes, I know, I've been trying to see him, but he's never around when I am. I'm not even sure he'll tell me either. I want to know what will happen to Sue. You're not going to keep her here indefinitely, are you?'

'Well, at some stage other arrangements will be made,' she says desperately.

'Yes, but *what*?'

'There are residential homes for people with PVS,' she says.

'PVS?' Jack says, screwing up his face.

'Persistent vegetative state,' says the nurse.

'*What?*' Jack sounds horrified.

'Look, I don't know, I'm just here to give your wife nursing care. You must see Dr Clegg – he's the one who'll make the decisions – or you can ask the ward sister, but I can't tell you anything, I don't *know* anything.' The nurse hurries out of the room.

'Good riddance!' Jack yells after her. He goes to Mum and takes her hand. 'Did you hear any of that, Sue? Don't you worry, darling. You aren't in this bloody PVS condition. I'm not going to put you in a home. You're going to come home with *us*, where you belong. You and me and our little boy.'

I hold my breath.

'And Ella,' he says. I sound very much an afterthought.

We barely talk on the way home. The house seems horribly empty. Samson wails forlornly.

'I'll feed him and you feed your guinea pig,' Jack says.

I feed Butterscotch, putting my hand right into his cage and stroking his head very gently as he nibbles away. 'Do you miss your mum, Butterscotch?' I ask.

I think of him aching for his warm soft mum every day, scurrying round and round his cage looking for her. I feel terrible. I'll try to make it up to him. I'll make his life as lovely as I can. I wrinkle my nose. I could make his cage much comfier.

'Jack, Butterscotch's cage is starting to smell,' I say, my nose twitching.

Jack lays Samson on the floor, changing his nappy. 'I know,' he says shortly. 'Hold *still*, Sammy.'

'It needs cleaning,' I say.

'Yes, of course it needs cleaning. He's your pet. You do it.'

I pause. I look at Butterscotch scrabbling. I look at his cage and all the dirty straw. 'I don't know *how*,' I say.

'Oh, for heaven's sake, don't be so hopeless,' says Jack.

That's just what I feel. Hope-less. I try to remember what the nurse said.

'What did that nurse say Mum had?' I ask.

'Oh, Ella. We're not taking any notice of that stupid nurse,' says Jack. 'There you are, Sam, all clean and tidy. You'll past muster, even if the rest of us won't. Now, we'll strap you in your little chair and you can kick your legs and whistle a happy tune while I start *our* tea and Ella clears out that wretched cage.'

'I *said*, I don't know how,' I say – but he can't divert me that easily. 'Jack, what does it mean? The veggie thing?'

'Don't call it that,' Jack says sharply. Then he takes a deep breath. 'She said "persistent vegetative state". It's a horrible term used to describe a person whose body is alive but whose brain isn't working.'

'Like Mum?' I whisper.

'No! *Not* like Mum. Don't you start, Ella. You're the one who always says she's going to get completely better.'

'Well, she is,' I say. I start pulling nasty straw that's sticky with black bits out onto the carpet.

'What are you *doing*? *Not* like that, with the guinea pig still in the cage. You need to find a cardboard box to put him in. Then put all the soiled straw and all those manky dandelion leaves and whatnot into a rubbish bag. When the cage is clean, get some fresh bedding and put the guinea pig back. Come on, Ella, it's not rocket science.'

'He's getting a bit bigger already,' I say, cradling Butterscotch in my cupped hands. 'It's a shame he has to be stuck in his cage all the time.'

'Well, when I've got a spare moment I'll make him a special pen in the garden so he can run about. But just at the moment I'm a bit pushed for time, seeing as I'm running backwards and forwards to your school and my school and the hospital, and we've still got to have our tea, and then I've got to mark a whole pile of homework and sort out my lesson plans for the week – so I'm not playing *Grand Designs* for guinea pigs right this minute.'

'Oh ha ha,' I mutter. I pull out an extra nasty clump of straw and drop it with a squeal. 'Yuck!'

'*Don't* drop it all over the carpet! Oh here, let me do it. Wash your hands – *thoroughly* – and then go and have a scrabble through Liz's frozen meals and stick one in the microwave. You *can* use the microwave, I take it?'

'Of course I can.'

'Just be careful taking it out when it's done.'

I cook our supper, Jack cleans out Butterscotch, and then we eat our meals on trays while we watch television. Jack flicks through all the channels irritably, rushing past several hospital soaps. Then he finds the Eden nature channel.

'*Whales!*' I shout.

It's a whole programme about predators, and I watch as Miss Anderson's food chains swim before my eyes: plankton, herrings, sea lions . . . and twelve humpback whales fishing together, spiralling through the air and diving down with vast splashes, hoovering up their supper. I wonder about phoning Sally to tell her to watch, but I don't think she'd really be interested.

I suddenly think of Joseph. I don't know his phone number, but his surname's Antscherl and there can't be many of them in the directory. I look it up and dial.

'Are you ringing Sally?' Jack asks.

'Nope.'

'Not your dad?'

'*Nope.*'

'Your boyfriend?' says Jack, acting silly, fluttering his eyelashes and making kissy-kissy noises.

I sigh at him.

'Mrs Antscherl? I'm Ella, I'm in Joseph's class at school. Please can I talk to him?'

Jack raises his eyebrows. 'It *is* a boyfriend!'

I stick my tongue out at him.

'Ella?' Joseph sounds astonished when he comes to the phone.

'Joseph, there's a programme right now on the Eden channel all about whales – do watch!'

'OK. Right. Well, thank you, Ella.'

I ring off.

Jack nods at me. 'Joseph, eh?'

'He likes whales too.'

'Well, it was sweet of you to phone him. You'll be able to discuss the programme together at school tomorrow.'

Oh dear. I wish I didn't have to go. It's Tuesday, and that means swimming down at the pool. I hate swimming. I tried to get out of it once, accidentally on purpose forgetting my swimsuit, but it didn't work. Miss Anderson keeps a couple of awful old-fashioned manky costumes in a locker and you have to wear one of them. Sally's brilliant at swimming. She can swim a whole *mile*, easy-peasy. She's in the top group for swimming, with Dory. Martha's in the middle group. I'm stuck in the bottom group, and I'm sadly *bottom* of that. I can't actually swim yet. I do lots of strokes, going faster and faster, until my arms and legs ache, but I don't really get anywhere. I'm terrified I'll start sinking so I keep my head sticking right up like a meerkat. The swimming coach tries to get us all to bob down under the water, but I hate it. The water stings my eyes and goes up my nose and gets inside my ears. The first time I ducked down, I came up crying and everyone laughed at me for being a baby – even Sally.

I'm still worrying about it when I go to bed. Whenever I had a worry keeping me awake, Mum would always *know*, even if I had the light off and lay still as still. She'd lie down on the bed beside me, snuggling into my pillow, and whisper, 'Come on, little worry, jump out of Ella's head.'

I would imagine my worry like a little buzzing fly. It would squeeze out of the creases in my fore-head and I'd say, 'It's out, it's out!'

Mum would run her hand over my face in the dark, pretending to chase it, and then she'd suddenly swat it. 'There, I've flattened it! The little worry's dead and gone.' It was always so weird because it *worked*. Mum hadn't solved anything – she often didn't know what the worry even *was* – but she made it go away.

I try to sort my worry myself. 'Come on, little worry, out you come,' I whisper, and then I try swatting at my own head. I swat too hard and bang my nose and it hurts – and it's all pointless, because the worry's still inside my head. It's not just the Tuesday swimming worry. There's the great big cockroach-size worry about Mum, and then all the horrid stinging worries about Jack and my dad, and then the biting-ant worries about Sally and Dory and Martha. I feel like one of those silly celebrities in the Australian bush with their heads stuck in a helmet of creepy-crawlies. I keep tossing and turning, trying not to cry out.

About midnight Jack opens my bedroom door and peers in. 'Are you OK, Ella?' he whispers.

I lie very still, breathing heavily, pretending to be asleep.

'I'll try to get to your school a bit earlier tomorrow, I promise.'

I still don't say a word – though perhaps I really want to.

'Oh well, night-night,' Jack says, and goes away.

I wonder if Mum is sometimes pretending with us. Maybe she can move a little, maybe she can even talk, but she's too tired or cross or scared to shift or speak. I don't know why. I don't know why I don't want to talk to Jack. I don't know *anything*. Yes, I do. I know a lot about whales. I run through all my whale facts in my mind.

I think of humpback whales swimming ten thousand miles every year to find a mate, singing their love songs. I remember the Latin name for humpback – *megaptera novaengliae* – and I whisper it over and over, like a magic spell. At last I fall asleep . . . and then I'm swimming through the turquoise ocean, deep down in the cool water, and it's not hard, it's not scary, I don't choke and splutter, I glide and arch and swoop with a flick of my flukes. I rise up to the surface and blow, and I leap up into the sunlight and then dive down down down again, swimming steadily, acting out my love for Mum, knowing she's waiting patiently for me to find her.

I wake up before I get to her, and I try hard to go back to sleep because it's such a beautiful dream. I was so very near Mum, and my heart is going to burst if I can't find her . . . but I can hear Samson crying and Jack's footsteps going up and down the stairs, and I know that it's time to get up.

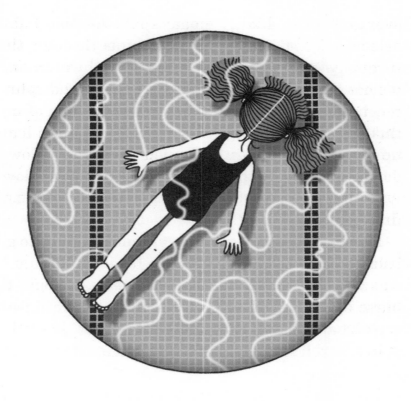

Chapter 13

It's Tuesday and it's swimming day – but now I wonder if it's quite so bad. I can still feel that wonderful gliding thrill of swimming through the ocean like a whale. Maybe that's the way it will be now. I'll swim all the way to the other side and back without stopping once, and I'll be put into the top group straight away. I'll be the best swimmer in the whole class, even better than Sally. Everyone says swimming is just a knack, a matter of confidence, just like riding a bike – and once you've learned you never forget. I've learned to swim properly now and I'll never forget.

I run into the bathroom, have a quick wash and then pull on my school clothes. I find Jack in the armchair downstairs, giving Samson his bottle.

'Morning, Jack, morning, Samson, morning, Butterscotch,' I chant.

I give Butterscotch fresh water, a bowl of nuggets, a few carrots and a dandelion salad. He squeaks appreciatively at this little feast.

'Would you like a cup of tea?' I ask Jack, putting the kettle on.

'Yes, please! My, you're in a cheery mood this morning, Ella. Regular little ray of sunshine. How lovely!'

I'm not sure whether he's being sarcastic or not, but I give him the benefit of the doubt and smile at him. I make us both a cup of tea and we sit Samson in his baby chair while we have our breakfast. Samson is in a good mood too, kicking his little legs and waving his arms around.

'He's excited because he likes going to Aunty

Mavis's house,' I say. 'I wish *I* was little enough to go there.'

'I wish I was too,' says Jack. He finishes his tea. 'Come on then, kids, let's get the show on the road. Have you got your school bag packed, Ella?'

'Yep. I've even remembered my towel and swimsuit because we go to the pool today.'

'Good girl! Are you *sure* you're Ella? You haven't locked her in a cupboard somewhere and taken her place?'

We get in the car and drop Samson off at Aunty Mavis's. She gives me a chocolate brownie to eat later, carefully wrapped up in foil. Sally loves anything chocolatey. We can share it on the coach on the way back from swimming.

I look for her as I go into the playground but I'm waylaid by Joseph.

'Hey, Ella, thanks for telling me about that programme! It was *great*, especially when all the humpbacks made that circle and fished together.'

We start talking whale-facts. Joseph says he's found two new whale books in the library.

'The school library? I looked, but I couldn't find anything.'

'No, the public library. We often go there on the way home from school. It's great – heaps bigger than the school one. You should come some time.'

'Yeah, I will.'

'After school? With me?'

'Well, I have to wait for my stepdad, and then we pick up my little brother from his childminder, and then we go home for tea, and *then* we go to the hospital to see my mum.'

'Oh. Well, maybe you could come and have tea with me some day?' Joseph asks. His brown eyes are very bright, though he blinks a lot because his fringe gets in them.

I reach out and make little scissor chops with my fingers. 'Your fringe needs cutting, just like mine.'

'Yes, I know, but I hate it all short and bristly. My dad keeps nagging me about it though. You know what dads are like.'

Do I? I suppose my dad would fuss about hair. Then I think of Jack cuddling Samson, nuzzling his cheek against Samson's soft dandelion-fluff wisps. I can't see him ever nagging Samson to get his hair cut if he didn't want to. Does that make him a good dad or a bad one? And should I say yes, I'll go to tea with Joseph and be his friend? I *like* Joseph and we enjoy talking about the same things – but none of the other girls have boys for their friends. And anyway, I've got Sally, haven't I?

I look round for Sally. There she is, arm in arm with Dory, heads together, talking earnestly.

There's Martha too, jumping right up on the playground wall and walking along it, which is dangerous and strictly forbidden, but she doesn't care – she just wants everyone to look at her and be impressed.

Miss Anderson comes into the playground and is distinctly *un*impressed. Martha is made to come down and severely told off, but she just laughs, pretending not to care – or maybe she really *doesn't* care.

I sometimes wish I could be like Martha.

We go into school for registration and I sit in my usual place beside Sally, and she asks me how Mum is and whether little Samson is sleeping OK. She *even* asks about Butterscotch and laughs when I do a guinea-pig imitation, twitching my nose and curling my hands in the air.

I start to think everything's fine. I wait before getting on the coach to go swimming, telling Joseph that I'd love to come round to his place to see his whale books. Then I jump up the steps of the coach. Dory has bagged the best seat at the front. She pats the place next to her . . . and Sally sits down beside her! I can't believe my eyes. Sally is sitting with Dory, not with me.

I stand stock-still, staring at them. 'Sally!' I whisper.

Sally wriggles, not quite looking me in the eye. 'Dory saved the seat for me,' she says.

'But you always sit next to me!'

'Yes, but *Dory* wanted to sit with me.' Sally takes a deep breath. 'Tell you what, you come and sit with us too.'

'But there are three of us. The seat's only for two.'

'It doesn't matter. We can squash up, can't we, Dory?' says Sally, smiling now she thinks she's solved the problem. 'There, we can *all* sit together now.'

But Mr Hodgkins, the horrible strict Year Six teacher who comes swimming with us, barges up from the back of the coach.

'What are you three silly little girls playing at? Come on, one of you get up and sit somewhere else.'

I look round for Miss Anderson, but she's busy talking to some girl who's forgotten her costume.

'We want to sit together, all three of us, Mr Hodgkins,' says Sally. She says it very sweetly, with a smile. Sally usually gets round all the teachers because she's got this soft little girly voice and she looks so pretty with her big eyes and blonde curly hair. But Mr Hodgkins doesn't smile back at her.

'You can't possibly sit three on a double seat. You won't be able to use your seat belts properly. Stop being so *silly*. One of you get up.' He gives me a little prod. 'Come on, you sit further down the coach.'

'But Sally's my best friend. I always sit with her.'

'For heaven's sake, you're not going on a day trip. It's a ten-minute drive. Now *move*, this instant!'

So I move, though it's so not fair – and there isn't anyone I can sit with. I look for Joseph, but he's sitting with Toby, so there *certainly* isn't room for another one on their seat – and anyway, the boys all sit together and the girls do too. There's only one seat left now, and, oh horror, it's the one next to Martha. I'm not not not sitting next to Martha. I'd sooner sit next to a rabid warthog. She clearly feels the same way too, spreading herself right over the seat and glaring at me.

'You, girl!' Mr Hodgkins bellows. 'Sit *down*.'

I sit right on the very edge of the seat.

'Get off! This is *my* seat,' says Martha, pushing me.

'You shut up. I can't help it. I don't *want* to sit next to you, but I've got to.'

'I don't know why you're bothering to come

swimming anyway, seeing as you *can't* swim, baby.'

'I can so swim,' I retort furiously.

'No, you can't! I've seen you puffing along with one foot on the bottom. You're absolutely hopeless. Everyone looks at you and *laughs*.'

'No they don't! They laugh at you because you look so stupid.' I try hard to think why she might look stupid. 'Yeah, your bum sticks out, especially when you swim, wiggle waggle, wiggle waggle.'

Bull's eye! Martha looks outraged.

'It does *not* stick out,' she says, and she pulls up her feet and kicks at me with her sandals. 'Get off my seat! Go on, get off!'

'You get off it, waggle-bum,' I say, and kick her back.

Then suddenly Mr Hodgkins's head is hovering over us, and his hands are pushing all our feet back on the floor.

'Will you two *behave*!' He glares at me in particular. 'If I have to speak to you one more time today, I'm sending you to see Mrs Raynor the moment you get back to school.'

I sit seething but silent until we get to the pool. Sally comes to find me in the changing rooms.

'Your face is all red, Ella,' she says. 'Are you OK?'

'No, I'm *not* OK. I had to sit with Martha because *you* sat with Dory,' I sniff.

'Oh dear. I'm sorry. But I did try to get you sitting with *us*,' Sally says.

'Will you sit with me on the way home?'

'Well . . .' Sally pauses. 'I wish I could, but I've just promised Dory—'

'Oh, see if I care. I don't want to sit with you anyway,' I say, and slam into a cubicle to get changed into my swimsuit.

I tear my clothes off in a rage and finish changing much more quickly than usual. I pad past the closed cubicle in my bare feet. I hear Sally talking to Dory behind one of the doors. She's whispering but I still hear.

'She's so *moody* now. She's just no fun at all. I know it's ever so sad about her mum – and *my* mum says I've got to be extra nice to her, and I am trying, but she gets so cross if I don't do everything she wants,' Sally whispers.

'I know, I know,' Dory whispers back. 'Martha's exactly the same.'

It's so unfair! I'm not a *bit* like Martha. I can't bear it that Sally's saying such awful things about me.

I stomp off to the side of the baths. The boys are larking around, trying to push each other in. The girls are clustered in little groups, looking like boiled eggs in their swimming hats. Martha is standing with her back to the wall, her face screwed up. Maybe she thinks she's really got a waggle-bottom. Well, good. She's so mean to me it's great to be mean back. Though she looks so sad staring at Dory and Sally as they saunter up, arm in arm. They start doing ridiculous stretching exercises, like they're Olympic athletes. I turn my back on them and look at the boys instead.

Joseph looks thinner without his clothes, his arms little sticks, his shoulders narrow, his neck too tiny to support his big head and unruly hair. He reminds me of Samson in a weird way. If there were just the two of us together I'd put my arm round him, he looks so little. Whereas Toby looks *big* – much bigger without his clothes – his belly huge, but he doesn't seem to mind at all. He's waddling around pretending to be a gorilla, thumping himself on his wobbly chest and growling.

Mr Hodgkins comes stomping along and tells him to stop messing about – but he ruffles Toby's hair. No one can be cross with Toby for long.

We have to divide into our groups, and there am I, stuck with all the doggy-paddle splash-and-scream beginners – and I'm the worst of the lot. We have to stay in the shallow end and do silly stuff like blowing bubbles in the water and kicking our legs while holding onto the side. I do this obediently for a while, but this isn't *swimming*. I want to see if my dream can come true, if I can glide through the water as easily and powerfully as a little whale. So while the swimming instructor is busy with silly Maddy, who breathes in instead of blowing out and is now having a choking fit, I suddenly duck right down in the water and push off from the side.

I glide. Yes, I'm gliding, I'm really slipping through the water – I'm not moving my arms or legs but I'm still swimming, I really am. I can do it, so long as I don't put my head up and start gasping. I must stay down down down, almost scraping my tummy on the pool mosaic floor. It's so easy, so simple. My chest's feeling tight now, but I don't need to breathe just yet. I can manage much longer. Whales can wait a whole hour before they come up to breathe. I want to stay down here in the dim turquoise depths. My heart is banging and my hands are scrabbling in the water, but I'm not giving in, I'm staying right where I am, I'm—

Something's got me! I'm being savagely attacked, hauled along, up into the air. There's sudden light and shouting and splashing, and then I'm thrown onto the hard tiles at the edge of the pool, and someone's thump-thump-thumping on my chest until I cough and splutter and a little sick dribbles out of my mouth. Then I'm wrapped up in a towel and carried out, and everyone's looking and pointing. I can't work out exactly what's happening, and I still feel sick. Where are my clothes? They're taking me outside and into a car and I'm just in my soaking swimsuit. Are they mad?

I struggle, and Miss Anderson holds me tightly and says, 'There, there, you're going to be fine, Ella, don't worry. I've got you safe.' I'm almost on her lap in the back of the car and she's got her arms right round me! But where are we going? Where is she taking me? Some strange man is driving us, whizzing along the roads and rushing through amber lights. Are they *kidnapping* me?

But then the roads start to look familiar, we turn down Milestone Road, and there's the great grey hospital looming at the end. Are they taking me to Mum?

We go in the A & E entrance. Miss Anderson is still holding me as if I'm a little baby. I'm being taken straight past all the waiting people into a little curtained cubicle, and there's a lady doctor – not lovely Dr Wilmot, I've never seen this one before.

'Oh, Doctor, she nearly drowned!' Miss Anderson says as the doctor takes my pulse and blood pressure and listens to my chest with her stethoscope.

I nearly *drowned*! I feel a thrill of excitement. But surely she's wrong. I was only under the water a minute or so. Whales stay under so much longer—

'Well, she seems reasonably all right now, if a bit damp and shivery! We'll keep an eye on her for a little while. Have her parents been told?'

'Well, that's part of the problem,' says Miss Anderson, and then she murmurs something to the doctor. They both peer at me anxiously.

I'm starting to feel anxious too. I am all right now, aren't I? I feel a bit strange and sick and shivery still, though I've got another blanket round me now, and a huge sheet of tinfoil so that I feel like a giant turkey. Every time I move, I crackle, so I lie as still as possible – but then I feel sick again and I have to sit up. I start retching, and the doctor gives me an odd cardboard bowl. I'm not very sick, but I feel so embarrassed doing it in front of Miss Anderson.

She's lovely to me though, holding my hair out of the way and rubbing my back. When I've finished and lie down again, she carries on stroking my shoulder and murmuring to me just like a mum. Oh, how I want *my* mum. I think I'm crying but my eyes are shut. I feel so tired. I just want to sleep a little . . .

Then someone's taking hold of me by the shoulders, shaking me, and I open my eyes. It's Jack! His face is grey-white, his eyes are bloodshot, he looks *awful*.

'Oh, Jack, is it Mum?' I gasp.

'No, no, you idiot, it's *you!*' says Jack. He flings his arms round me and hugs me hard.

We never hug — we mostly never even touch — yet here's Jack practically lying on me, his tousled hair tickling my face. I want to push him away. He's not my dad, he's only my stepdad, and I don't like him, I've never liked him — but he's all I've got, and my arms go round his neck and I hang on tight.

'Ella, you can't swim, can you?' says Jack, his voice muffled against my head.

'No, not really. Well, just a little bit.'

'But they said you deliberately went under the water — and stayed under . . . as if — as if you were trying to drown,' Jack says.

'What? No, I wasn't trying to *drown* — though I nearly did, they said.'

'So what on earth were you playing at?'

'I was playing at being a whale,' I say truthfully.

'Oh, for God's *sake* — you and your wretched whales!' says Jack, and he starts shaking.

'Are you . . . crying?' I whisper.

'I'm mostly *laughing*, because you're such an idiot. Don't you *dare* play silly tricks like that again. I just about had a heart attack when they phoned me at school. What would I have done if you *had* drowned? How could I ever tell your mum?'

'Don't let's tell her now – she might worry so,' I say, suddenly very ashamed.

'You bet she'll worry, so we *won't* tell her. But you promise me you'll never ever do anything as daft again?'

'I promise. Jack, can we go upstairs and see Mum now – not to say anything, just to see her.'

'I don't see why not, when they've given you another check-up to make sure you're OK. Though look at you! You can't go dripping down all the corridors in your swimming gear. What's happened to your clothes?'

Luckily Miss Anderson has had the presence of mind to bring them with her. She has another whispered conversation with Jack while I'm getting dressed. Then she comes and sits beside me.

'Ella, your dad says it was just a silly accident. Is that right?'

'Yes,' I say, in a very tiny voice. 'I truly wasn't trying to drown myself, Miss Anderson. I was just trying to swim underwater like a whale.'

'Well, don't ever do that again! You scared us all terribly.'

'Aren't I going to be allowed to go swimming again, Miss Anderson?' I ask hopefully.

'Yes, but we'll be watching you like hawks, and woe betide you if you try any tricks like that ever again!' she says. 'Ella, I know it's a very bad time for you at the moment, but you do know you can always come and have a little chat with me whenever you need to?'

'Yes, Miss Anderson,' I say – but the only person I *really* want to chat to is my mum.

But Jack's right, I can't tell her about nearly drowning because if she hears that, she'll start worrying so badly. So when the doctors say I'm perfectly OK and Jack and I go up to Mum, I don't breathe a word about it. I just stand by Mum's head and whisper, 'I-love-you-I-love-you-I-love-you,' into her ear. My hair is still damp and it trickles on Mum's face.

'Sorry, Mum, am I getting you all wet? I was just pretending to be a whale,' I say.

Jack frowns at me.

'So if I'm wet like a whale, I can sing you my special love song,' I say. 'I told you about the humpback who sang for twenty-two hours, didn't I? I wonder if he found a special lady love after all that time? I do hope so. If I sing you a love song for twenty-two hours – breaking it up into little bits, ten minutes here, twenty minutes there – will you wake up then? Will you open your eyes and smile at me and tell me you love me back?'

Mum sighs. She really sighs. I hear her clearly. I look at Jack. He's heard her too.

'Sue?' he says urgently, gripping her hand.

She doesn't move. Her eyes stay shut. She doesn't make any more sounds. But we both know what we heard.

'Don't be too excited, Ella. The nurses all say it doesn't really mean anything. It's just something she does involuntarily. All their machines show she's deeply unconscious.'

'She's not going to talk to machines, is she?' I say. 'She's trying to talk to *us*, Jack.'

'I hope so.'

'And we'll go on and on talking to her.'

'Of course we will,' says Jack.

'Can we stay a bit longer now?'

'Well – I've left my class totally in the lurch – but yes, why not.'

So we sit one on each side of Mum, and we're allowed to stay even when the nurses wash her and wipe her eyes and check all her tubes and give her a clean nightgown.

'Mum's got a really pretty new nightie at home. Can she wear that one day?' I ask.

'Yes, of course she can, dear,' says the nicest nurse.

She's called Niamh and she's got lovely short hair and a smiley face. Some of the nurses treat Mum just like she's part of the hospital bed; some of them treat her like a doll, which is even worse; but Niamh treats Mum like a proper person. She's always very gentle with her, and talks softly to her all the time. 'Now, Sue, I'm just going to peer into your eyes. It won't take a minute. There now. You've got lovely blue eyes and such long dark lashes. I bet you don't ever need to fuss with mascara.'

When she takes Mum's pulse and blood pressure, she holds her hand afterwards, giving her a little massage, smoothing her fingers out, and takes infinite pains to get Mum lying in a comfortable position.

'Get a move on, Niamh, Dr Clegg's due any minute,' says one of the nurses, rushing past.

Jack sits up straight. 'Dr Clegg? He's Sue's consultant, right? Good, there's all sorts of things I want to ask him.'

Niamh pulls a face. 'You'll be lucky,' she says. 'I think you'll have to make an appointment.'

248

'Yes, but I could just have a few words with him now.'

'Well, you can try, but I rather think his wife has to make an appointment to ask him what he wants for his supper. He's that kind of fellow.'

We see what she means when Dr Clegg parades down the ward, little entourage grovelling behind him. Lovely Dr Wilmot is there, and she smiles at Jack and me and mouths hello. Dr Clegg is a tall thin man with a long nose. It's very easy for him to look down it. His mouth is thin too and doesn't look as if it knows how to smile.

'I wasn't aware that we'd changed our visiting hours,' he says crisply, standing at the foot of Mum's bed.

'We were at the hospital anyway this morning, Ella fetched up in A & E,' says Jack, standing up and bravely offering his hand to Dr Clegg. 'I'm Jack Winters, Sue's husband. I'd like to ask you—'

'Yes, yes, Mr Winters, we'll have a proper meeting to discuss your wife's condition. You can make an appointment through my secretary.'

'Yes, I know, but as we're both here now, can you tell me if my wife's made any progress whatsoever, and just what sort of treatment you've got in mind for her.'

Dr Clegg sighs. 'Your wife is in a stable

condition. There's no sign of any chest infection, no pressure ulcers – the nurses are clearly doing an excellent job.'

The nurses flutter happily.

Dr Clegg nods and seems about to move on.

'And her treatment?' Jack says. 'Why isn't she having *any* treatment?'

'What sort of treatment did you have in mind, Mr Winters?' Dr Clegg asks icily.

Jack stands his ground. 'Well, I'm not sure, obviously, because I'm not a medical man. I don't know if there are any kind of new drugs you can give her?'

Dr Clegg makes an irritated little puffing sound with his thin lips.

'And what about more extensive physiotherapy?' Jack says desperately. 'Something to help get her moving? Or a special therapist to help her learn to talk again?'

'Mr Winters, I'm not sure you quite understand. Very sadly, your wife isn't responding to any sort of stimulation. She's in a profound state of unconsciousness.'

'Not always. She sighs sometimes, as if she really is responding,' I say.

Dr Clegg glances at me. 'I don't really think this is the right sort of conversation to have in front of a small child,' he says, looking at Jack reproach-fully.

'But Sue does sigh. I'm sure she's aware of us sometimes, especially when the baby's near her.'

'These are involuntary responses. She might well move occasionally, even open her eyes – but these aren't significant signs. We've been monitor-ing your wife scrupulously.' Dr Clegg seizes Mum's charts. 'This refers to the Glasgow Coma Scale, a fifteen-point scale for assessing levels of consciousness. We evaluate three different behav-ioural responses – eye opening, verbal response and motor response. I'm afraid your wife has scored very disappointingly – and there's no per-ceptible change as the days progress. At some stage we need to make a proper private appoint-ment to discuss future plans.'

'It sounds as if you've given up on her. Well, I'm not going to. I'm not putting her in a home!' says Jack.

'We will offer you help in coming to what will clearly be a difficult decision,' says Dr Clegg. He nods curtly and moves on.

Dr Wilmot looks agonized. She pats Jack's shoulder, squeezes my hand, but walks on too. Jack and I are left with Mum. We're both shivering, as if Mr Clegg has thrown buckets of cold water all over us.

'Don't take any notice of that horrible man, Mum. He doesn't know anything,' I say.

'That's right, Sue. Come on, baby, you wake up right this minute and prove him wrong,' says Jack.

We clutch Mum and will her to wake – but she stays silent and serene in her own faraway world. We want to stay with her for ever, but my tummy has started making silly rumbling gurgles.

'Here, it's way past lunch time, Ella – and you were sick, weren't you, so you must be totally empty. Let's go and get something to eat,' says Jack.

We go to the canteen on the ground floor, but it reeks of old chip fat and the sad pervasive smell of the hospital.

'We'll go out to eat,' says Jack. 'Come on, Ella, we'll be wicked, we'll have a pizza.'

We go to the restaurant and I choose a Hawaiian pizza because I love pineapple. In fact Jack orders one for me with *double* pineapple. Sally had her birthday in this pizza place and she chose a Hawaiian too. Did she invite Dory to her party? I think she was there, but I didn't really notice her then. Sally's little brother Benjy came and kept pretending to be a puppy dog, begging for scraps from all our plates. He even got under the table and starting licking our legs, which was pretty disgusting. Sally's mum told him to come out of there sharpish, and he stood up and bumped his head and made all our knives and forks clatter.

I wonder if Samson is going to grow up to be as irritating. No, we'll teach him to sit up properly in a chair, and if he's interested in dogs, I'll help him do a special project on them. Jack can teach him stuff too. I expect he's quite a good teacher. I know they all like him at Garton Road. And Mum . . . and Mum . . . Will Mum ever be able to teach him anything?

I chew and chew but I can't seem to manage to get through my mouthful of pizza. I can't even swallow the lovely sweet golden pineapple. I feel a tear spurt down my cheek and stab at it quickly with my napkin, hoping Jack won't see.

'It's all right,' he says quietly. 'You don't have to finish it.'

'It's lovely, especially the extra pineapple, it's just—'

'I know. I'm not making much headway myself.'

'Jack, if Mum doesn't get better—'

'Hey, hey. We're not giving up hope. Take no notice of that Dr Clegg. He might fancy himself like crazy but he's not God. He doesn't know our

Sue. She's such a fierce little fighter. I reckon she'll pull through. Even if she can't get completely better, I know she'll come out of this coma. Some people are in comas for *months* and then recover.'

'Yes, I know. I've got all the newspaper printouts from Joseph. But, Jack, *if* Mum doesn't get better, *will* she have to go in a home?'

Jack puts down his knife and fork. 'The only home your mum is going in is *ours*. I'll care for her myself if necessary.'

'Oh, Jack! And I'll care for her too. We can wash her and dress her and change her just like the nurses, can't we?'

'And I expect we'll be able to have nurses come in every day to sort out any medical stuff. The only thing is, I'll have to give up going to school,' says Jack.

'Ooh! Can *I* give up going to school too?'

'No, silly, you have to go, it's the law. But if I give up work it means we'll be very poor – poorer than we are already. We'll probably get some benefits but there'll be four of us to keep.'

'Five, counting Butterscotch.'

'Ah, good point. Not that he costs much, funny little fellow. Perhaps we'll all go on a diet of dandelions and guinea-pig nuggets.'

'I could earn a bit of money for us. I could deliver

papers or – or run errands for old ladies, or – or design homemade birthday cards.'

'Thank you, Ella. Those are lovely offers – though I'm not sure girls your age are allowed to earn money. I *am* sure you're going to have to miss out on a lot though – new clothes, games, treats, holidays—'

'I don't care,' I lie. 'Just so long as Mum's home with us so I can go and cuddle up to her whenever I want.'

'Well, that's exactly the way I feel too,' says Jack.

He takes my hand and squeezes it. I cling onto him tightly and squeeze back.

Chapter 14

We're fighting once more the very next day. It's all Jack's fault. He's late picking me up *again*. I stand in the playground waiting and waiting and waiting. I have a new whale book to look at. Miss Anderson brought it into school specially for me, so at first I don't notice just how late it's getting. Then Miss Anderson herself comes across the playground looking worried.

'Ella? I've been keeping an eye on you. Where's your dad?'

'I don't know.' I see the time and start to panic. 'Oh, Miss Anderson, what's happened to him?'

'Now, now, calm down. I'm sure he's fine. Maybe something's cropped up. Tell you what, he's probably left a message with the school secretary. I'll go and have a word. You wait here, OK?'

She hurries off and I march up and down anxiously. Miss Anderson is back in less than a minute.

'Oh dear, no message. Did he say he might be late?'

'He's always a little bit late.'

'Well, this is silly. It's not good for you, just hanging around the playground all by yourself. Why on earth doesn't your dad fix you up to go to after-school club?'

'I don't know,' I mumble, though I *do* know: I've told Jack hundreds of times I'd sooner perforate my head with pins and eat cold sick than go to after-school club with Martha.

'Well, never mind. I'll have a word with your dad about it when he comes,' says Miss Anderson.

I shudder.

'Oh dear, you're shivering! Shall I put my jacket round your shoulders? We don't want you getting a chill, especially after yesterday.'

'I'm fine, Miss Anderson,' I say, but I pretend to shiver a bit more because I love it when she fusses over me like a mum.

She puts her hand on my shoulder and starts asking me all sorts of questions about whales, marvelling when I mostly know the answers. I'm not daft, I know she's doing it to distract me – she's not *really* impressed that I know that sperm whales can dive a whole mile deep, that blue whales weigh a hundred tons, that some baleen whales can live as long as ninety years. She does look a bit startled when I tell her about the twenty-two-hour love song of the humpback.

'Twenty-two *hours*? Are you sure you don't mean twenty-two minutes?'

'Absolutely positive. Though mostly they just sing for ten or fifteen minutes. They dive down about fifteen metres and just hang there, totally still, and sing.'

'What does it sound like, this song?'

'I'm not really sure. It says in the books that it's kind of moans and groans, which doesn't sound very – very—'

'Melodic?' says Miss Anderson.

'Maybe it just sounds funny underwater. Our ears can't hear it properly. The books say that it's only the males who can sing, but I think the females can too. I don't see why not – they're *bigger* than the males. They haven't been heard, but perhaps they've got such high-pitched voices, like sopranos, that we can't hear them at all, though really they're singing away like crazy. Do you think that's possible, Miss Anderson? All those whale experts, they don't always know everything, do they?'

'Indeed they don't.'

'Experts can sometimes be entirely mistaken, can't they?' I say. 'Even very senior ones.'

Miss Anderson squeezes my shoulder. I think she's guessed what I'm talking about now. 'Everyone can occasionally make mistakes, Ella,' she says. 'Even me!'

Then we hear the *chug-chug-chug* of our old car and Jack comes jumping out, running through the gate.

'I'm sorry!' he says. 'Total crisis! One of our oh-so-lovely parents attacked a member of staff. I had to help her deal with it. She got slapped across the face.'

'Oh dear!' says Miss Anderson. 'I hope that doesn't ever happen to me! But Ella was getting a bit worked up and worried. You're forty minutes late.'

'Yes, yes, I'm sorry.'

'I can see it's a huge problem, getting all the way over here – but isn't it easily solved? Why don't you enrol her in our after-school club?'

Jack looks at me. I shake my head violently. *He takes no notice!*

'Yes, I think that's the most sensible idea. Shall we nip along now, Ella, and get it all fixed up?'

'*No!*' I say, agonized.

'I'll fix it all for you so Ella can start tomorrow,' says Miss Anderson.

'That's so good of you,' says Jack.

The moment we're in the car I explode. 'I'm not *going!*'

'Now, come on, Ella, it's the only sensible option.'

'It's not sensible at all! I hate hate hate after-school club, you *know* I do. You said I didn't need to go again. *Mum* said.'

'Yes, yes, and I thought I could cope, but I clearly can't. We're forever having crises at Garton Road and there's no way of predicting them. I can't have you standing there all lost and lonely in the play-ground.'

'I *wasn't* lost and lonely, I was having the most interesting conversation about whales with Miss Anderson. I was *fine*. I don't mind if I have to wait. I just mind about after-school club.'

'So what exactly do they do there that is so horrible? I thought you all played games and had a snack and watched cartoons? Why is that such torture?'

'Martha's there – and I don't like her.'

'Oh, for heaven's sake, Ella, don't be so wet. If you don't like Martha, stay out of her way. At least you'll be safe and sensibly occupied at after-school club and I won't have to worry so much.'

'I won't be the slightest bit safe at after-school club. Martha will get me. She hates me because I told on her, and I think she blames me because Dory's not friends with her any more. She can't do anything in school because Miss Anderson looks out for me, but those ladies who run the after-school club are useless, they won't stop her. She'll kill me.'

'Oh, Ella! How is she going to kill you? Attack you with a machine gun? Hurl a hand grenade at you? Impale you with a bayonet? Exactly how many weapons of destruction does she have at her disposal?'

'Oh, very funny. You don't know what she's *like*.'

'No, but I'm very curious to find out why an ordinary small girl can be so terrifying. Or maybe she isn't ordinary or small. Does she have super powers? Can she chop you in two with her cleaver arms, kick you to bits with her size-twelve feet? Is she six metres high so she can sit on you with her enormous bum and squash you flat?'

He's trying to make me laugh but I'm not having it.

'She *says* such mean things.'

'Oh, Ella, *you* can be Queen of Mean when you want. Don't tell me you can't match this Martha. If she says something mean, retaliate. You're not a little shrinking violet. Stand up to her!'

We break off our argument because we've arrived at Aunty Mavis's. Samson is fast asleep, his little thumb in his mouth.

'Shame to waken him just yet,' says Aunty Mavis. 'Sit yourselves down for a few minutes. You both look hot and frazzled.'

So we sit on Aunty Mavis's comfy old sofa, and she brings us each a glass of homemade lemonade and a cherry flapjack.

Lily and Meggie are playing with Noah's ark wooden animals. Jack helps pair them up in a long line, trumpeting like an elephant, roaring like a tiger, hissing like a snake. Then he puts the twins at the end of the long line.

'You're a matching pair. What kind of animals are you? Are you . . . little monkeys?'

Lily and Meggie shake their heads, giggling.

'Are you . . . great big hippopotamuses?'

They start squealing with laughter as he runs through all the animals he can think of. I watch a little sourly, still worrying about Martha.

'Hey there, chickie,' says Auntie Mavis. She sits down on the sofa beside me and then reaches out and pulls me onto her lap. I know I'm much too old for this sort of cuddle, but it feels so *good* to snuggle against her warm cardigan and have her arms go round me tight.

'How's my special big girl?' she says.

I don't want to be big at all. I want to be as little as the twins and Samson, and then I could stay with Aunty Mavis and I wouldn't have to go to school, let alone after-school club.

The next day I tell myself that Miss Anderson might have forgotten all about fixing it up. She doesn't *always* remember things. She doesn't mention it all the way through school and I think it's fine. Jack isn't going to be picking me up until five o'clock but I don't care. I'll hide in the girls' toilets so people won't see I'm waiting. I've got my whale book and I've even got provisions. Toby secretly shared his bumper chocolate bar with Joseph and me while we were working on our Tudor project. He said all that thinking about food was making him feel starving. I ate one square to show I was very grateful, but hid the rest in my school bag. I was so worried about after-school club I didn't have much appetite, even for chocolate.

The bell goes for the end of school, and Miss Anderson stands up and says goodbye to us, and then she starts packing her bag up, goes out of the door – oh glory, she really *has* forgotten! I rush out of the room – but, oh no, she's standing in the corridor, waiting for me.

'I thought I'd take you over to after-school club, Ella. I've fixed it all up with Mrs Matthews and Miss Herbert.'

My heart is thudding. I feel sick. 'Thanks, Miss Anderson, but it's OK, I know where it is. I'll go by myself,' I gabble, thinking, *Oh no I won't*.

Maybe she can see inside my head.

'I'll take you,' she repeats, smiling at me.

So she walks me round to the hall as if I'm one of the infants. She even stops on the way and asks me if I need to go to the toilet. This gives me an idea. I spend a very long time in the toilet, until Miss Anderson comes into the room, calling me.

'Are you all right in there, Ella?'

'No, Miss Anderson,' I say, flushing the lavatory and coming out. I try to look as weak and white as possible. 'I've just been sick,' I announce.

'Oh dear,' says Miss Anderson. 'Perhaps it was

the chocolate you ate while you were doing your Tudor project.'

How did she *know*? Toby passed the chocolate bar under the desk ever so discreetly. Teachers can be so spooky at times, the way they know stuff.

'Perhaps I'd better go and lie down on that couch in Mrs Andrews's office until my stepdad comes for me,' I say.

'No, if you don't feel well you need someone keeping an eye on you, and Mrs Andrews will be going home soon. Come on.'

'But I can't go to after-school club – I might be sick again. And I might infect all the others with my sick bug. Imagine if we all started vomiting simultaneously.'

'I think your imagination is a little too much in evidence at times, Ella,' says Miss Anderson. She takes me by the shoulder and steers me out of the girls' toilets. There's nothing I can do. We go plod plod plod down the corridors to the hall.

Miss Anderson takes me right up to Mrs Matthews. 'This is Ella, Mrs Matthews,' she says.

'Ah yes, the little girl you told me about. Yes, I remember you, Ella. You came for a few days last term, didn't you?'

I remember Mrs Matthews too. She's got very bright blonde hair even though she's an old lady, and she puts her face very close to yours when she talks, and sometimes little bits of her spit spray your face.

'I'll look after you, Ella, don't worry,' she says. She puts her finger under my chin and taps. 'Chin up, that's my motto. Now, come and have something to eat.'

'Ella feels a bit sick, Mrs Matthews,' says Miss Anderson. 'She might not want anything right now.'

'Oh dear, have you got the collywobbles, Ella?' says Mrs Matthews loudly, like I'm three – and deaf.

I put my head down and pretend I'm not there.

'Bye, Ella,' says Miss Anderson.

I'm not even going to reply. It's all her fault I'm here. She pats my shoulder and then goes. And I'm left there, with spraying Mrs Matthews, a whole load of little kids I don't know, some of the big kids I'm not keen on – and Martha.

She comes swaggering up, her chin jutting.

'Ah, Martha, you're in the same class as Ella, aren't you, darling?' says Mrs Matthews. 'Can you show her the routine, see if she wants anything to eat? She might not be very hungry because she's feeling a little bit sick.'

Martha's eyes gleam. 'Yes, I'll look after Ella,

Mrs Matthews,' she says ominously. Then she hisses at me, 'Oh, poor little baby Ella has to have all the teachers fuss-fuss-fussing. And you suck up to them so, going all dopey and big-eyed and telling tales. No wonder you feel sick. You make *me* feel sick just looking at you. Right, here's the food. Get a plate. You're allowed two sandwiches, egg or Marmite, and a glass of orange squash.'

I help myself and go to sit at a table. Martha follows me, and stands watching while I nibble and sip. She pulls a disgusted face.

'Yuck! I can't believe you've just eaten that. It's not *really* egg, it's cold sick, and they never use real Marmite, they just smear bread with dog's muck. And fancy drinking that squash! Any fool can see it's wee-wee.'

She's just being stupid. Of course I know she's not serious – and yet I want to spit out my Marmite sandwich right this minute, and the squash in my mug looks horribly convincingly like wee. I heave and Martha laughs.

'You are *such* a baby,' she says. 'No wonder Sally can't stick going round with you any more. It's all dribble moan whine, poor little me, boo-hoo. It's *your* fault Dory's gone off with Sally and left me without my best friend.'

'That's rubbish. Dory doesn't want to be your

friend any more. It's *your* fault,' I hiss back at her.

'You are *so* pathetic, Ella-Smella. Yeah, you *do* smell, yuck yuck yuck,' she says, holding her horrible little snub nose.

I'm immediately stricken, wondering if I *do* smell. Life is such a rush now I don't always have time for baths – and I know my hair needs washing very badly, especially since it got all sticky with chlorine in the swimming pool. I think Martha's just being hateful. After all, I *know* the sandwiches aren't made with sick and dog's muck. But I'm not *sure*.

Mrs Matthews puts on a cartoon for us on the big screen at the end of the hall, and we all sit cross-legged and watch. Martha sits beside me, and hidden in the crush of children she reaches out with her hands and gives me a horrible Chinese burn on my wrist. I try to give her one back, but the other lady, Miss Herbert, is behind us and sees.

'What are you up to, Ella? Don't do that, dear. You come and sit over here.' She makes me go and sit with some of the kids in Mr Hawkins's class. I'm glad to get away from Martha, but I hate it that Miss Herbert thinks *I'm* the one who likes to torture people.

I hunch up small, breathing in deeply and anxiously to see if I *do* smell. I can't get interested in the silly cartoon. It seems to be about pirate mice.

One of them is forced to walk the plank and falls into the sea, and then a huge whale comes swimming along and swallows him whole, and I start to get interested – but the whale is drawn all wrong, and inside him he has a whole suite of rooms where the pirate mouse sets up residence. Then the mouse discovers that the whale can sing, and I get hopeful that I might hear what a real whale sounds like – but this cartoon whale throws back his great head and sings Italian opera, which I suppose is quite amusing, but very silly too. Everyone else is laughing but I don't find anything really funny nowadays.

The cartoon finishes and Mrs Matthews snaps on the light and produces six bouncy balls. She announces that we're all going to play team games so we can let off steam. Oh no, I hate team games at the best of times – and this is the *worst*.

Martha is one of the team leaders and she hurls the ball at me. I put my hands up but can't catch it in time. It bangs my head so hard I feel it's going to snap straight off my neck.

'Whoops! Sorry, Ella, that was an accident,' Martha calls cheerily for Mrs Matthews's benefit.

It was accidentally *on purpose*. I've gone all shivery wondering what she's going to do next. We have to stand with our legs wide apart while the head of the line throws the ball down, and Martha manages to make it bounce painfully onto my kneecap. When *I'm* at the head of the line, I try to throw it to hurt her, but I've always been a bit rubbish at ball games and can't throw hard enough.

We have to suffer these team games for *ages* – and then at last we're allowed to stop and sit down properly at tables. The little ones are given paper and crayons. The older ones are allowed to get on with their homework or read a book.

I've got some spellings to learn but I can't be bothered with them. I get out my latest whale book and my whale project. It's fatter than ever, fifty-eight pages now. I've never written anything as long. I start flicking through, watching the whales swim quietly through my own hand-coloured turquoise and cobalt seas – and then a hand stabs at the page like a giant squid on the attack.

'Push *off*, Martha,' I say through clenched teeth.

'No, let me see. I want to look. Oh God, it's so *boring*, whale after whale. Can't you do anything *else*?'

'I like whales,' I say.

'Yes, but what's it all for? It's not like it's a school project.'

'It's just for me, though I've shown it to Joseph and he likes it.'

Martha snorts derisively. 'That sad geek!'

'He's not the slightest bit sad or geeky. He hap-pens to be the most interesting, intelligent boy – but you wouldn't appreciate that, seeing as you're not interesting *or* intelligent. Now shove off, and leave my project *alone.*'

But her hateful fingers still scrabble at my book, and she turns over more of the pages, practically tearing them. She gets to the title page, where I've drawn the word WHALES with a big illuminated letter W, with tiny whales swimming up and down in this enclosed ocean. She pretends to read: '*Whales, by Ella Very Babyish and Boring Lakeland.*'

She flicks the page over. 'What's this?' She pauses at my dedication page. '*To my dear mother Sue with all my love,*' she reads out.

'Shut up! That's private.'

'You've dedicated your book to your *mother*? Well, that's plain stupid. How can she read it if she's stuck in this coma?'

'She won't always be in a coma.'

'Yeah, but even if she comes *out* of this coma, she won't be able to read your silly whale book.'

'Yes she will!'

'No, Sally's mum told Dory's mum. *Your* mum's never going to be able to do anything. She won't be able to walk or talk. She'll just be a vegetable.'

'Shut *up*!'

'She'll be Poor Mummy Parsnip. Or Sad Mummy Sprout. Or Batty Mummy Broccoli.'

I snatch my project, lift it high, and hit Martha hard with it on the top of her head.

She stares at me, stunned. Then she snatches it back from me, her face flooding crimson. She takes hold of the pages and rips and rips and rips. I scream and wrestle with her. She scratches me down my face, I punch her right on the nose – and then we're torn apart. Mrs Matthews hauls me away, her arms round my waist. Miss Herbert has hold of Martha. All the other children are on their feet, staring and squealing excitedly.

'Now, settle *down*, children! Get on with your homework!' Mrs Matthews shouts, showering the top of my head with spit.

Then she staggers with me to the top of the hall while Miss Herbert drags Martha there too.

'How *dare* you two behave like animals!' says Mrs Matthews. 'I *won't* have that kind of violent behaviour at after-school club. Hitting and scratching each other like hooligans! Just look at you!'

Martha's cut my cheek and I've made her nose bleed. We stand there, hot and panting, glaring at each other. I see the crumpled page in Martha's clenched fist. I see the other pages strewn in her wake and I burst into floods of tears.

'Now then, Ella, I don't think you're hurt *that* badly,' says Mrs Matthews. 'Look at Martha's poor nose – and *she's* not crying.'

'Yes, because Ella's a baby, and she thinks she won't get told off if she goes boo-hoo-hoo,' says Martha, wiping her nose with the back of her hand and smearing blood across her mouth.

'Here, here!' Miss Herbert comes running with tissues for both of us.

'Now tell me *why* you started this ridiculous fight,' Mrs Matthews demands.

'*I* didn't start it,' says Martha.

'Ella hit her right on the head with her book – *bonk*!' says one of the little boys, sounding awed.

'Is that right, Martha? Did Ella hit you with her book?'

'*I* don't tell tales,' says Martha.

'Yes, well, that's the right attitude. But, Martha, even if someone hits you—'

'Bonk on the head!' says the little boy.

'Yes, that's enough Simon. You mind your own business,' says Mrs Matthews. 'Even if someone hits you, you do *not* hit them back. Ella's got a really nasty scratch on her poor cheek. Honestly,

what a pair of sillies you are! Ella, it's very dangerous to hit someone on the head—'

'*Bonk!*' says Simon.

'*Simon!* Go away! It's not only dangerous, Ella,
it's very silly, because look what you've done, your
book's all torn and spoiled now. I hope that's not a
homework project.'

'I wish it was, but it's my whale book!' I sob.

'Yeah, that's all you do – wail, wail, wail!' says
Martha. 'You make me sick.'

'Now stop that. I'm very disappointed in both of
you. I will not tolerate this behaviour. You two sit
on these two chairs in front of me where I can keep
my eye on you.'

'Please can I gather up the pages of my whale
book first?' I ask.

At least she lets me do that. I sob harder when I
see just how much Martha has ruined. But it's not
just my whale book. I feel as if she's torn and
defiled my mum. I hear her ugly words over and
over again. It's as if she's pelted my mum with all
those rotten vegetables – and I can't bear it.

'Now now,' says Mrs Matthews irritably. 'Do stop
crying, Ella. You've just got a scratch. Here's Miss
Herbert coming with the medical box. We'll pop
some antiseptic on and then you'll be as right as
rain.'

Miss Herbert dabs at me and mops Martha's nose. Then we sit on our chairs. The other children all stare at us. Martha crosses her eyes and sticks out her tongue at them. I just sniffle and stroke my poor torn book. After a long while some of the mums start to arrive to collect their kids.

Martha starts fidgeting now, her eyes going flicker flicker, watching the door. 'Can I go and sit at a table now, miss?' she asks as Miss Herbert rushes past.

Miss Herbert looks at Mrs Matthews.

'What's that? No, Martha, you're to sit there, in disgrace.'

'But my mum will be here soon,' says Martha.

'Exactly,' says Mrs Matthews.

Martha bites her lip. She looks as if she might start crying too.

Oh, if only *my* mum could come. I wouldn't care if she told me off. She'd probably fuss about me fighting but she'd want to know *why*. Then, when she'd stopped being cross, she'd put her arms round me tight and give me a hug and make it all better.

Martha's mum comes tap-tapping across the parquet floor, holding hands with her small sister. They are both little and fair and pretty, not a bit like Martha, who is big and dark and plain.

Martha's mum isn't much taller than Martha herself, even though she's wearing really high heels. She doesn't look like a *scary* mum – but Martha flinches as she comes marching up.

'What are you sitting there for, Martha?' she says.

'Ah, Mrs Michaels, I'm afraid there's been a little argument between these two girls. In fact it turned into fisticuffs and we had to separate them.'

Mrs Michaels sucks in her lips so that they're one straight line. My heart starts hammering inside my chest. She's starting to look just as mean as her daughter now. What's she going to do to me when she finds out I hit Martha on the head and punched her on the nose?

She doesn't say *anything* to me. She's just looking at Martha. 'I'm just about sick of you and your behaviour, Martha,' she hisses.

'Has Martha been naughty again, Mummy?' the little sister says smugly.

'Yes, she has! Fighting!' Mrs Michaels takes hold of Martha's arm and pulls her off her chair. 'Just you wait till I tell your dad! He'll give you such a whack!'

'He's *not* my dad,' Martha mumbles. She doesn't just look sulky. She looks scared. I suddenly understand Martha much better. I still hate her – but I can't help feeling a little bit sorry for her too.

I'm also much more sorry for me, sitting here nursing my ruined book. I'm not scared of *my* step-dad, but my tummy goes tight when I think of him coming to collect me.

Here he is, dashing in, peering around anxiously. Then he spots me. He waves and comes rushing up. 'Hi, Ella. What are you doing sitting here all by yourself?' he asks.

'Well might you ask,' says Mrs Matthews, bustling up. She's practically frothing at the mouth she's so eager to tell tales on me. 'There was a very nasty dispute between Ella and one of the other girls.'

'Don't tell me. Martha?' says Jack.

'Yes, Martha!' says Mrs Matthews, surprised. 'I didn't realize this was an ongoing thing. I'd hoped the two would play together nicely, but oh dear, no!'

'Well, I've never met Martha, but I'd quite like to have a word with her,' says Jack. 'I don't think she's been very kind to Ella recently. I know Ella's been a bit worried about her, haven't you, sweetheart?' He goes to give me a little chuck under my chin, and then stops.

'What's that mark on your face? Did Martha do that?' He looks at Mrs Matthews angrily. 'I thought you were supposed to be keeping an eye on her?'

'Miss Herbert and I can't be everywhere at once,' she says coldly.

'I appreciate that, but it's worrying when one little girl suddenly starts attacking another one. Poor Ella here is obviously frightened of this Martha, and with good reason. That's a really nasty-looking scratch.'

'I think you'll find it was Ella who started the fight. She hit Martha hard on the head with her folder, and then they both started scrapping, and Ella punched Martha on the nose and made it bleed.'

'Ella!' says Jack.

'I appreciate Ella's going through a bad time with her mother so ill – Miss Anderson explained all about it – but I can't have all this fighting.'

'Oh dear, I'm very sorry. Ella, apologize to Mrs Matthews at once,' says Jack. His voice sounds very strange and strained. Perhaps he's getting really angry now.

I mumble that I'm sorry to Mrs Matthews.

'That's all right, dear. Just don't let it happen again.'

'Come along, Ella,' says Jack, giving my arm a little tug. He's very red in the face. 'Outside.'

Oh dear, what's he going to *do*? Is he going to shout? Is he going to think up some awful punishment? Is he going to whack me?

We get outside into the playground. Jack's face is practically purple. He starts spluttering – and then he's totally whooping with laughter. I stare at him in astonishment.

'Oh dear! I'm sorry! I'm not laughing at you, Ella, it's just – oh, Lordy, you *really* punched Martha on the nose? You mustn't *ever* punch anyone. What on earth made you turn into a mini Mike Tyson?'

'She said horrid things about Mum. She said she was a vegetable.'

'Oh God. Did she really say that? Well, maybe I'm glad you punched her – though don't do it again.'

'And she ripped up my whale book,' I say.

'Oh no! You've spent such ages on it. How *horrible* of her. Dear goodness, *I* feel like going and punching her now. Let's start up a We-Can't-Stand-Martha club, eh?'

'Good idea, Jack. And Mum can join too.'

'And little Sam.'

'And Butterscotch.'

'Yep, all our family. Well, let's pick up Sam, feed both our little boys, and go and see Mum.'

Chapter 15

When we get back home from the hospital, there are three messages beeping on the telephone.

'Oh God, what's all this?' says Jack.

The first message is from my dad. I listen, my heart thumping, wondering if he's going to invite me for the weekend after all. No, it's not an invite.

'Hi, Ella, this is your dad. I hope you're doing OK, sweetheart. I want you to know I'm thinking about you all the time. I'm going to come and see you again really soon. I'm a bit tied up at the weekends just now.'

'With Tina,' I mutter.

'But hopefully there'll be a window of opportunity asap.'

'What?' says Jack. He calls Dad a very rude word. He says it under his breath but I hear. I don't really mind. I actually agree with him.

'Meanwhile, take care. I hope little . . . Butterball is doing fine. Bye-bye, darling.'

'Butter*scotch*. He can't even remember his name right. And he didn't ask after Mum!'

'Still, he's obviously concerned about you, Ella. It was good of him to phone,' says Jack, though I can tell he doesn't mean it.

He presses the button for the next message. It's Liz.

'Hey, you two. I'm doing another big shop tomorrow. What do you fancy for a treat? Any special requests, food – or drink-wise? And my love life is a bit rubbish at the moment, so do you two want to come over on Saturday evening for a few drinks and a pizza? Whoops, I've forgotten the baby. Bring

him too, naturally. Though I expect he's a bit young
for a can of Coke and a hunk of garlic bread. How's
he doing, poor little scrap? And how's my Sue? How
are you coping, Jack? And Ella, remember if you
need any girly advice or a chat about men or make-
up, I'm your woman.'

I burst out laughing. 'I'm not into men and make-up yet!'

'I know. I think she's joking. She's a good friend after all, old Liz,' says Jack.

The third message is for me. It's Joseph!

'Hello, Ella, I hope you're all right. I expect you're
at the hospital seeing your mum. Anyway, my mum
says can we meet you from school tomorrow and
take you home to my place for tea? I can show
you all my whale stuff, and then we can have tea,
and then your dad could come and collect you
about seven, if that's OK. Do say yes, it would be
such fun.'

'I can say yes, can't I?' I ask Jack.

'Of course. He sounds very nice – and dead keen. Maybe you'd better have that men and make-up chat with Liz after all,' he says.

'Joseph isn't like a boyfriend, silly.'

'Who are you calling silly?' says Jack, but he's deliberately pulling a silly face. 'Now, let me get on with my marking.'

'Jack, if I go to tea with Joseph, I don't have to go to after-school club, do I?'

'No, I suppose not. They'd probably ban you anyway.'

'So I don't ever have to go again?' I say delightedly.

'No, hang on, you've *got* to go. We'll just have to grovel to Mrs Matthews. And listen, Ella, keep away from Martha, do you hear me? No more fighting.'

'It was you who told me to stand up to her.'

'Yes, well, maybe that was a stupid suggestion. I'm glad it worked once, but I can't have you kicking off like that again. The school is worried enough about you as it is. You just keep your head down and behave. Ignore Martha. If she opens that big mouth of hers and starts sounding off, pretend you've got little flaps over your ears so you can't hear a word. Block her out. OK?'

'OK.'

'Right then. Marking time. And why don't you see what you can salvage of your whale project? You can use my special sellotape if some of the pages are ripped.'

I sit down, take all the pages out of my file, and do my best to smooth them out and fix them. 'It's just going to look total rubbish now,' I say sorrowfully.

'Well, you can always redo the worst pages.'

'That blooming Martha. I'd like to rip *her* in half,' I mutter.

I think about her. I think about her stepfather.

'Jack, are grown-ups allowed to hit children nowadays?'

'No – though it's very tempting at times.' He sees me staring. 'I'm *joking*.'

'*Do* some grown-ups hit kids, though?'

'Yes, of course they do. Though it's very wrong.'

'What's a whack? Is it like a smack?'

'I don't know. Maybe.'

'You wouldn't ever give me a whack, would you, Jack?'

'What? No, of course not.'

'I'm glad *you're* my stepdad,' I mutter, sticking another torn page with sellotape.

Now Jack's staring at me. 'That's the nicest thing you've ever said to me,' he said.

I think about giving him a hug, but that might be going a bit too far.

'Shall I phone Joseph back then, and say it's a definite yes for tomorrow?'

'Yep, and I'll have a word with his mum.'

Samson starts wailing fretfully while Jack's on the phone to Mrs Antscherl. I pick him up and change his nappy and then get him ready for bed, putting him in his little spouting whale sleepsuit.

'There now, who's a nice clean boy, all ready to snuggle up in your cot and go to sleep?' I say.

I put Samson's mucky day clothes in the washing machine, and then I wander round with him on my hip, collecting up the rest of his grubby clothes and some of my stuff and Jack's, and get the load started.

'Hey, you'll be qualifying for the Best Daughter of the Year awards if you keep this up,' says Jack. 'Here, let me take over, sweetheart. You have a little time on your whale book. Or have you got homework?'

'No,' I say quickly. Then I sigh. 'Yes, but it's spelling, and I h-a-t-e spelling.'

'I'll help you,' says Jack.

He sings silly little songs to help me remember the words: 'Remember two As in separate, I can spell it, isn't that great! Attention has three Ts, if you please! Deceive will deceive you unless you sing with me, *I before E* except *after C*!' As we sing, we munch the rest of Toby's chocolate.

Guess what! I get ten out of ten for my spelling test the next day, the first time *ever*. Joseph gets ten out of ten too, but that's only to be expected.

'Well done, Ella,' says Miss Anderson. Then she adds quietly, just for me to hear, 'I'm surprised you had time to learn your spellings last night. I hear you had quite an eventful time at after-school club.'

I look down.

'Yes, well may you hang your head. I feel thoroughly ashamed of you and Martha. Why don't you stop all this nonsense and make friends?'

Miss Anderson must be quite mad. I hate Martha and Martha hates me. She's weirdly quiet today, sulking on one side of Dory. Sally and Dory are going whisper whisper whisper, giggle giggle giggle, and it feels a bit lonely being stuck beside them – but Joseph taps me on the back and passes me a little note:

I'm so pleased you're coming to tea. I hope you like macaroni cheese! And salad and fruit jelly and chocolate fudge. I made the fudge and it truly tastes terrific, Joseph xx

I write him a little note back:

I'm looking forward to going to tea with you. It all sounds yummy! Ella xx

I'm not usually a kissy-kissy person, but it might seem rude if I didn't return the compliment to Joseph. I pass it to him. Toby looks a little left out, so I pass *him* a note:

Thank you for the chocolate. I did enjoy it. Ella xx

Toby writes back:

Your welcum and I have MOORE in my school bag, Toby xx

Toby only got one out of ten for his spelling test.

The three of us are soon circulating notes like crazy, and it's great fun. Toby shares some of his chocolate with us at break time, but keeps a few squares back for us to eat when we work on our Tudor food project together.

I dash into the girls' toilets just before the bell goes. There's Martha sitting in a sink, moodily swinging her legs and glaring at all the little kids scuttling in and out. She glances at me and makes a very rude sign at me with her finger. I make it back at her and charge into a toilet cubicle. She's still sitting there when I come out and wash my hands.

'Watch out, stupid baby, you're splashing me,' she growls.

'Well, you shouldn't be sitting there, should you?' I say. I pause. The bell goes but I don't hurry away. 'Martha?'

'What?'

'Did you get whacked last night?'

She blinks at me. 'How did you know?'

'I just wondered. Did it hurt a lot?'

Martha shrugs. 'What do you think? But I don't

care. I got my own back on that pig. I spat in his beer and he didn't notice and drank it all. He's such a loser. He's not my real dad, he's just my stepdad.'

'I've got a stepdad.'

'Is he a pig too?'

'Yes, totally,' I say, and I make snorty noises.

Martha giggles.

'Well, he's not *always* a pig. In fact he can be quite nice sometimes,' I say, a little guiltily.

'Mine's never nice, he wouldn't know how. I hate him,' says Martha, and she looks as if she might cry.

My tummy's churning. If she was Sally or even Dory I'd put my arms round her.

'Still, you've got your mum,' I say.

'I can't stick her either,' Martha mumbles. 'She's mean to me too.'

Now I'm truly shocked. 'My mum's never been mean to me ever,' I say.

There's a little silence. Then, 'Well, your mum *can't* be mean, can she? If she's just lying there like a vegetable. Like a cabbage.'

'Stop it!'

It's as if a great white light has flashed inside my head. Martha is being horrid now simply because it makes her stop feeling so unhappy.

'Like a carrot, like an onion.'

I can't *stand* her saying all this vegetable stuff. I want to slap her hard. But I also feel sorry for her.

'This is crazy, Martha. Don't let's fight all over again. Let's surprise everyone and make friends instead.'

'I wouldn't be friends with you if you were the last person on earth,' says Martha – but she jumps out of her washbasin. 'You mean, like *best* friends?' she says, wrinkling her nose incredulously.

'Just *friend* friends,' I say.

'So do you think Sally's still your best friend?' Martha asks.

'Nope.'

'Don't you *mind*?'

'Yes, but I've got another best friend now.'

'Who is it, then? You *haven't*!'

'I have so. Joseph's my best friend.'

'Now I *know* you're crazy. Joseph's a *boy* – and he's a total geeky freak.'

'Well, I like him,' I say.

'Oh *please*. He gives me the creeps. Mind you, *you* give me the creeps too,' says Martha.

'Creepy-creepy-creepy creep,' I say, tickling her.

She tickles me back until we're both shrieking with laughter.

'What are you girls playing at?'

Oh heavens, it's *Mrs Raynor*. Now we're for it. She comes right into the toilets, crossing her arms and shaking her head.

'I can't believe it! Ella and Martha *again*! I've just had a report that you both behaved abominably at after-school club, *fighting* – and now here you are, a full five minutes after the bell has gone, leaping about and laughing like hyenas!'

She pauses. Martha and I stand very still. What is she going to do? Mrs Raynor is terribly strict. We're surely going to be severely punished. She's still shaking her head.

'Make up your minds, girls,' she says. 'Yesterday you seemed like deadly enemies, now you're acting as if you're friends. Which is it?'

'Both!' we say in unison.

'Girls!' says Mrs Raynor. 'I give up. Run off to your classroom now and stop giving me grief, do you hear?'

We run, unable to believe our luck. Miss Anderson *is* cross with us though, and gives us a right old telling off, but when it's over I settle down with Joseph and Toby, doing our Tudor project. They work on a description of the kitchen in a Tudor palace while I draw a picture of a great big hog roasting on a complicated spit. There's a little kitchen boy turning the handle and a big fat cook making an enormous pie with little bird beaks poking through the pastry. Then I draw Joseph and Toby in those funny Tudor-trousers like puffy rompers, and me in a ruff and a sticking-out skirt. We're all sitting at the table, sharing a honey cake – while in real life we sit in our school uniform with our mouths full of Toby's chocolate.

I think Miss Anderson maybe knows about the chocolate again, but she's pretending not to see. Maybe she's tired of telling me off today.

I try extra hard in lessons, wanting to please her. I stick my hand up every time I know the answer to any question. I try even harder in our art lesson. Miss Anderson shares out some wonderful brightly coloured dough, pink and yellow and red and blue, and gives us an assortment of wheels and sticks, and tells us to invent a child's toy. I decide I'll make a little toy for Samson, a pull-along whale on wheels. I'd ideally like a lump of black dough and a little white for the markings, but I have to make do with blue. I fashion a humpback whale, taking great care with its long flippers, making little nobbles on its head, and marking a pattern underneath its tail.

'That's *very* good, Ella,' says Miss Anderson. 'Is it a blue whale?'

'Well, it's actually a humpback, but I haven't got the right colours.'

'It's beautiful.'

'Can I take it home? It's a present for my little brother Samson.'

'Well, I'd like to put it on display for a while. But you can take it home at the end of term. I'm sure Samson will love it when he's a bit older. Listen, as you're so good at making things with dough, maybe I can give you a little piece to play with when you go to after-school club? It will keep your hands busy so you won't bop poor Martha on the nose.'

I giggle.

'I'd love some dough but I won't need it today, because I'm not going to after-school club.'

'Oh dear. Mrs Matthews hasn't banned you, has she?'

'I think she'd *like* to! No, it's not that. I'm going to tea with Joseph.'

'Oh, that's good.' Miss Anderson sounds really pleased.

When she goes to look at someone else's model, Sally moves her chair away from Dory, nearer to me.

'Did you say you're going to tea with *Joseph*?' she says, sounding astonished.

'Yes.'

'*Why?*'

'Because I like him. And he's going to show me his books about whales.'

Sally rolls her eyes. She carries on making her pink dough doll. It's a very basic doll, and the head keeps falling off its puny little neck.

'Oh, drat this wretched thing,' she says. 'Listen, Ella, *I* was going to ask you to tea. Mum said you could come for a sleepover.'

'That would be lovely,' I say.

'Maybe Dory can come too?' Sally suggests.

I feel that would not be anywhere *near* as lovely, but I keep smiling. 'Fine.'

'Well, come tonight then. You can get out of going to tea with Joseph. You don't want to go to his house, it'll be dead boring,' says Sally.

'No, it won't. I want to go.'

'Look, you're not *his* friend, you're mine,' says Sally, looking peeved.

I want to yell, *Make your mind up!* At her. But I *still* stay smiling. 'It's all arranged for tonight. I even know what we're having for tea. But maybe I can come to your house another time?'

I'm trying to be Miss Sweetness-and-Light, keeping friends with everybody. I shall end up going to tea with Martha at this rate. No, maybe not.

I'm going to tea with *Joseph* – and in the last lesson before going-home time I start to worry about it a little bit. Joseph talks in a very precise voice. Even though he looks a bit scruffy, with untidy hair and crumpled school shirts, I have a feeling he's very posh. Perhaps he lives in a really big house. I have a sudden image of Joseph and me sitting at a very long polished table with a complicated set of knives and forks and spoons in front of us, being served our macaroni cheese from a silver platter by a maid in uniform. And what about his mother, Mrs Antscherl? I start imagining her like Miss Raynor, our head teacher, wearing a neat grey suit and a silk scarf, raising her eyebrows if I say anything silly.

It's a wonderful relief to meet the real Mrs Antscherl. She's plump and smiling, with long, very curly hair. She's wearing a skirt with little mirrors sewn all over it so that she twinkles as she walks. She gives me a big hug as if she's known me for ages.

'I'm so glad you're coming to tea, Ella. It's such a treat for Joseph. He talks about you non-stop.'

'Mum!' says Joseph, going pink.

Their car is comfortingly small and old, with books and maps and sweet wrappers on the floor. Their house *is* big and posh, with three floors and a basement, but it's not grand at all. There are untidy bookshelves everywhere, with further books spilling into every corner, even in piles going up the stairs. The sagging sofa and armchairs in the living room are covered with bright throws and lots of cushions – there's one with little mirrors just like Mrs Antscherl's skirt. We sit there for ten minutes while we have juice and chocolate raisins, and chat to Mrs Antscherl. Then she goes off to the kitchen and we go down to the basement.

It's like a giant playroom just for Joseph, with all *his* books, and his computer, and an entire set of encyclopaedias. There's an old-fashioned train set laid out all over the floor, and a wooden Noah's ark too, a special old one with carefully carved animals – heaps of them, at least fifty pairs.

'There's a Noah's ark at Aunty Mavis's house – she looks after my baby brother – but it's nowhere near as big as this one,' I say.

'It was my mum's when she was little – and the train set was my dad's. *I* don't really play with them. I like reading best,' says Joseph, but he obligingly shows me how the train set works.

'Can we take the littlest Noah's ark animals on a train trip?' I ask. 'We could pretend they're a travelling circus, a special troup of performing animals.' I grab a handful out of the ark. 'Look, here are two performing rabbits who can turn somer-saults, and *these* are little birds who are excellent trapeze artists.'

'You are so mad, Ella,' says Joseph happily. 'OK, OK, put them in that open carriage there, and we'll take them for a ride.'

I've never played with a train set before and it's great fun, especially when we have two trains on the line and have to divert them to avoid a major collision and tragic animal extinction.

'There are no whales in the ark, not even little dolphins,' I say.

'I expect they swam along *beside* the ark,' says Joseph. 'Shall we look at my whale books now?'

He's got such *wonderful* books – not just about whales, about everything under the sun.

'You don't need to go to the public library, you've got an entire library here,' I say when he shows me his library books too.

'I'd like a *real* library of my own one day,' says Joseph.

'Well, maybe if I work some more on my whale project, it'll get long enough to be made into a proper book and you can keep it in your library.;

'In its own special glass case, and only very important people can borrow it – i.e. *me*!' says Joseph. 'Let's have a look at it now.'

'Martha tore up a lot of it,' I say mournfully.

'Martha's a really scary girl. I hate it when she picks on you. Ella, do you think I should stick up for you more?'

'No, I can stick up for myself. Well, sometimes. Look, here it is. I tried sticking the ripped pages with sellotape but they don't look very good.'

'Why don't you rewrite them?'

'Well, it will take such *ages*.'

'I'll help you. I've got paper exactly that size. I'll do all the writing if you like, and you can do the drawing. You could come round to tea heaps and heaps and we could work on it together. Would you like that?'

'Oh *yes*!'

I settle down to redrawing the title page, with an even more elaborate letter W. Joseph doesn't just have good felt tips with tiny points – he has *coloured inks*! I've never used these before and they are totally brilliant, especially the gold. My title page is going to look almost like a *real* illuminated manuscript in a museum.

Joseph doesn't just copy out a page or two, willy-nilly. He's getting my project *organized*, shifting all the pages around into chapters on humpbacks, killer whales, blue whales, etc.

'We could also do a chapter on the history of

whales. And whales in captivity. And all sorts of typical whale behaviour – hunting and feeding together, like we saw in that film on television.'

Just for a moment I wonder if I mind Joseph taking over like this. It's becoming very much a *joint* project now. But it will only have *one* illustrator. I'm very glad Joseph isn't so great at drawing.

We work happily until Joseph's mum calls us for tea. She's set it all out on the big wooden table in their kitchen: macaroni cheese, salad, fruit jelly and chocolate fudge, just as Joseph promised. Mrs Antscherl gives us great big helpings, but only serves herself a small portion of salad. But later, as we're chatting, she absent-mindedly helps herself to the macaroni cheese left in the serving dish – and then pops several chocolate fudges into her mouth, one after another. She sees me looking.

'I know, I know! I'm rubbish at sticking to my diet. It's so unfair, Ella. Joseph and his dad eat humungously and stay as thin as pins, and I pile on the pounds just *looking* at fudge.' She laughs and pops another chunk in her mouth. '*And* eating it.'

'My mum's the same,' I say. 'Well, she *was*. She can't really eat properly now. She has a feeding tube.'

Mrs Antscherl reaches out and gives my hand a squeeze. 'It must be so sad and worrying for you.

Joseph's told me all about it. Your mum's still in a coma?'

'Yes, but she will get better one day,' I say quickly.

'I do hope so,' says Mrs Antscherl.

'I'd quite like to be a doctor when I grow up,' says Joseph. 'Or a surgeon – one who does terribly tricky and delicate operations on people's brains to make them function properly. Or maybe I could be a research scientist and find out *why* some people's brains don't work.'

'What do you want to do when you grow up, Ella?'

'Mm, I don't know. I like drawing so maybe I could be an illustrator.'

'I think you should be a marine biologist,' says Joseph.

'What's that?'

'It's a person who knows about everything in all the oceans. So you could research whales. Mum, Ella and I are working on a new whale project together, seeing as her old one got partially destroyed.'

'Oh dear. How did that happen?'

'I had an argument with another girl at after-school club,' I say. 'It's so lovely today – I don't have to go because I'm having tea here.'

'Well, perhaps you can come here on a regular basis. I'll have a word with your dad when he comes to collect you,' says Mrs Antscherl.

'Are you *serious*? I wasn't hinting or anything,' I say (though perhaps I *was*, just a little bit).

'I know. But it would be a big treat for Joseph to have someone to chat to, especially when I'm busy marking.'

'Oh yes!' says Joseph.

'Are you a teacher, then? My mum was always doing marking. *And* my stepdad.'

'I teach students part-time, so I have to mark great long essays.'

'I bet they're not as long as Ella's original whale project, Mum. It was fifty-eight pages, and even I haven't written anything that long.'

'It wasn't all writing though. There were lots of drawings,' I say modestly.

'Yes, Ella's fabulous at drawing. She's illustrating our new whale project – and she's done all the pictures for our Tudor project at school. She's especially good at drawing people in Tudor costumes.'

'But I like drawing whales best,' I say.

'After tea I'd simply love to have a look at this famous project,' says Mrs Antscherl.

We eat until there's nothing left, not even one square of fudge, and then we all go down to the basement together. Mrs Antscherl sits cross-legged on the floor just like a child and we show her the newly assembled project. She looks at it at length in a very satisfying manner, taking her time, commenting on each and every picture, reading quite a lot of the words. She pauses when she comes to the section on humpback whales.

'Ah, whale song! It says here that one humpback was recorded singing nonstop for twenty-two *hours*!'

'Yes, that's my absolute favourite fact. I don't know what it actually sounds like though, whale song. I know it's not like *our* singing.'

'No, it's very strange, but very magical and soothing.'

'You've heard it?'

'Yes. In fact I used to have a CD of whale song when I did relaxation classes before Joseph was born. I'll go and see if I can find it.'

'Oh my goodness!' I say, so thrilled my voice has gone all husky.

'Don't get too excited,' Joseph says gently. 'We've got so much stuff in our house we often lose things for years.'

But Mrs Antscherl comes running back into the room, triumphantly waving a CD. 'Here we are!'

She inserts it into a little CD player on the desk.

There's a pause, and then the strangest, oddest musical sound starts, low and eerie and rhythmic, utterly unlike anything I've ever heard before. I listen, transfixed, trying to work out whether there's a pattern to the singing. Birds sing the same song over and over, but whales sing differently – and yet it doesn't sound as if it's random notes. Sometimes there are great soulful bellows, sometimes soft murmurs, as the whale sings earnestly, with great purpose. There's obviously a mysterious meaning to his song.

'Well, what do you think?' Mrs Antscherl whispers.

'It's wonderful!' I say.

She looks at Joseph. 'Do you mind if we give the CD to Ella, chum?'

'I think that's a lovely idea, Mum!'

'Oh no – I couldn't possibly – but I'd absolutely *love* it!' I burble.

Chapter 16

I play the CD all the time at home.

'For pity's sake,' says Jack. 'I already have to put up with the baby crying and the guinea pig squeaking. Do I really have to listen to your pet whales burbling and burping all night long?'

'Yes you do!' I say. 'I want to play it to Mum too. I'm sure she'll find it so soothing. Mrs Antscherl actually used it for her relaxation class, she said, so I know Mum would find it relaxing too. She needs to blot out all those horrid hospital sounds, the squeaking trolleys and the rattling cups and the click and hum of all the machines. Can we take our CD player into the hospital?'

'I suppose we can try,' says Jack. 'Though I'm not sure there's anywhere to plug it in.'

It turns out we don't need to try to lug it to the hospital. When we go round to Liz's on Saturday evening, she's got more presents for us. (We've got presents for her too. Jack's brought her a bottle of wine and I've drawn her a special card of very fashionable ladies with high heels and big hand-bags. Samson's given her a present as well: a little photo of himself wearing his spouting-whale suit, looking *so* cute.)

Liz has bought us more food – and a special new present for Mum. 'You unwrap it, Ella,' she says.

It's a little light rectangle in a bag.

'Oh, Liz, an iPod!' I say.

'Wow! A very upmarket, state-of-the-art, expensive iPod!' says Jack.

'I thought you could plug it in for Sue – and if

she *is* awake at all, it will help to pass the time. It must be so *boring* for her, just stuck lying there in that awful hospital. You don't think it's too crazy an idea then?'

'It's a *wonderful* idea, Aunty Liz! Mum will love it!' I say.

'You two can take it back home and download all Sue's favourite tunes on it.'

'We could download my whale music!' I squeak. 'That would soothe her. Oh please, let's do the whale music!'

'You're a funny kid, Ella,' says Liz, laughing at me. '*Whale* music?'

'It's so kind and thoughtful of you, Liz. You're a great friend,' says Jack, raising his wine glass to her. 'Why don't you come and visit Sue tomorrow? Then you can give her the iPod yourself.'

'I'd like to – but I just can't bear it. I've got as far as the hospital car park twice and then chickened out,' says Liz. 'You two are valiant, trekking all the way there every day, with the baby too.'

'Mum might be coming home soon,' I say.

'What? You don't mean she's come out of the coma?' Liz gasps.

'No, no, it's just the hospital seem to have written her off,' Jack says bitterly. 'They're suggesting I move her to some kind of institution – but we're not going to do that, are we, Ella? Mum's coming home with us. But we've got to have the house adapted, with a special bed and a hoist.'

'Oh, Jack,' says Liz. 'Does that mean you'll have to give up work?'

'That's fine. We'll manage,' says Jack, but his voice cracks.

He gets up to go to Liz's bathroom. I think he's gone to have a little private cry. Samson starts crying too. We've given him his bottle but he knows he's not in his own house and he can't settle down to sleep.

'Oh dear, poor baby,' says Liz. She takes a deep breath and then plunges her hands into his carry-cot and plucks him out. She holds him very gingerly, almost at arm's length. Samson drools unhappily. He doesn't feel at all safe.

'Snuggle him against you, Aunty Liz,' I say.

Liz looks down at her cream silk blouse.

'Here,' I say, and I take Samson and hold him close, his head peeping over my shoulder. 'There now, let's stop that silly crying,' I say, and start walking him around the room, showing him all Liz's ornaments and photos.

'You're very good with him, Ella,' says Liz. 'Your

mum would be so proud of you.' She sounds as if she might start crying herself.

I pause at a photo on the mantlepiece. It's Mum and Liz when they were younger, with their arms round each other. They're wearing very thick make-up, their smiling mouths almost black in the photo. They're wearing worryingly short skirts and fishnet stockings and very high heels.

'Did you and Mum used to go out like that?' I ask, astonished.

'What? Oh, that was some silly tarts and tramps dance. My God, look at the state of us!'

I stare at Mum in the photo. She's pulling a silly face, sticking out her tongue. It seems so strange to see her clowning around like that. I'm so used to seeing her face blank and still, just like a mask. It really scares me. Mum has only been in a coma for a couple of weeks and yet that's the way I think of her now, as if she's always been lying immobile, like Snow White in her glass coffin.

Is that the only way little Samson will think of her? No, because I'll tell him all about her and what she's really like. Perhaps I can make him a Mum project, with pages and pages of descriptions: Mum running along the beach building sand-castles, whirling me round and round; Mum racing me down the road; Mum pushing me on the swings; Mum mock-wrestling with me in bed on Sunday mornings and then cuddling me close and telling me a story.

It's very late when we get home from Liz's, but Jack lets me play my whale CD very softly while he feeds Samson again and I get ready for bed. It's the same CD, the same whales, but they sound different now, faraway and so sad, their song a mournful lament. I cry as I listen. Perhaps it will be too sad for Mum? I worry about it until Jack knocks on my door and puts his head round.

'Samson's gone out like a light,' he whispers. 'Are you and your whales settling down too?'

'Yes,' I say from under the duvet.

'Ella.' He comes nearer. 'Oh, Ella.' He sits down on the side of the bed. I nestle against him and he strokes my hair. 'It's sometimes good to cry,' he whispers.

'I'm worrying that the whale music is too sad for Mum,' I say. 'I don't want to make *her* cry.'

'Perhaps it will good for her too,' says Jack. 'I'll put it on her iPod in the morning and we'll see how she reacts. You try to go to sleep now. Night-night.'

'Night, Jack,' I say.

He kisses the bit of my head peeping out from under the duvet. I don't move – but I make a kissing noise back at him.

After breakfast on Sunday he sits at his computer with the iPod, frowning and muttering – Jack's not very good at technology – but thank goodness he works out how to download the whale song at last.

'Shall we put some of Mum's other favourites on too? Do you think she'd like some Take That? Or what about the *Mamma Mia* songs? She always loved singing along to them.'

'It'll be a bit muddly if it's all jumbled up together. Shall we try just the whales first and see if she likes them?'

We go to the hospital first thing after lunch. It's crowded out with visitors carrying bunches of flowers and baskets of fruit, bottles of squash and chocolates, magazines and books. It's always so hard knowing we can't bring Mum anything to eat or drink, not even anything to look at – but this time we have the iPod of whale music with us.

Mum is lying quietly on her back. Her hair is looking pretty, very shiny, spread out across her pillow. One of the nurses must have washed it this morning.

'How's my lovely girl today?' Jack whispers, kissing Mum's cheek. 'Ella's got a special surprise for you.'

I take the iPod, lay it beside Mum on the pillow, press the button and insert the earphones very gently into her ears. She gives a little start at my touch – and then sighs.

'Oh, Jack! Did you see, did you hear?' I gabble.

'Yes! Yes, she moved. Just a little bit, but she moved – and she sighed too.'

'She likes my whale song, she really likes it! We'll play it for her every day, and we'll ask Niamh and all the nicer nurses to play it for her too when they're on duty. Mum can have her own love song playing in her head all the time,' I say.

So we plug it in for her every time we visit – and every single time she starts and sighs. When we next see Dr Wilmot, Jack excitedly shows her the way Mum reacts.

'Look at her! You saw that, didn't you? You tell that Dr Clegg!'

'Yes, I do think Sue moved a little,' Dr Wilmot says gently.

'Aren't you going to write it down on her chart?'

'Perhaps – perhaps it was just a little involuntary reaction to the headphones?' Dr Wilmot suggests.

'No, it wasn't! It was deliberate. And she sighed too. She does that every time. Isn't that proof that she's becoming aware of things?' says Jack.

'She likes listening to the whales, I know she does,' I say.

Dr Wilmot nods and smiles, but we can see she doesn't believe us. When she's finished checking up on Mum and goes away down the ward, Jack and I sit on either side of the bed, holding Mum's hands, whispering our own love songs to her.

The next day we come in the evening, bringing Samson in his carrycot. Mum lies quietly, her eyes shut, her mouth slightly open, very very still. The iPod is on her bedside locker, its wire dangling.

'I wish they'd leave it plugged in,' I say. 'I want Mum to be listening all the time we're not here. I wonder if she's listened for twenty-two hours yet: Mum, listen.' I sit very close to her, my mouth by her ear. 'Did I ever tell you the longest recorded whale love song lasted twenty-two hours?'

'I think you have told her, Ella. You've certainly told everyone else,' says Jack. 'You and your whales!'

'Jack's always teasing me, Mum. But I shall ignore him,' I say loftily. 'Have you had a good day? Joseph and Toby and I handed in our Tudor food project today, and Miss Anderson said it looked incredible. Her exact words. Sally and Dory and Martha aren't anywhere near finished their costume project, and none of them can draw for toffee, so their project doesn't look very good at all. Sally asked if I could maybe draw them some of the court costumes, and so I started drawing a lady-in-waiting, putting in lots of little embroidered details, and Sally and Dory were saying how good it was, but then Martha nudged me hard and I got scribble all over the lady-in-waiting's sleeves. Typical Martha. But I just sighed at her. She can't seem to help being spiteful sometimes.

'Then Joseph's mum came and collected us from school, and Joseph and I made fudge together, which was such fun and it tastes brilliant. I wish you could have a tiny little taste yourself. I'd rub some against your lips but I'm scared it might choke you. I ate lots, and so did Joseph and Joseph's mum – but I kept some back and put it in a little paper bag and tied it with a ribbon, and then, when Jack came back to collect me, I gave it to Aunty Mavis. She's always giving me lovely treats to eat so I thought it would be nice to give her something in return. She had a piece of fudge, and gave a tiny bit to Lily and Meggie, and they thought it was lovely too. Aunty Mavis even asked me for the recipe!

'So it's been a good day so far for me, Mum. How about you making it a very very very special day? I'll plug in your whale music and you move a little bit more, sigh really deeply, and then we'll know you're listening. Will you do that for me, Mum?' I say it every time.

'Show them, Sue. Wake up properly and show them, sweetheart. We know you're still our Sue, and we love you so. I need you, Ella needs you, and our little Sam especially needs his mum,' Jack whispers. He says this every time.

Samson murmurs in his cot, as if he's talking to Mum too.

I start my whales singing and put the earphones into Mum's ears. She moves. She jerks her head. She sighs – not softly. A real irritable sigh – the sigh she used to make if I'd done something silly, when she'd put her hands on her hips and roll her eyes.

'No more moany whales!' she mumbles.

We stare at her. Jack clutches my hand.

'Oh, Mum!' I whisper, my throat dry. 'Oh, Mum, you spoke!'

She speaks. She opens her beautiful blue eyes and looks at us. I put my face close, my nose touching Mum's. I cry, and a tear runs down Mum's cheek too. Jack kisses her, and her lips pucker as she tries to kiss him back. Samson lies in the crook of her arm and her fingers move to stroke him.

'I'm so very happy for you,' says Dr Wilmot, and she cries too.

Mum's coming back to us, slowly but surely, nearer to normal every day.

Everyone cries a river of joyful tears, while the whales go on singing their mysterious love songs down in the deep blue ocean.